GREEN IS MY SKY

Aidan A. Quigley

First published 1983 by Avoca Publications, Avoca Avenue, Dublin.

Typesetting/Design by Litharne Ltd.

Printed and bound by BPCC Design & Print Ltd.

Copyright 1983 A.A. Quigley.

ISBN 0 9509206 0 6.

Front cover — oil painting by author of *Gloster Gladiator Fighter.*
Back cover — Aer Lingus photograph of Boeing 747.
Cover design — Brian Keating.

Dedication:

*To Stephanie and our family,
and to all who work in
aviation for Ireland.*

ACKNOWLEDGEMENTS

The following publications and sources were used for reference in the preparation of portions of this book:

THE CONQUEST OF THE ATLANTIC BY AIR. Charles Dixon.
HISTORY OF CLIFDEN 1810-1860. Kathleen Villiers-Tuthill.
SLEEP AND BODY RHYTHM DISTURBANCE IN LONG RANGE AVIATION.
Frank H. Hawkins F.R.Ae.S.
RAILWAY INVOLVEMENT IN AIR TRANSPORT IN THE BRITISH ISLES.
1929-39. John King.
THE IRISH AIR CORPS. Anthony P. Kearns.
THE THREE MUSKETEERS OF THE AIR. George F. Dunay.
BREMEN. IRELAND — AMERICA 1928. Col. J.C. Fitzmaurice.
The Military Archives of the Irish Army.
The National Library.
The Irish Times.
The Connacht Tribune.
Aer Lingus.

The Mercier Press of Cork gave me permission to use material of mine previously published by them, and Colonel W.J. Keane, and the late Colonel W.P. Delamer and Captain J.C. Kelly-Rogers wre most helpful in recalling for me early events in Irish aviation.

Finally, my grateful thanks to a lifelong colleague of army and Aer Lingus days for his suggestions and his proof reading of the original text, Captain Thomas P. McKeown.

Aidan A. Quigley.
Dublin. 1983.

CONTENTS

HIGH FLIGHT

Oh, I have slipped the surly bonds of earth
And danced the skies on laughter-silvered wings;
Sunward I've climbed, and joined the tumbling mirth
Of sun-split clouds... and done a hundred things
You have not dreamed of... wheeled and soared and swung.
High in the sunlit silence. Hov'ring there,
I've chased the shouting wind along, and flung
My eager craft through footless halls of air.
Up, up the long, delirious, burning blue
I've topped the windswept heights with easy grace
Where never lark, or even eagle flew.
And, while with silent, lifting mind I've trod
The high untrespassed sanctity of space,
Put out my hand, and touched the face of God.

Pilot Officer G. Magee.
412 Sqn. RCAF.
Killed in action, 11 December 1941.

FOREWORD

Ireland — a small country lying in the Atlantic ocean to the west of the European mainland possesses an equitable climate, and its geographical features and location have made it an ideal centre for domestic and international air traffic.

Its historical background in, and its contribution to aviation are extensive and ongoing, but its writings about it are modest and almost non existent. Practically nothing has really been penned about Irish aviation; in the bookstores of the world, there are millions of books and periodicals dealing with every aspect of the civil and military aeronautics of all of the nations — except Ireland.

This book then contains extensive coverage of the history of Irish military and civil aviation, personal reminiscences of forty one years of flying — jet lag, papal flights, army days, youth in the west of Ireland, and a look into the past from the papers of my grandfather, Frank Sherry who was the manager of the Providence Woollen Mills, Foxford, Co. Mayo, from 1891 until his death in 1949.

ATLANTIC CROSSING 1928 is a description of the pilots, the plane and the events that took place during the first crossing of the North Atlantic from Europe to North America by an aeroplane. Lindberg had flown from New York to Paris the previous year, but a number of aviators perished in the more difficult task of endeavouring to fly the ocean from east to west. The crew of the BREMEN which made the record flight were the two Germans, Captain Hermann Koehl and Baron Guenther von Huenefeld; Commandant James C. Fitzmaurice, officer commanding the Irish Army Air Corps was the co-pilot, and the flight took off from the Irish military aerodrome at Baldonnel in County Dublin.

Captain Bartley O'Connor features in three stories in the chapter: SOME MATTERS IN CONTRAST. These separate events are totally fictitious, but Bartley's background is not. I did have a pilot friend who was psychic, Bartley was not his name, and he did have these odd happenings in his home. My own experience in these matters would seem to indicate the presence of something unusual in an apartment block in which once we lived.

I drew the name "Vaalkar" from my imagination, but having ventured unwarily into the supernatural, I find myself slightly caught with it. A pilot colleague told me that he was flying a passenger jet in Africa, and was retailing my yarn to his French co-pilot, who asked him to repeat the name of the Russian cosmonaut. 'Vaalkar,' said my friend quite loudly — and one of the windscreens of the jet shattered.

Chapter One

ATLANTIC CROSSING

Ocean waves toss in endless array,
Wild winds are flecking the waters in spray,
But high near the sun with gossamer string,
A jet plane is flying on tranquil wing.

The wind was blowing across the runway, and the co-pilot had positioned the control column to prevent the wing from rising in the crosswind. The captain opened up the throttles slowly and released the brakes, held the steering as they started to gain momentum — slowly at first, with just a flicker on the airspeed indicator, until the engines are pushing us forward with tremendous force. At 80 knots the rushing air has given the Boeing complete directional command with its rudder and the captain was able to transfer his left hand from the steering to the flying controls — up to this point the co-pilot had been assisting him from his side.

As the acceleration continued the co-pilot called: 'Rotate,' and the pilot eased the stick back and the 747 came clear of the runway.

Here it always seems as if a big jet is unsure of itself, just as if it was expelled from the womb of earth and the runway its umbilical cord, yet the hesitation is only momentary as the thrust pushes it clear. The undercarriage retracts rapidly but the flaps, those necessary lift devices, take almost ten miles before they have fully retracted and are stowed neatly away, not to be used again until the next landing.

At 1630 hours the jumbo jet set course and climbed out west for its cruising level of 31,000 feet, and in that comfortable aeroplane were 4 pilots, 16 hostesses, and 338 passengers; the normal crew was three pilots but I was supernumerary. The radios in the cockpit picked up continuous communications chatter, and in the cabin the hostesses prepared for a busy afternoon. The voice of the air traffic controller, who had given us climb out instructions, was familiar to me, and he was a Mayo man too; we had both flown Hurricanes in the same unit........

In 1943, No. 1 Fighter Squadron was stationed in Shannon, and I had the opportunity to fly many times up over the countryside that I loved so well. As a boy, I had not realised that the town of Foxford stood on a plain and thus from the air was difficult to pinpoint. Nephin however, that pyramid like mountain, caught the eye with its set piece lakes, Conn and Cullin, and drew you towards it. I had pushed the nose of the Hurricane fighter down over Granny Healy's at Pontoon, and then went low over the waters of Cullin. From the railway bridge, where we used to shoot wild geese, the run to Foxford was less than a minute, and I went up steeply at the town and barrel rolled until the repetitive manoeuvre exhausted the climb and I levelled off and looked down in pleasure at the scene below.

The town clung tightly to the banks of the Moy, and the woollen mill with its large chimney and clock tower dominated the picture, and I could see that the river that gave birth to it all, did indeed flow in slow majesty, with generous sweeps and easy grace, along the ten miles to Ballina. But that same river had other moods too, and in winter ire it flooded many of the fields along its banks, and if the farmer was late with his second crop of hay the waters in their overflow would swirl around the contours of the ground and make islands of the haycocks, and rot them where they lay. The fields and the farms were despoiled by the continual winter inundation; the hungry waters of the river perpetually drained away their very lifeblood and deposited it along the banks as muddy waste whilst its substance flowed down to the sea. Some consolation was the fact that the marshy ground was alive with geese and duck.

Time and "progress" caught up with that lovely river Moy, when public and political pressure eventually forced the government to implement the "Moy Drainage Scheme." The project went ahead and drained the Moy, but it turned the river into an almost dried up summer stream with steep earthen banks, and with its granite, blasted brutally from the bed, piled in indiscriminate heaps all along the banks, whose generous sweeps had brought it with easy grace those ten delightful miles to Ballina. Lough Cullin was destroyed as a fishing ground — reduced to a shallow lake with its surface covered with a million exposed rocks, and the two large mills on the river — Foxford and Murphy's flour mill in Ballina lost their water power. Ironically, it was said at the time, that many farmers whose land was drained found the contractor's wages more alluring and went to work for them.

1640 Hours.

'Shamrock 109 — change to Shannon Area. Squawk A0325 with height read out.'

The co-pilot set up the frequency on the transponder.

Senior hostess enters the cockpit and says that she is making a pot of strong tea for today's important men. I relished the thought as I interested myself in the radio reports.

'Area Control request the Shamrock to report level at 310, and to call passing 220.'

'George Able Yankee Lima Juliet from Bristol Lulsgate — estimating Tuskar Rock at 03.'

'Aer Lingus 765 by Clonmel requesting descent.'

'Aer Lingus 765 clear descent to 70. Call leaving 240.'

I knew the pilot of 765, he had flown Lysanders in the Air Corps........

We flew quite frequently as target aircraft for the anti-aircraft batteries. The Ack Ack called the exercise a "burst short," since their shells, devoid of shrapnel, were fused to explode at a safe height below the Lysander.

I was flying up the Dublin coast on a sunny afternoon, accurately maintaining the desired 10,000 feet for the batteries; the warm sunlight was streaming through the large cockpit windows of the plane, and I was admiring the deep tan of my left arm which was leisurely draped along the padded rest. The shell bursts were far below but something seemed to have disturbed the fairly steady tempo of the barrage; as we turned back for the last run along the range line I saw a German Ju-88 coming in from the east. I knew that if he had seen me he would not have gone through the process of closing courteously to identify the markings; a Lysander was a type in common service with the RAF. We quickly sought the refuge of a fat cumulus cloud, and when its misty sanctuary finally expelled us, he was nowhere to be seen.

1646 Hours
'Lufthansa 467 checking receiver on emergency frequency 121.5.'

A small fly, trapped in an alien environment was crawling across the vast windscreen of our jumbo, a screen that is composed of glass laminations over three inches thick. The insect had been there during the cockpit check on the ground, and although the pilots had heard its frantic buzzing, and the interruption when it collided with the glass, they could not locate it to remove it.

How tiny things and inconsequential sounds pluck the strings of memory. The buzzing sound brought me back to Foxford, and that delightful walk down the Green where the road by the river followed the gracious sweep of the Moy. I used to walk there with my mother of an evening and the grassy banks and meadows nearby were alive with the sounds of the bees. I visit her grave every summer, in the old cemetry at Craggagh, and the tranquillity of that lonely place is a haven for those little creatures searching for honey amongst the wild roses and mountain flowers that bloom all around; there the meadow grass is uncut and high, and the bees buzz louder and the silence is greater.

1649 Hours.
Cabin supervisor calls on the cockpit telephone, and asks the third pilot to come down to the first class section and check out the refrigerator at the horse shoe bar.

'GAYLJ Calling Shannon — estimating Tuskar now on the hour.'

Co-pilot of Shamrock 109 reported to Shannon, that EI-ASJ was passing through Flight Level 220 (22,000 feet). Shannon acknowledged and asked him to call High Level Control on 135.6.

Lufthansa 467 confirms that his receiver is OK. The German voice is guttural and heavily accentuated........

When World War Two was ending, each BBC radio bulletin brought new and dramatic announcements: 'The Germans in Holland have surrendered and remaining troops in Denmark in contact with Allied Headquarters to arrange immediate capitulation.'

The morning at Gormanston was misty with a drift of fog banks from the sea, and the cloud base was 200 feet as the unmistakable roar of a German bomber thundered across the wakening camp and

14

lost itself to the west where the ceiling was lower, and it had climbed to avoid collision with the rising ground. They made a landing from the fourth sweep: the latest model of the Ju-88 — a fast truck with a mounted machine gun tore out from the apron to meet the aircraft.

The crew switched the engines off, slid back the cockpit hatches and got out of the aeroplane; they were wearing Luftwaffe uniforms with the ugly bum freezer jackets. The pilot, a sergeant major, had facial scars; blue eyed and blond, he looked a tough customer and he wore the German decoration, the Iron Cross; his two companions, one a gunner, the other a navigator, did not have the moulded and dedicated look of their pilot.

We eyed them with suspicion as the sergeant major stood in front of our CO and saluted; the German explained to the commandant, in good English, that German forces in Denmark had surrendered, and his squadron had been given the choice by the commander of flying their machines to neutral countries before the truce was valid. Forty aircraft of Gruppe L-30789 at Grove, near Aalborg in Denmark had been filled with fuel and were lined up for patrol missions — the wing was a night attack unit engaged against British naval minelayers; but throughout the early hours of this night, instead of the usual pursuit of British shipping, the crews were in a totally confused state; they knew what was happening but were determined not to surrender their machines to the Danish Resistance. 'The Danes were cowards' according to the Ju-88 pilot, Oberfeldwebel Herbert Giesecke. They considered amongst themselves the various options of flying out to neutral countries as proposed by their CO, or of even going to Prague and Bohemia to fight the Russians. Time was running out for Giesecke and his crew, but by 0515 hours they had made their decision — they bade sad farewell to the others, some had already taken off for unknown destinations; the Oberfeldwebel gave the two 1700 hp. Jumo radials full throttle and the Ju-88 raced into the dawn — destination neutral Ireland. The flight was relatively uneventful — gun button safetied, fast and very low, and admiring the scenery of the English countryside in the light of the dawn, for the first time. One RAF airfield was lit, and Herbert switched on his lights as they made a low pass; he later attempted a landing at an aerodrome near Liverpool but overshot as he realised his mistake, this time with the gun button pressed.

We gave them breakfast, and then brought them to a guarded barbed wire protected billet, where they remained for a few days before being taken to GHQ for interrogation, High ranking German officers were reported to be fleeing from Europe in the guise of ordinary flight crew, and speculation was rife in England that the

Gormanston 1945. JU-88G with Oberfeldwebel Herbert Giesecke and his crew.   Photo – Colonel E.J. Wills and Military Archives.

Gormanston Ju-88 had on board "Lord Haw Haw" — Joyce, the Irishman who had broadcast propaganda for Germany; even Commander Locker Lampson, Conservative MP for Handsworth, put down a question in the house for the Prime Minister, Mr Churchill, as to whether 'the German aircraft that recently landed in Eire, contained Hitler or other German renegades?' Our sergeant major and his two crewmen proved to be genuine; they were subsequently interned in the Curragh, the huge military complex situated in the plains of County Kildare.

During their stay at Gormanston, we got to know them well, and Herbert Gieseke the pilot, evidenced the tragedy, the futility and the suffering that is total war. Married to a South African girl — he had been living there before the conflict; his brother-in-law was a major in the South African Airforce. Being a Berliner by birth, he returned to Germany in 1939 and joined the Luftwaffe, but he was shot down behind the Russian lines in the Crimea, and with two companions, survived on a diet of berries and herbs for six weeks before reaching German controlled territory — by that time he had developed diabetes. Invalided out of the airforce he went back to Berlin and practised as an architect — understandably there was little business, and when the Luftwaffe ran short of experienced pilots, they were pleased to have him back. A telegram was sent to him from Gormanston to Queenie, his wife, telling her of his safety; and he told me that he had never seen his baby girl — she arrived some time after he had sailed for the wars.

When they were at Gormanston, I never quite found out what they thought we had in store for them; they requested permission to run up the engines of the Junkers each morning — a request we found totally in character with good airmanship, but whilst we allowed them to run the engines, we had taken the precaution of pointedly draining off most of the fuel in their presence, and removing the armament. The engines had a most unusual sound as they raced them to their peak: they had fuel injection, which was unique at that time. The navigation equipment resembled a ticker tape machine, and it rolled out with monotonous precision each day, the exact latitude and longitude of Gormanston Camp. That JU-88G was almost the epitome of German aircraft design, and was the ultimate in the many variants which had emerged in a production series that had totalled over 15,000. Immense range, fighter handling characteristics, large bomb carrying capacity, and fitted with "Naxos 2" on the top of the fuselage enabling it to home on RAF bomber radars, and "Flensburg" which locked on to enemy anti-radar devices. Sadly we were to see Lt. Commander Brown, a British navy test pilot, fly this magnificent machine away.

One of the crewmen of the "88", Unteroffizier Horst Walter Schmidt subsequently wrote to me from the Curragh:

German Internment Camp,
Curragh.
6 July 1945.

Dear Lt. Quigley,

It's a long time since we left Gormanston and I should say I won't forget the time staying up there. Here all is quite different. Herbert and me are amusing ourselves building lampshades and making at least a couple of bob a week. Bernhard is working on the turf and depends more or less on the weather. We heard that you are interested in buying a flying dress from us. Myself, I am prepared to sell the leather jacket, the leather trousers and the flying boots. I don't know whether £12 will be too much, but the things are in very good condition. You know perhaps somebody else who is interested to buy Herbert's leather trousers, and his silk flying jacket as well as his boots?

In any case I would be very much obliged to hear from you again. Will you give our kindest regards to all of you,
I remain-ever yours,
Horst Schmidt

I bought his flying helmet, but lost contact with him. I found his letter amongst my papers a few years ago, and wrote to the German Red Cross in an endeavour to contact him, but they never replied.

The inside of a German aircraft smelt rather oddly, and it possibly came from the amount of artificial or "ersatz" material that was used in the manufacture of the interior fittings and the instrumentation. Perhaps the smell was just peculiarly German in the way that various odours associate themselves with different races. There was a dump of crashed German aircraft at Baldonnel — mostly Heinkels and Junkers, and the air around was heavy with this unusual chemical smell. The dump contained very many interesting objects of military hardware, including a machine pistol — minus its stock which had been burned in the crash, but which was still in very good condition. We had the ammunition in our stores, and a sergeant friend of mine had just completed a new stock, when orders came to hand up any articles or equipment taken from the dump — I lost my pistol.

Towards the end of the war, as described elsewhere in the book, our neutral skies were filled with the aircraft of the participating nationalities, and many crashed around the countryside. As they did in World War One, the Germans attempted to blow them up or set them on fire, but the British and the Americans generally left their machines intact, and most of them were handed back to the Allies at the border by our crash units.

This handing back of military equipment has its parallel in the fact that, after the disastrous retreat and evacuation at Dunkirk during the early stages of the war, when huge quantities of equipment were left on the beaches, Hitler conveyed a message to De Valera through the German ambassador in Dublin, that, since the Irish army's equipment was similar to the British, the Irish government could have all the hardware captured at Dunkirk, provided they came to collect it!

1654 Hours

At 25,000 feet the third pilot adjusted the engine power to 1.4 engine pressure ratio. The outside air temperature was -30 degrees Centigrade and the speed 366 knots; the rate of climb was now 700 feet per minute.

Captain called Shannon with the estimated time of arrival at 54 North and 15 West. He gave a time of 1711 hours as the automatic inertial navigation computer read 17 minutes to the next position.

An Aer Lingus BAC 1-11 is asked to change to Shannon High Level Approach. I recognised the pilot's voice as Hammy's........

Captain Ivan B. Hammond was affectionately known to all from general manager to hangar sweeper as "Hammy". He was a self made aviator and he had come up through the system the hard way: he earned his money from a mediocre job and then handed it over for flying lessons and aviation night school. He flew with Aer Lingus from 1936, and unlike some pilots from those years, Ivan progressed with the newly developing art of blind flying and all that went with it in cockpit instrumentation and radio aid expertise.

He had evolved his flying style in his own way, and if his techniques were different from others, I can never remember him making a bad landing. I sat in the co-pilot's seat of a DC-3 and watched him in strange places seek out radio bearings like a terrier searching for a bone; once he locked on to them he held — whatever the weather. With the wipers pummelling back and forwards across the smeared windows, Ivan would also have his side panel open, peering expectantly into the darkness waiting for the approach lights to come up, as we broke from the low cloud and swept in from the gloom to the landing area.

After the touch down was completed and we bumped across the grass to the apron, I would hear 'OK, you can take her back to Dublin, Sonny.'

1658 Hours.

Alitalia 649 reported squawking A0322 at Flight Level 310. He was estimating Lee at 1706; Cork was his next position.

Shannon replied: 'After Cork clear to proceed direct to 54 degrees North and 15 degrees West.'

A Swissair 747 asked for permission to remain at Flight Level 310 for a further 10 minutes as he was too heavy for 350.

Frank, the co-pilot undid his safety harness and said to the captain: 'OK Skipper if I go aft and siphon the python?'

He is a great man for dry jokes; he established his reputation many years ago when he asked a multi-chinned company official if he had to use a book marker when he was having his breakfast.

As distinct from my grandfather, there were two Uncle Franks in my family: one was a traveller with the woollen mills, and he was without the slightest shadow of a doubt, the finest story teller in the west of Ireland; the other was a fireman on the airport fire tender, and although I had not spoken to him for years before the incident, I welcomed his anxious face peering in at me from the side window of a wounded DC-3, a long time ago.

This flight was taking off for Paris, and was but a short distance down the runway, when the co-pilot mistook something that I had said to be a command to retract the undercarriage — he pulled the lever. Such an accidental selection could not occur in a modern aeroplane, because an interference mechanism, operated by switches that sense the weight at the trucks, physically prevents a premature retraction whilst the machine is on the ground. The gear came up, unexpectedly to me, and the DC-3 sagged slowly to its knees and graunched to a halt along the concrete. The propellers bit into the runway and bent backwards; there was no fire and little damage except to the props themselves, nobody had panicked and there were no injuries — but there was my humiliation and Uncle Frank's helmeted face anxiously peering in at me through the windscreen.

The older Uncle Frank had very expressive hands, and a ritual was always involved in the way in which he lit a cigarette and removed it from his mouth. Very positively up and back went the head, in went the cigarette and so it was lit. The removal required, first of all, the full distension of the fingers of the right hand before they ever reached the face, then with slow ceremony the palm went flat on the side of the cheek, and the fingers squeezed slowly together with equal panache to gather the fag — now was the danger time, that's if you didn't know Uncle Frank. He carefully transferred the cigarette to his left hand, and the palm of the right smote you with some force on the chest — now you were off on the story.

1700 Hours.

'Shannon, Saturn 955 — Flight Level 370, estimating Cork at 1702 hours.'

'Saturn 955, expect Flight Level 410, squawk A0331.'

'Alitalia 640 requesting High Frequencies in use?'

'Alitalia 640 — you are on the wrong frequency, call Shanwick on 127.9.'

'Saturn 955, this is Shannon, I am not receiving your transponder, squawk now on A0367'........

I flew Hawker Hind 67 for the first time in May 1941. The Hind had been intended for two roles: a trainer and a medium day bomber; it had outlived its usefulness as a bomber, but it was an excellent trainer and was engined with a powerful Rolls Royce Kestrel. The aeroplane was one of a long line of Hawker biplanes that culminated in that famous monoplane fighter of Battle of Britain drama, the Hurricane.

The wings and body of the Hind were constructed with formers of tubular metal, upon which linen fabric was stretched tightly, stitched in position, and then sprayed with special cellulose dope; both the wings and the tailplane were braced with strong wire and stays. There was a rear cockpit from which an observer could fire a Lewis machine gun.

Fabric stretched upon metal was quite a common method of saving weight in early British warplanes even in World War Two. An important twin engined bomber that was very different to shoot down was the Wellington — it had stretched fabric on a special and unique geodetic aluminium alloy frame. Nevertheless this did not prevent American service pilots from calling it "the cloth bomber."

Despite the deficiencies of the Hawker Hind, the Air Corps used it for dive bombing exercises with small smoke bombs suspended from racks beneath each wing. It was impossible to manoeuvre the machine into anything resembling a steep diving angle, but yet the engine went into a diabolical sounding whine, the slipstream almost tore the goggles from the face, and the pilot was left wondering when the fabric was going to shred from the wings or their very structure collapse from the strain of the attack.

In the terrifying dive you glued your eyes to the long tubular Aldis sight, and it was easy to imagine that the tar barrel on the water below was terrified too, because it kept weaving back and forward across the sight glass. Your right hand was tugging and yanking an ancient lever, which through a system of gates, like an old gear shift, eventually conveyed its movement to the bomb release mechanism under the wing. The target was safe from me because most of the bombs fell hundreds of yards away, and the last one tumbled down near the observation post as I flew over it for the subsequent landing.

1703 Hours.

Captain picks up the microphone and reports to Shannon: 'Level at 310, speed Mach .84.'

Control replied: 'Roger, call again at 15 West.'

'Shannon, this is Air Corps helicopter 42 reporting over Cashel'........

The military manoeuvres of 1942 ranged over the mountains around the Suir and the Blackwater rivers, and our army co-operation squadron operated from a landing strip near Cashel. I flew a Lysander: a high wing monoplane specifically designed for reconnaissance and army work. The flight commander lost no time in familiarising us with the area, and in the early dawn the flight went out in formation; we skirted the edge of the Galtees and swept down the Blackwater between Fermoy and Lismore.

The valley was still in slumber, and only a random spiral of smoke identified the presence of a unit not yet identifiable as friend or foe. The morning sun lay low on the horizon, and beamed its slanting rays into the glen, the shafts of light were etched with blue as they filtered down into the misty dampness of the rivers environment. Heather patches, glistening rocky outcrops, vivid splashes of yellow furze, stunted trees, and all the glorious tinting of changing greens slipped by the large cockpit windows as we banked over the mountains away to the south, and went out low over the water at Ballycotton. The winding coast fell rapidly away behind us, and I knew that my rear gunner was contemplating the receding shores of his beloved County Cork.

We flew over the sea at 300 feet and the flight commander signalled to open out. My wing mate on the other side came into view and we exchanged greetings, his black identification number glistened in the sun behind the orange and green roundel near the tail. We were all bobbing up and down in the warm air, and the propeller discs were changing and weaving as their spinning blades tossed the sunlight into the circular patterns.

Another signal came from the lead aircraft, and I pushed the throttle up to come in tight on the turn and, as the other two tilted below, we turned around and went back to the coast. This time we came in high, climbing up through cotton cloud puffs only to file into line astern as we came diving down on a mountain road. We had caught an enemy column on the move: troop filled lorries, Bren gun carriers and armoured cars deployed in every direction, and before all that chaos had sorted itself all out we hugged the contours of the

Comaragh mountains to finally bump safely across the rough grass surface of our landing field near the foot of Slievenamon.

1704 Hours.

'Swissair 168 — over Cork at Flight Level 310, can now accept Flight Level 350.'

'Swissair 168 — report leaving 310. Be advised Swissair 168 — aircraft reported light to moderate turbulence on your track to 15 West at 350.'

1706 Hours.

TWA Reports light chop — light turbulence at 350.

1708 Hours.

'Shannon — this is Air France 017 at Flight Level 310, estimating Cork at 1724.'

'Air France 017, squawk A0336 and report Cork. Clear 340 on Delta track.'

The co-pilot had slid the green glare shield across the windscreen to protect his eyes against the sun, and the shiny surface of the perspex mirrored my face in an odd far away reflection. I was a boy once again, sitting on a half cut turf bank on a summer's day and gazing down into the still waters of a bog pool; I bobbed my head around and a small face moved amongst the reflection of little puffy clouds and a bright blue sky. Now and then the image was rippled by a water beetle zig zagging across the blue panorama; it disappeared among the reeds and then scurried out again from a different direction, and I wondered if it was the same insect. I threw in little pieces of turf, and the blue sky with the small face and the white clouds see-sawed up and down, until all was still once more and other water beetles appeared and scuttled about like their companion.

My chum called me, but I snuggled further down into the heather and lay still and listened to the bees. 'Come on,' he shouted, 'the hay float is waiting for us, and we have to bring the can of tea and sandwiches down to the men in the meadow.'

When we got there Willie Kennedy ga 'e us a puff from his clay pipe.

1711 Hours.

Co-pilot reports: 'Shamrock 109 by 15 West at Flight Level 310 and estimating 55 North and 20 West at 1738.'

Shannon told him to change to Shanwick on 127.9 and request his High Frequency assignment.

The third pilot logged the fuel readings and made an adjustment to the engine power.

1713 Hours.

Captain dials PA-PA on the cabin public address system and then speaks to the passengers. As he does so the co-pilot starts singing a bawdy ballad; captain digs him across the cockpit with his elbow and continues talking into the telephone.

1717 Hours.

Crew saw a contrail up ahead: it was from another aeroplane and its blip was painting on their radar screen at a distance of 30 miles. Soon the contrail disappeared, but a little glistening silver dot remained in the clear blue sky.

1720 Hours.

Hostess comes into the cockpit and reports that it is too warm in Zone 2. She asks the third pilot for a cigarette and then says that a passenger, who insists that he has permission to visit the cockpit, is making a bloody nuisance of himself since they left Shannon. Captain says: 'Keep the nut in the cabin.'

'I like your new uniform, Maura', remarked the captain. 'Bloody gorgeous', said Frank, 'you were like a crowd of green fairies in the tights'........

The first handmade suit that I ever wore was in 1940, and it was the uniform of an officer in the army. It was tailored in Dublin by an old firm of military outfitters, who for many years had catered for the needs of the British garrisons in Ireland. It seemed strange though that at that time, in 1940, some of their uniforms still on the stocks were of the formal type, with scarlets and blues and embroidered gold epaulettes; they were obviously intended for peace time functions.

The elderly cutter had this in mind as he measured me for a pair of Bedford cord breeches — these were worn for ceremonial purposes. He recalled, that just as some of the soldiers in the early stages of the Boer war were easy targets in their red tunics, young medicals from Dublin were commissioned in World War One, and sent to Flanders in light coloured breeches 'They were picked off' said the cutter 'by German soldiers wearing glasses.' He had made the breeches, but some of the young officers were dead in France before they could pay the tailor.

1741 Hours.

Position 55 North and 20 West — three minutes late; speed is 404 knots, windspeed reads 100 knots from a direction of 245 degrees true.

Third pilot again jots down instrument readings and notes the position of the power levers.

More tea arrives in the cockpit.

24

1750 Hours.

Co-pilot listens to Canadian weather broadcasts, and writes down the forecasts and the actuals for Gander, Goose and Montreal.

'Did you hear that, Skipper?' — Frank removed his earphones and continued: 'Temperature at Montreal is 33, and snowing heavily. Gander has ice patches on the runways with braking action reported as fair. That's a bit early for that sort of jazz don't you think?'........

Many of the winters at Foxford used to bring a heavy frost, and the flooded fields above the town provided an admirable skating rink. There were few sets of skates, so most people made their fun by resorting to the local method of sliding along the ice. It was essential to wear a pair of heavy boots with soles well studded with flat headed cobbler's nails. A brush handle, spiked at the end with a long nail, and stroked like a canoe paddle, propelled the wielder along the ice at a modest speed.

1810 Hours.

'This is New York with terminal forecasts for period ending 0200 hours.' Frank logged it down.

1827 Hours.

Position 55 North and 30 West passed to Gander radio.

Hostess with the shapely legs brings in four cups of clear soup.

Neat cardboard folder, which the third pilot had prepared for the crew to monitor fuel burn-off, slips off pedestal onto cockpit floor; captain picks it up and only now sees reverse side which is impeccably printed:

"Dalton's Compleat Thirde Pilote — guide to Apollo 109 fuel conservations in the Mach .84 mode, with all four burning — after burn shut off."

1855 Hours.

Cabin supervisor takes crew order for meals. Captain and co-pilot order different food to guard against possible stomach upsets.

The captain told the co-pilot that when they returned on the weekend, he was going down to Leenane in County Galway for a week's sea fishing in Killary.

Uncle Frank told me that when he was nineteen years old, he sat on an upturned porter barrel in a pub beside Killary, and drank pints with a sailor of the mighty British Atlantic fleet. The battleship was anchored a few hundred yards away in the inlet, because Killary is one of the finest deep water anchorages in Western Europe.

1956 Hours.

Position 50 West. In touch with Gander on Very High Frequency.

'Gander clears the Shamrock 109 to the Kennedy airport on North American route 57; Flight Level 350 not available — climb to and maintain 330, squawk A2100 on transponder and ident.'

The frequency was set up on the transponder and the little black button pressed. This momentarily duplicated the strobe on the Canadian radar screen and positively identified Shamrock 109. 2001 Hours.

Air France reports turbulence........

Msr. Francois Storez was the Aer Lingus representative in Paris, and he was located at the Le Bourget airport; tall, goodlooking, balding and excitable — the excitable piece of his Gallic character being really a "put on" for his audience. Storez was not only beloved by all of the Aer Lingus crews, but by all of Ireland as well, because to them he was "Mister France." Any Irish person journeying through the Continent, and not necessarily by air, who encountered difficulty got in touch with Francois.

In 1958 I was sent to Lourdes to confer with the French civil and military aviation authorities in the preparation of procedures and facilities at the Tarbes airport, which the Irish airline had brought into prominence by the operation of its many pilgrim flights. Storez accompanied me as an aide.

He was the product of an old French military family, and his grandfather had been an instructor in the St. Cyr Military Academy with Marshal Petain. He had the education and the ability to become a cadet in the Armée de l'Air, but those sinister influences of pre-war France, which had destroyed her military potential: the masonic lodges, corrupt politicians and incompetent senior officers, prevented him from securing a cadetship. He enlisted in the French Air Force as a private, and by the time the war arrived he was a sergeant.

For six months after the fall of Poland, the armies on the Western Front remained motionless, the "Sitzkrieg" or "Phoney War" as it was called, was the calm before the storm. 'Every cloud that passed over the moon,' recalled Storez, 'was a German parachutist or a fifth columnist,' and the French military had to react accordingly. 'I had command of a jeep' said Francois, but our rifles were so big, early World War One vintage, that they had to be strapped on the back of the vehicle, and the ammunition was wrapped in greasproof paper, carrying instructions to the effect that it was not to be used except by the orders of an officer of the rank of captain or above.'

'Imagine the scene,' said he, as he manhandled a Lourdes bar stool to represent his jeep, and manoeuvred me in front of the "jeep" to represent the parachutist.

'STOP!' said Storez to the parachutist, 'Please to do nuzzing 'till I get my riefal from ze back of ze jeep!' By now all of the bar were laughing, as he went through the motions of untying the cumbersome weapon from the back of the "jeep." Now moving in front of the bar stool in a very brusque, confident military fashion and with his rifle at the ready he challenged, as he did on all those moonlit French nights years before, 'Halte — put up ze hands!'

As his unit vacated its base before the advancing Germans, vast stocks of petrol remained behind, and Francois, of his own accord, returned with his patrol to destroy the fuel dump. Nearby was a hangar, containing tonnes of propaganda leaflets which the Armée de l'Air had intended to drop on the Germans, the leaflets read: SURRENDER BEFORE THE MIGHT OF THE ALLIED ARMIES........

'I only had time to get the fuel dump' said Storez, 'but how ze Boche must haf laughed.'........

2017 Hours.

Flight conditions very smooth at 33,000 feet. Engine fuel consumption was now $10\frac{1}{4}$ tonnes per hour.

2025 Hours.

Captain had his meal. The food was tastefully arranged on a small tray, which he had placed on his lap. He had pushed his seat back from the controls.

Cabin supervisor took the technical log and sat in the spare cockpit seat. She wrote in her snags, and as she went along she discussed them with the third pilot; when they had finished with the snags he sipped one of the cups of coffee which she had brought into the cockpit, and he spoke to her about her recent holiday in the Caribbean........

The 'Blue Danube' sounded delightful as the music swelled and ebbed and paused, and then rushed on passionately as Strauss had intended; every instrument gave of its sound in turn when the rest of the orchestra faded, and then the individuality of the violin, piano or cello and the brass became predominant. The melody hung magically in the tropical air, and only the officers of the regiment and the rustle of the dancers were missing.

The waltz tempo increased to its climax, and quite abruptly, with no lazy notes or late finishers, the music stopped. There was no regiment, nor would there ever be one; there was no conductor either, and no sheet music to bedeck dimly lit stands; we were 4000 miles from Vienna, the musicians were West Indians, and all the instruments were steel drums.

This unusual method of making music originated in Trinidad during World War Two. There the military had discarded the many metal barrels in which they had stored their fuel and oil supplies; the enterprising locals made them into musical drums — steel drums; hence the name — steel band.

2027 Hours.

'Gander Control now clears Shamrock 109 to climb to and maintain Flight Level 350. Cleared Inertial Navigation direct to Kennebunk; in ten minutes change to Moncton Control.'

Crew inserted the direct route to Kennebunk in the navigation computers.

Co-pilot disengaged the height lock and dialled in 35,000 feet on the altitude select, and at the same time he moved the pitch control to start the aeroplane in the climb; the third pilot had leaned forward to adjust the throttles to give climb power, and he said to me, 'what ever happened that strange flight of the Walrus from Rineanna during the war?........

On the morning of Friday, 9 Jan. 1942, a conference was being held at the Rineanna headquarters of the Reconnaissance and Medium Bombing Squadron. The meeting had been called by the CO of the 7th. Brigade, who was anxious to discuss the results of the area night attack exercises, carried out the previous evening. The discussion was in full swing when, at 1200 hrs the throaty roar of a Bristol Pegasus engine filled the room — the roar came from Walrus 18, an amphibious biplane of the Coastal Patrol Squadron. The Pegasus had no exhaust manifold, but each cylinder discharged its gases individually and noisily, the flame output being particularly spectacular at night; fortunately the engine was a "pusher," installed behind the wings with the propeller facing towards the tail; a slow cumbersome biplane, but it had a very useful patrol range of some 600 miles. When that sound hit the conference, the assembled officers were not to know that a young officer, dissatisfied with the inactivity of the neutral state, was on his way, with a crew of three to join in the wars.

The pilot had apparently ordered a ground crew to ready the machine for flight, and in the normal sequence of events he would have run the engine up, but before the NCO in charge realized what was happening, the Walrus went to full throttle and was gone. The night attack conference broke up in disorder: Baldonnel was alerted and a flight of Lysanders was placed on standby. Meanwhile, at Helvic Head in Waterford at 1232 hrs, the observer reported to Command HQRS, that, 'A biplane, altitude 6000 feet, was moving south in good visibility.' That was Walrus 18, tranquilly flying south to join the wars, and at 1630 hrs. it landed at the RAF aerodrome of St. Eval in Cornwall. The crew were automatically interned and the aircraft impounded, but they were, almost immediately returned to Ireland.

28

The distance from Rineanna on the Shannon to St. Eval in Cornwall is 200 miles, and with the Walrus cruising speed of 100 mph this would entail a normal flight time of just over 2 hours — yet the machine was airborne for 4½ hours. This gave rise to the speculation that the pilot's intention was to land in occupied France and that, perhaps, navigational difficulties forced him to drift over to the sanctuary of the Welsh coastline and the eventual landing in Cornwall.

The Irish government was embarrassed over the affair — the routine charge of "desertion" was preferred against the crew, and the young officer was found guilty of: "The offence of desertion, conduct to the prejudice of good order and military discipline, absence without leave and losing by neglect arms and ammunition," — his revolver and some rounds of ammunition. He was dismissed the Forces and sentenced to 18 months imprisonment, but was released after 6 months by order of the Minister of Justice.

Two Air Corps pilots and an airman were sent to Cornwall to retrieve the Walrus and its equipment, and to fly it back to Baldonnel. To cater for expenses which would be incurred, the adjutant at Air Corps HQRS. had authorized an advance payment for each officer of £7, and £4 for the soldier. In the event, the British had booked the party into the Russel Hotel in London, and a similar high quality establishment in Cornwall. The RAF liaison officer, Pilot Officer Cooper-Driver was most charming and helpful, and chaperoned the party via Paddington station all the way down to New Quay in Cornwall. That other papal pilot (circa 1979) who was the co-pilot on the return flight of the Walrus, left his gas mask in a bedroom of the Hotel Russel; Cooper-Driver undertook to recover it and have it returned, via the 'Eire High Commissioner's Office in London'.

In the matter of Walrus 18, the Department of Defence subsequently billed the state for the fuel and oil involved — 70 gallons of high octane petroleum — £10.10s, and nine shillings and nine pence for three gallons of oil. The second lieutenant who stole the Walrus got into the war eventually, and he served with some distinction in the RAF as a sergeant pilot on fighters in the Mediterranean theatre of operations.

2045 Hours.

Captain finished his meal of chicken; co-pilot now has his steak. Third pilot places his food tray on the shelf in front of his instrument panel.

The sun, which had beamed through the cockpit windows with such unrelenting brilliance, sank down into a crimson bed of clouds, and shrouded the contrail of Lufthansa up ahead with a fiery glow. The four trails of chilled white condensation had poured out from the engines as separate streams to some distance behind the aeroplane, where now they combined to form two; half a mile further back it was one, and all the time the setting sun daubed the twirled rings of the jet efflux with darkening red........

John Cosgrove was a kindly man, and his job was working with the convent horses — two enormous Clydesdales. When the animals required to be shod he brought them to the blacksmith whose premises were near our house. John and the two horses were always followed by a plethora of small boys, and I was usually well to the fore.

The forge was dark and dusty, with a worn stone hearth in which burned the coke and coal. The blacksmith thrust the lengths of shoe iron into the glowing mass and levered on the bellows, until the hissing air angered the coals and changed their colour from dull red to searing white; the metal in turn responded by turning crimson.

The smith took the piece out with a tongs and held it on the anvil, striking it resounding blows with his hammer until the outer crust flaked off with the impact and the iron bent to his skill. Another thrust into the fire, more clanging with the hammer as he punched the nail holes into the hot shoe; now he had the horse's hoof gripped between his legs, prizing off the old shoe and pressing the smouldering surface of the new one into the foot to make a perfect fit. The pungent smell of the scorching filled the forge, and mixed with the steam which clouded up from the trough of cold water, into which he had plunged the newly made horseshoe. The fitting was easy and we were allowed to hold the nails.

The forge, and the ground outside was littered with metalwork of every kind: ploughshares, tractor parts, car springs, wooden wheel spokes and metal rims, donkey carts and sidecars.
2054 Hours.

A flickering anti-collision light just overhead was now all that was luminous of Lufthansa 467.

*   *   *

The Irish jumbo flew on into the west and down over Kennebunk and into the New York control area........
2213 Hours.

'Shamrock 109 descend to Flight Level 200 (20,000 feet), squawk A1500'........

The air traffic controller's voice came through the muted loud speakers: 'Shamrock 109. I have a target: he is in your nine o'clock position and passing one thousand feet below.'

'Positive contact,' replied the captain — 'I have the DC10 in sight'........

Uncle Frank senior was an authority on aircraft identification during World War 2; his descriptions may have been colloquial, but at the same time they were strikingly accurate in depicting what he actually saw. Many a Ju-88 nosing its way around the Irish coast was correctly spotted by Uncle Frank as a 'Single wing German bummer,' and our antiquated biplanes were dubbed by him with equal authority as 'Wan engined double wingers.'

What Uncle Frank did not know, and neither did the Irish authorities until late in the war, that German reconnaissance planes, and their submarines, laid a number of weather reporting stations in the waters around the Irish coast.

The apparatus resembled a torpedo in size and shape, and they floated vertically in permanent positions and lay low in the sea; at set hours a mechanism opened the top of the cylinder and extended sensing probes; a radio transmitter then relayed the local temperature, pressure, humidity, wind direction and speed. When the observations were completed the probes retracted, the cover closed and the stations hugged the surface of the water, unseen by the Irish coast watchers. Their presence was only detected when one broke from its moorings and was washed up on the coast.

Uncle Frank never knew what a radio sounding balloon was, but like many other country people at the time, he saw them and correctly deduced that they were 'some new fangled yoke connected with the war.'

Both the Allies and the Germans used these devices extensively for sampling distant weather conditions; when released they drifted with the wind and relayed information similar to their counter-parts in the sea. Eventually the radio balloon ascended to such a height that it burst in the upper atmosphere, but not before it had transmitted a considerable amount of valuable information from normally inaccessible skies.

Were Uncle Frank alive today, his comments would be equally colourful, and then his outstretched palm would strike you on the chest and he'd say: 'Never mind about all those new fangled yokes wait until I tell you what happened to the German commercial traveller and the donkey on the road to Kenmore........
2230 Hours.

'Shamrock 109 change to New York Approach' — they were now being manoeuvred by radar for landing.
2235 Hours.

Captain ordered: 'Descent Approach Check.'

Crew progressed through the listed items.

Captain called: 'Flaps One.' Co-pilot made the required selection, but after 30 seconds both he and the third pilot said:- "No joy Skipper — something's wrong.'

Captain replied: 'Go ahead with the alternate system.'

Third pilot opened the ABNORMAL AND EMERGENCY checklist and went down through the details with the other pilot. He glanced at the captain and said: OK Skipper-stop worrying about it; you just fly away and leave the problem to us.'

2237 Hours.

'Shamrock 109 — what's your speed. I told you to slow down to 180 knots.'

'Sorry New York — we have a problem with the flaps.'

'OK Shamrock — do you want emergency equipment standing by?'

'Negative New York we will be able to commence normal approach in five minutes.'

'OK Shamrock 109. I'll vector you out of the traffic pattern; turn right to a heading of 340 degrees'........

Ten minutes later the big jet was safely on the ground. It was 5.47 pm. local time.

Chapter Two

ROOTS

Beautiful yet barren west –
rain washed in history.

Percy French, a celebrated Irish entertainer of some years ago, in one of his recitations recalled 'the bog below Belmullet in the County of Mayo.' I grew up near there in the 1930's in the small town of Foxford — it was a haven of prosperity in an otherwise depressed area. The town possessed a woollen mill and two schools, national and convent, and there was even the sophistication of a music academy.

The money from the factory was good, but it was paid by a differential scheme, and in practice this meant that two men could do precisely the same work at a loom, but the man with a wife and family would earn more than the bachelor. At Christmas, those employees in need received blankets or suitlengths of tweed or serge from the mill. It was a system which catered for the needs of this Irish country town, as Ireland and Foxford with her emerged from the twilight of the unwanted imperial marriage, to mother her two children: national freedom and industrial enlightenment.

Foxford had been a designated "black potato" area; the blight came regularly and destroyed the crop. Land was poor and unfruitful, and the only possessions apart from poteen and talk was an abundance of turf and water. However, while nature would not provide comfortable living conditions, the Irish Sisters of Charity could. A decade before the turn of the century they came to this small village and they built their woollen factory on the river bank just below the Moy bridge, there the mill race fed the turbines with a swift flow of energy in bounteous supply. The waters as we knew them then tumbled and cascaded over half mile of rough riverbed below the bridge until, their vigour dissipated, they ran through the eel weirs and spread out to a deep flowing river. It ribboned its way down the Green and around a small island or two and then, as if it had a sense of intelligence in realising its energy was spent, it gathered itself in slow majesty to flow with easy grace and generous sweeps the ten miles to Ballina.

My grandfather, Frank Sherry, was a foreman in Mr. Smith's woollen mill in Tyrone — in a wee town called Caledon, and in 1891 he had been sent by that good man to be the manager of the new mill being built by the sisters in Foxford Co. Mayo. He died in 1949, but we discovered in his desk, notes and writings dating from 1891 until the year of his death. He vividly recalls his arrival in Foxford:

'When I left Tyrone, I left a fertile county where there was poverty enough, but not such poverty as can abound in an infertile region where there is no possible source of income but the unwilling soil. I was young and not interested in economic questions, possibly I did not attach much importance to the fact that the nuns were starting the mills to help the poor. I came to Foxford because Mr. Smith had offered my services, and I came ready to do my best at work which I knew and liked. Only by degrees did I come to see what a task had been undertaken.'

Mr. Smith had evidently appreciated all the circumstances, for from his first letter to Mother Morrogh-Bernard, the superior, when she had written for advice and he had replied, 'Madam — are you aware that you have written to a Protestant and an Orangeman?' he then proceeded to point out the helplessness of the project. But he had somehow been won over to see the poor of Foxford as the nun saw them, and offered all the help in his power. Grandfather continued with his reminiscences:

'I was part of the help, and he brought me to Foxford himself.

34

We arrived at 2am, on a December morning, and I saw the west first as snow spread country, silent and lonely, set among high white hills. I wasted few glances on it for I was weary of the long journey. We went to a hotel and slept late that morning and breakfasted alone on good eggs and bacon.

I never recall that first morning in Foxford without smiling at a cryptic remark of Mr. Smith, a cat, attracted by the savoury odour of the bacon, jumped up on the table in close proximity to our breakfast rasher. "Hold on there, I'm from the north" said Mr Smith, as if a cat on the breakfast table was somewhat of a western custom of which he did not approve. I rather fancy the cat murmured "sorry" as he dropped to the floor at once.

After breakfast we ploughed our way through snow drifts to the mill, where the contractors were at work erecting a shed. To say that we came to the mill is putting it nicely — we really came to a place where, if God willed, there might one day be a mill. At the moment there was snow, slush, mud and one shed, plus the great spirit of a nun, backed by the approval of the Mother General of the order, and a deep unquestioning trust in divine providence. That was December 1891.

Perhaps some of you, reading this imagine that you know what the homes of the poor in the west of Ireland were like. You picture a humble cottage with crumbling walls and broken thatch, not believing perhaps that the mud cabin existed outside of tales of Irish peasant life. Believe me, those hills I view every day were studded with cairns of stones and heaps of earth, chimneyless, windowless, in which six or seven or nine or ten people lived in such poverty as can scarcely be imagined today. They existed in squalor — how could it be otherwise.

When the nuns started a school and few pupils came, some of the sisters went out to see why; the reason was simple — the children were half naked. Clothes had to be found, and then breakfasts, because starving children do not make apt pupils. I saw these things and saw them remedied and knew that the nuns in the humble convent, which was merely two cottages knocked together had very little themselves.

However, I was on loan from Caledon, and my task was merely to help in starting a woollen industry........'

Little had changed in the west of Ireland, since almost one hundred years before my grandfather came to Foxford, and Captain Jean Louis Jobet of the Second Battalion of Grenadiers in Humbert's army wrote:

'One thing that surprised us greatly at this time was the extreme poverty that we encountered everywhere we looked in

Ireland. Never has there been a more wretched country; the men women and children go about half naked, with no shelter other than their poor cramped huts which do little to protect them from the ravages of the weather. And to make matters worse, they share these flimsy dwellings with all their farmyard animals. Their staple diet is made up of potatoes and sour milk, hardly ever any bread and rarely any meat. But the wretchedness of these people is less a result of the barren land, than to the extreme ignorance and great apathy in which they wallow. Their lot would be less hard if they were more industrious, but they are so used to their way of life that they do not even recognise their own wretchedness.

Nearly all of these quasi savages are Catholics, and their tedious fanaticism is really pitiable. When we passed their disgusting cottages — in which we never set foot, except to glance inside, as one would glance at something repulsive — they would throw themselves in front of us, falling at our feet with their faces in the mud and reciting long prayers for our success. All of them, men and women, wore wide filthy scapulars around their necks, as well as chaplets or rosaries.

There is a shocking contrast between this class of Irishmen, which makes the majority of the population, and the easy life style of the gentry, who are nearly all very rich. The latter are surrounded by luxury and abundance, while the former are in thrall to a poverty that I have not even begun to describe. This is the reason for the inevitable hatred of the lower classes for the rich, whom they see as an insult to them in their poverty. So it is no surprise that this great disparity in life styles, exacerbated by religious fanaticism should have produced the rebellion that has troubled Ireland for so long........'

Jobet would not have known that one of the main reasons for housing the animals in the dwellings was to provide heat for the occupants, nor would he have known that their bedding was shared with them also — rushes or straw. He went on with his compatriots and their Irish auxiliaries to drive the British out of Castlebar, but the French were later defeated at Ballinamuck and were repatriated to France with the customary honours of war of that time. The rebel Irish paid the penalty; the events at Castlebar were dubbed: "The Races of Castlebar", to commemorate the speed with which the British evacuated the town; a street there was named "Staball Street," a district near Foxford acquired the unlikely name of "Alleylecampaign," and the unfortunate peasants of County Mayo sank back into the bog and their apathy.

One hundred years after those events my grandfather carried out his assigned task extremely well, and he remained in Foxford.

That mill that he had helped to build, aptly called Providence Woollen Mills, was to prosper and manufacture high quality products for global markets, but World War One in the interval had imposed curtailment of wool supplies, and he went to Dublin in 1916 to arrange, amongst other things, an overdraft with the Bank of Ireland, to enable the factory to lay in stocks. Unwittingly he arrived in the middle of the rebellion:

'We prepared for the Spring Show at Ballsbridge, which was to go ahead in spite of the war. In fact life in Ireland was very little disturbed by the European upheaval. Dublin restaurants served saccharine tablets instead of sugar, and there were certain restrictions as to the amount of food that could be served with afternoon tea!

Butter was half a crown a pound, which was considered an appalling price and was scarce into the bargain. Tea was plentiful, and the system of giving sugar when tea was purchased enabled the people to a get a reasonable quantity of sugar by buying tea beyond their needs. Eggs were dear, but in an agricultural country where other foods were available, the high price of butter and eggs was not altogether a calamity.

In only one particular aspect was Ireland tragically concerned in the first world war. Every day Irishmen marched singing to the North Wall en route for France or far Gallipoli, and every day the newspapers printed long columns of casualties that brought grief to many an Irish home. Yet on the surface, life in Ireland was little disturbed and I set out for Ballsbridge as usual on Easter Sunday in April 1916 — we arranged our goods for the show, and walked out again on Easter Monday expecting a busy week.

As we went, we noticed men at windows in many houses but took no particular notice. When we arrived we were told that there would be no show. Dublin was in insurrection and the men we had idly observed were snipers. We got back to the hotel, the Shelbourne in Stephen's Green without incident. However, insurrection or no we had the responsibility of the valuable goods we had left in Ballsbridge, so on Tuesday we made our way out then once more and packed and covered the exhibits as well as possible.

On emerging we found it impossible to get back the way we had come, because of the intense sniping. Finally we made a long detour by way of Donnybrook and got back to the hotel which faced the enclosed park — St. Stephen's Green, which the insurrectionists had occupied. The moments when we had to walk past the park before we reached the hotel were somewhat nerve racking, for besides the force inside the park railings, there were snipers on the roofs and at any moment a military sortie might be made from a side street.

On Wednesday we again sought Ballsbridge; I don't know if we were beginning to like danger or had to finish packing our goods — anyway we went. I think in fact that we did not realize the danger, for that day we stood on the high parapet outside the Show Grounds and watched British military march into Dublin in battle array; they had landed at Dun Laoghaire — Kingstown as it was then known, and had marched so far unmolested. How foolhardy we were can be judged from the fact that, less than a quarter of a mile from where we stood calmly surveying the scene, a pitched battle took place between snipers in houses and roofs and the military. It has been called the "Battle of Mount Street" and there were many casualties on both sides.

On another detour we bypassed St. Stephen's Green and emerged at the point where Grafton Street joined it; this meant that we had to traverse one side of the Green to reach our hotel. We were getting ready to face the ordeal when a volley of shots came from a nearby club. As we were obviously the target we hastily changed our plans and went down Grafton Street to approach the hotel from a different direction. This street, usually thronged by elegant shoppers and the elite in search of lunch or tea, was empty except for a party of men intent on looting a broken shop window. We carefully ignored them and by devious ways arrived at the side door of our hotel, knocked discreetly and were admitted. We were not able to put our noses outside until Saturday afternoon.

We could have no lights on at night, but from the darkened rooms listened to the sound of shooting and saw reflection of fires, for many buildings were in flames. By day we watched discreetly from the windows and saw many incidents of the fight in Stephen's Green — it is not pleasant to see men shot before your eyes. When we came out from the Shelbourne we could scarcely move a few yards withot a "Halt, Hands Up!" from British military posts, and we were continually searched for firearms.

Altogether it formed rather a memorable visit to Dublin and the last scenes that we saw were not calculated to send us home in a bright mood. Tall, splendid looking men, who would have done credit to any army were being marched in hundreds to prison, after a surrender — they walked between double files of soldiers. Some of them went over the sea to English prisons, some to Irish ones. Perhaps, unknowing, I saw men who were going to die before the firing squad and whose names live on. They impressed me anyhow, and I came back, sadly to Foxford after that exciting week........'

The unhappy history of Ireland was to continue unabated, and the events of 1916 became the prelude to the War of Independence and the final tragedy of all — the Civil War. Foxford and its families did not emerge unscathed from the bitter events of that troubled era. The papers of Frank Sherry reflect and evoke the pathos of those times:

'Easter Week seemed to me as to many others probably to be yet another of the brave but hopeless bids for freedom which have marked the course of Irish history, and it seemed all over and done with when the executions took place and the other men were marched off to British jails or internment camps. It was not the end of course, it was the beginning and we in Foxford did not entirely escape our share of the troubles that followed.

In Parnell's time, Mother Morrogh Bernard had said "I have no politics" and she spoke as head of Providence Mills; that remained true, the mill never allowed a man's or woman's politics to interfere with his or her natural right to work and a fair wage. To enable people to live decently was the reason for founding the mill and she loved and served all the people as a whole. With her clear judgement and her love of justice she could and did understand national feeling and could not be indifferent to the peoples' troubles. The task however was to steer an industrial enterprise through the emotional and economic troubles that mark periods of national unrest and she did it with rare tact, without ever losing her dignity or interfering unnecessarily and yet without compromising with injustice.

I remember the day in her own office that I stood by her side as manager, as a tall suave officer of the English army called on some pertinent business. The superior was old then, the small frame bent and feeble. The officer saw before him an old and probably timid nun, "don't be affraid Mother" he encouraged her as he entered — the direct glance of her blue eyes met his, "young man" she said, "I am afraid of nothing but sin," — the military gentleman was rendered speechless.

As she stood up to attempted intimidation in the Parnell days, so she protested when her workers were ill treated in the Black and Tan times — it meant little to her that whole power of an empire was behind the men who did the wrong.

There had been some trouble in the district, roads had been trenched to hamper the movements of the Crown forces, and bridges broken — one night a party of Black and Tans descended on the place and seized young men and forced them to fill in the trenches; that was the sort of thing that normally occurred in many places and is worthy of no particular note, but worse followed. Three of our mill workers were taken with others to the bridge over the Moy, that same bridge where Mother Morrogh Bernard first paused

39

to dream of an industry in Foxford — the men were stripped and painted orange and green and flung into the river which at that point runs swiftly over a rocky bed — shots were fired down at them, but by scrambling, swimming and hiding they managed to keep alive. One of them hid under the bridge for hours, clinging precariously; in the end they made their way to different houses where they received attention and assistance.

It was all over, but injustice had been done and innocent men had suffered. In spite of all counsels of prudence, the superior protested vigorously; people spoke to her of reprisals of the possible effects of getting into the military's bad books; but she would not be deterred, her people had been illused; in the sequel the men were compensated.

I might not be telling these tales now if a bullet had taken a slightly lower course one early morning. It was during that same Black and Tan period that I awoke that morning and heard the sound of shots; I went to the window of my bedroom which faces the dwelling house attached to the police barracks — I saw at once what was happening. The local IRA were launching an attack on the barracks, and before I could draw my head in, a bullet (probably not intended for me) passed just over my head and lodged in the bedroom wall.

At a later date we had a visit from two Black and Tans who entered my house at 7 am. one day and searched every inch of it and gave particular attention to the papers in my desk: it was quite a formidable task but availed them nothing.

If they hoped for some seditious document or something that would connect us with the IRA activities they were disappointed. I had no politics, I had a job to do and gave all my attention to it because it seemed to me worth doing well. I could see in the lives and homes of the people the reflection of what the coming of Providence Mills meant to the district. Ceaseless work and ceaseless care were necessary to keep that effort going, especially in such unquiet times, and I thought I was not serving my country too badly if I did my ordinary day's work. I could look back to the potatoes and Indian Meal diet of the people in earlier days and contrast it with the still modest but more varied table that wage earning had made possible. I could in quiet moments recapture the smell of the mud cabins where the pig and poultry dwelt with the poor family, not because the poor approved of that arrangement but because they had no better way and were too harassed, sick and sad, to plan better ways. I could remember the manure heaps where the vegetable gardens are now. I had gone into the homes where a sick man or woman lay on hay or even rushes on the floor.......'

Whilst Frank Sherry, that conscientious and hard working Northerner laboured in his small mill with his workers, Ireland's destiny was being decided in a room at 22 Hans Place, London SW. where the Irish delegation to the treaty negotiations met for the last time and agreed to sign the document, after agonising days of indecision and differences. The mill manager's papers reveal the effects that treaty was to have on Ireland:

'I have yet to meet the man or woman who likes to recall the events that followed the signing of the Treaty with England on 6 Dec. 1921. Almost before the ink was dry — to borrow a phrase connected with another Treaty — conflicting opinions were being hotly expressed. The Dublin papers which printed the full text of the treaty were studied intently in our little town, as no doubt they were elsewhere and there were those who said it was a good settlement of a dispute that had gone on for seven hundred years and seemed at times impossible of settlement. It looked to moderate opinion as if our problems had been solved — our representatives had signed certain Articles of Agreement, which if they did not give quite what a number of people wanted, gave much more than the most optimistic Home Ruler had ever hoped for. Many of us thought that peace in our time had come.

There were others who did not see the Articles of Agreement in any such light and there was talk of a certain amount of pressure brought to bear to force the Irish representatives to sign. Dail Eireann, the national parliament, ratified the treaty and the hopes of peaceful times seemed to revive — but it was not to be; we saw the country split into two armed camps. By 1922 civil war had us in its grip and civil war was an ugly thing not merely for the material damage caused, but because it stirs up unholy feelings of hate against our neighbour. There was a certain amount of activity in our district and one night our sleep was broken by the sound of an explosion. In the morning we learned that the railway bridge had been blown up, and for thirty days no letters or parcels reached or left Foxford. To a business concern that state of things can be very serious as our daily mail both ways was heavy, and we could hardly imagine ourselves getting through the day without our usual incoming and outgoing orders, not to mention the necessity to keep in touch with various firms who supplied our wants in raw materials and the many requirements of a flourishing factory.

Yet, we had scarcely any need to consider what we should do; the workers were always and had always been the first consideration; we would not have dreamed of leaving a loom idle while it could be kept moving to maintain a man or woman at work. We did not lose even one hour's time, we worked a full day every day and the products of the looms were piled up upon the shelves. How long they might be there in the disturbed state of things we had no idea, but the mills had been opened to give employment and we went on giving it. We piled up the webs of material and there were moments when I looked at the laden shelves and wondered would we ever empty them, or would the process go on until we reached the roof. Actually, we learned from that period the wisdom of accumulating stocks — when the inevitable influx of orders came after the period of stagnation, we were able to supply the goods immediately and the customers were pleased. From that time forward we always carried big stocks and have found it a sound policy.

We had our drama of the Civil War. One day a young man who was a member of the Free State Army, as the government forces were then called, came into our wareroom. He talked a while to one of our men — they were in a gay mood and after some laughing conversation they both left together. The Republican Forces — the Irregulars, who were in opposition to the Treaty were active in North Mayo; the two men, who left our mills as if they were going on a picnic, went to intercept them with others — only a short time afterwards both were killed and we had two sad funerals to the local cemetery. I have always remembered their laughing departure as if bound for some happy event........'

The member of the "Free State Army" that called to the woollen mills on that fateful morning was Captain Tom Healy, commander of the army garrison then based in the ex-RIC barracks in Foxford, and he had come to the mill to seek the help of his former comrade in arms of the pre-Truce IRA, Volunteer Sean Higgins; they had both been members of the 2nd. Battalion of the North Mayo Brigade; in fact Sean Higgins was one of the six Foxford men who had been dumped into the River Moy by the Black and Tans in May of the previous year.

Captain Healy led his troops out of Foxford in gay spirits to engage the enemy, but fifty three miles away on a lonely winding road at Glenamoy near Bangor Erris, four Irregular snipers had taken up position at Gortleetha Lodge, whilst the main body of the large Flying Column with machine guns placed themselves in an ideal ambush site with a full field of fire, on the mountain overlooking the road. The advance guard of the army troops made their way up towards Gortleetha, and Tom Healy and Sean Higgins fell dead with four other soldiers from the first volley on Saturday 16 September 1922........

The engagement at Glenamoy was a defeat for the newly

formed army of the Irish Free State, and the Republican brigade involved in the action submitted this report to their divisional adjutant:

'On 14th. inst. the major general with a small party ambushed a body of 50 Free State forces between Ballycastle and Belderrig at Glenossra Lodge. The advance guard of Free State troops was captured without a shot and 16 rifles were taken. The main body retreated to Ballina for reinforcements. Arriving on the morning of 16th. Sept. at daylight, they moved towards Gortleetha Lodge assuming the general had an outpost there, whereas his full column were in the vicinity. Four of our snipers were placed in position at Gortleetha Lodge and the main body took up an ambush position on the mountain overloking the road and covering the enemy from whatever position he chose to advance. The advance guard of 16 Free State troops moved down the road towards Gortleetha and were accounted for by the 4 snipers who killed 6 and wounded 3 seriously and 3 or 4 others. The main body of Free State forces advanced across country and engaged our troops. After three and a half hours engagement, they surrendered; 35 prisoners were taken excluding the 6 killed. We captured 80 rifles, approximately 100 bombs and some revolvers. Suffered no casualties.'

When the Treaty was signed on 6 December 1921 and the Irish Free State established, deep divisions of opinion and allegiance arose within the newly formed army commands; the pre Truce IRA became two armies, and as a division or a brigade took its character from the majority of the men in it, the members opposed to them would leave and join a unit where their own views prevailed; three out of the four Western Divisions became anti-Treaty, opposing the forces of the newly established state. The horror had begun, civil war: brother against brother, comrade against comrade in the final convulsion of tortured emotions and passionate ideological beliefs; there were many other military actions in Mayo, where the Free State army were the victors with the casualties on the Republican side. The conflict was to continue until the anti-Treaty forces were defeated in the field, and by 12 May 1923 the cataclysm was over.

It is to the eternal credit of the hundreds and thousands of Irish men and women who were involved on either side in the tumultuous events of those years, that those two fine institutions of the state, born in such distress — the Army and the Garda Siochana, were able to transcend politics and establish themselves as pillars of the Republic of Ireland, serving with total loyalty successive Irish governments of every political hue.

The intensity of the feelings generated by the Civil War, the tragedy and the poignancy is enshrined in a letter written at the time to the Mayo newspaper, "The Western People" by Tom Healy's mother — Granny Healy, that wonderful woman; she was trying to get in touch with the Irregular commandant who set up the ambush:

Angler's Hotel
Pontoon

An open letter to the Western People.

Owing to the Post Office strike and not knowing your present address I am addressing you through the Press. If, in the terrible shock I received on hearing of the death of my son I said unkind things, pray forgive me. Next I thank you or the man instructed by you who shot him and hope God will forgive you as I do. It was hard to lose him so young but God is the best judge and welcome be his holy will. I left a message for you at Glenossra Lodge but don't know if you received it. It was to ask you if you would kindly return to me the rifle, revolver and other things he wore when he was shot — not for use but as a souvenir to be kept here. I am sure you could spare them for me. We went down to the scene of the tragedy to put a cross to mark the spot where he fell, and to take up the green sod soaked with his blood to lay it on his father's grave in Foxford cemetery. To the parents of the other boys who fell there I offer my sympathy — may God give them grace to bear the cross.

Next, I would ask you to instruct your men to respect the people here. They are afraid to open the door at night if any one knocks. It is a shame to see so many young lives taken. You leaders say you love Ireland — why turn it into a shambles. I pity the poor boys who are led away by you — they should be at home helping their parents to build up a comfortable dwelling for them and not to be burning other homes.

I thank all the friends for their kindness to me and mine in need, and I forgive my enemies and those of poor Ireland,

Sarah Healy.

The tragedy of Tom Healy's passing was lessened to some small degree by the discovery, after his death, of one of his light hearted pranks. Some of the citizens of Foxford, fearing their community was not being adequately protected, voiced their concern to the garrison commander; twenty four hours later, the belfry of the Protestant church in the centre of the town was bristling with guns of every calibre, covering all approaches. When they were being removed much later, it was discovered that they were old iron pipes of every conceivable diameter and length.

*　　*　　*

44

Nature, which had been so cruel to its people in providing sustenance, relented in endowing the land around Foxford with a majestic and rugged beauty. Nephin mountain was to the west where it heaved itself almost three thousand feet into the sky; its symmetrical shape stood behind Loughs Conn and Cullin. In the long winters it scowled when misty rain clung to its majestic head, or when the rolling grey clouds before the atlantic winds buffeted its mass, but on a summer's day it stood like an Egyptian pyramid in bright and proud relief, jealously guarding the beauty of its lakes and yawning with soft pleasure in the warmth of the sun.

Pontoon on Lough Cullin was the focal point of nature's artistry and the ANGLER'S HOTEL was its centrepiece. The hotel was set between Granny Healy's garden of rhododendron bushes and shrubs and the rising ground to Coryosla, it faced the rush cluttered bay, already too deeply invaded by sand, the boat slip was over to the left, and the full panorama of the lough was dotted with rocks; those that lay beneath the surface were known in size and depth to every gillie.

They were all fishermen in Foxford, the young and the old, and whilst most of them tried their luck from the picturesque foam flecked on pools or the weirs or the silent water down the Green, the dedicated plied the long waters to the lakes. The men that fished from the falls or the bridge were never to be seen up the town or down the Green; each had a time to fish; some early in the morning before work, others late at night. The professionals used the handmade fly, but the majority picked their bait from the rocks as required or stocked it away the day before in a nail pricked cocoa tin. Many stretches of water were privately owned, and the salmon poached from them were acquired by a variety of methods; simple fishing, or other less orthodox but more rewarding techniques.

As in every rural community the people in Foxford knew everything of each other. News was eagerly received, relished, digested, and finally passed on to the next, suffering little in the telling. Every pattern of behaviour was known and felt, and each daily sight or sound conveyed not only a meaning but a character. Each member of the community had a role to fill, no matter how small: the opening or closing of doors, the clamour of cows coming down the street, the tone of a car horn and the way it was blown, the tremolo whistle, the half known song, the noisy bicycle, the barking dog, the rattling trap, the laughing lilt of a woman's voice, the metallic clank of the pump and every morning, particularly in the vicinity of our house as they made their way to the brook — the loud and very clear quackle of Baby Glover's ducks. All of these noises were part of the life and roles of the people, and an absence or an irregularity within the pattern was an indication of something wrong.

Baby Glover was the daughter of a carpenter, and her brother Victor was the Church of Ireland schoolteacher whose classroom was part of their dwelling. They lived across the street from us and my mother and her sisters had grown up with the Glover girls. Baby never married, but she was an eternal romantic and the finest cook in Ireland; the open hearth fire in her kitchen was always alive with smouldering hand won turf, and their food was cooked upon it in three legged cast iron pots, either suspended over the fire or buried in the embers beneath. Porter cake, two inch glazed apple tarts, turkeys, geese, hams — the crescendo came at Christmas. There was a small Protestant community in the Foxford of those years and their pastor was Canon McQuaide, a tall distinguished looking clergyman who always wore the typical ministerial gaiters; the canon was a saintly man and his charity extended in good measure to his less fortunate Catholic neighbours. The rectory and the gardens were typical of Irish Protestant husbandry, and those gardens contained in serried rows every fruit and vegetable known to man; there was a tennis court, and when we played there, each set was followed by bowls of Mrs. McQuaide's loganberries and raspberries smothered in cream from Victor Glover's dairy.

In 1895, just four years after the mill had opened, changes had come about in Foxford. My grandfather recorded:

'Changes take place without our noticing. A block of houses rising in a familiar street soon makes it difficult to remember what that street previously looked like. So it is that I have to pause and reconstruct mentally the Foxford of early days; the low convent looking out on the fair green, the straggling street of houses that knew neither modern sanitation nor had dreamt of bathrooms, the little wooden chapel, the wooden school, the modest mill buildings.

'I recall well the arrival of the first piano ever seen in the village; it came in 1895 and was a great source of interest. I remember the terrible problem presented by the necessity of hauling a boiler from Castlebar for use in the mill. It was dragged by horses unused to team work and at first it simply seemed immovable, only when Lord Lucan lent us three horses for the job did we make any progress. One of the horses was said to the oldest horse in Ireland at that time; it was reputed to be 39 years of age and they say it slept standing supporting itself against a stone wall. It pulled its weight however when our boiler was on the way!'

The year of 1898 was that of a very bad harvest and he wrote:

'There were other visitors to the mill — Lord and Lady Cadogan came, also Sir Francis Cruise and a young girl whose beauty I have

46

not seen equalled or even approached. She arrived one day on an outside car, not as might have been supposed from her elegant appearance, to see if we had anything alluring for her to purchase, but as a sympathiser with the poor and the downtrodden. It was the year 1898 - once again the crops had failed and many parts of the country were in distress and the poor West most of all. The young girl who came personally to inquire into the troubles of the poor was Maud Gonne. She was the loveliest person I ever saw.

'Things were indeed bad that year and on my Sunday surveys; I saw some pitiable sights. I went into a little house in Quinmore, which with Rininanny was one of the districts worse affected. There was sheer starvation in that home, and in it I saw the most awful sight I ever witnessed - two little girls, aged perhaps six or seven and evidently suffering from acute starvation, were rolling on the floor like dogs and grimacing horribly'. The man who did most at that time to try to alleviate such suffering was Michael Davitt — he died in 1906, and the grandfather attended the funeral:

'That year I attended in Foxford, a historic funeral - that of Michael Davitt. As a leader of the Land League Agitation, he sacrificed himself unselfishly. He had, as a boy, seen his father and mother evicted from their home in Straide, and the bitter memory remained during the years of exile, when his parents were forced to emigrate to Lancashire to make a living. He himself worked, when a mere child, in a Lancashire cotton mill, tending a loom, and in the course of that employment lost an arm through being caught in a machine. He grew to manhood with a vivid memory of the hardships of the poor and set himself to redress the grievances of one sorely tried section of the Irish people, the small farmers from whome he had sprung. His efforts landed him in an English prison cell and he did a long term of penal servitude but his release saw him once more busy. On the site of his home in Straide - he called on men to band themselves together to demand fair rents and security of tenure. It was the beginning of the Land League. That is the story in brief, of the man whose body came to Foxford station in May of 1906. A hearse conveyed the remains by road to Straide; I attended the funeral and saw John Redmond, amongst the many prominent men. But I did not see there the small farmers for whom Davitt and his like had won a succession of Land Bills that gave them security and fair dealing. At least I saw some of them, but not in the cortege - they were lookers-on standing in the ditches........'

Foxford in my own time was a typical Mayo town and turf was still the common fuel, there were brown stains on the gable ends of the houses, stains which grew over the years as the tarry deposits from the turf smoke seeped through the walls and lifted the plaster into round brown moulds. Like every other small boy I knew each stain as I knew the precise number of telephone cables on the poles, and on many a day I watched in fascination from my bedroom window as the water droplets gathered pendulously on the lines near the wire insulators; they grew fat by feeding on their neighbours and then, with pear distended bellies and a tenuous elongated connection to the wire, they slid down the incline from the cup finally losing their grip to tumble and burst on the roadway far below. Those telephone cables went straight up to our unpretentious little post office, here was the other haven of security to the town and the neighbourhood, because dollars arrived from boys in America, and pounds from the men working in England and the migrant potato pickers of Scotland.

Those potato pickers were known as "tatty hokers" and they came mainly from the west of Ireland, and particularly from the island of Achill. Boys and girls and men of all ages traditionally went to Scotland in June for the potato harvest - they returned in dribs and drabs until December; they were following the custom of previous generations of their families until by 1937 it was estimated that 6000 pickers were crossing over to Scotland from the west each year. I went to school with some of those boys and girls and I knew the deprivation of the land and the living from whence they came:

> Barren bogland: watery waste with rampant rock-
> Inheritance of alien curse.
> Cromwell, Clanricarde, countless scion from Ardrahan-
> With privilege and purse.

> Gnarled hands, weathered face,
> Broken knees in potato mire,
> Broken spirit at Scottish ire,
> Broken body in bothy fire.

The houses, or "bothys" in which the workers were accommodated were in many cases no better than animal stalls, and it was in one of those filthy dwellings in Kirkintilloch, Dumbartonshire, that tragedy struck in the early hours of 23 September 1937. A number of young boys, accompanied by their sisters had gone to Scotland for the potato harvest; they were lying asleep on beds of straw upstairs in the bothy, their sisters were downstairs - the building went on fire and ten young Achill men were trapped above and burnt to death.

Frank Sherry's writings refer to the post office of his day, and whilst he was describing it, his thoughts were rambling over new ways and old:

'Man is a vain creature: to each it seems that the universe

48

revolves around him. Each plays his or her little part in the centre of the stage, forgetting that every other player thinks that the limelight is for him. Well, after all life is like that: each man's life is his drama, in which he plays the principal part. It has to be that way, because God gave each of us a soul. I have paused here to wonder is it worth while to set down the thoughts that come to a man when he looks back over the years that are gone.

In recalling memories it is easy to bore people with incessant laments for old times. Yet, I feel that the old times for all their hardships had much good in them, but I am willing to admit that the new times have their compensations. I am glad that the lot of the worker has improved; I am glad that rural housing conditions have got very far away from the mud cabin, but I am not so sure that these things are appreciated - is the worker of to-day much happier with shorter hours and the half holiday? He has, I think, partly forgotten how to be happy.

Here in Foxford we still make our own amusements, we have no cinema, though they are accessible. We have plays and concerts and our own talent furnishes them and that is good for us.

While many small towns are sunk in apathy we are lively. Strangers notice the busy activity of our little Post Office - from its appearance one would imagine that half a dozen letters a day would be its full compliment and that telephone or telegrams were yet unknown. But the little old fashioned shop, with its rustic air, hums with business and the switchboard girl has her work cut out for her. Some day they will build a sedate edifice with 'POST OFFICE' in stucco on the front of it and it will be a pity because the wee shop has a character all of its own. It might almost be a showpiece for tourists - it is exactly what a Hollywood producer might present as a rural post office in Ireland, without even dreaming that it has been true to life. Its activities mirror the bustle and briskness that a thriving industry brings to a neighbourhood.

Any of the towns and villages of Ireland could be made equally brisk by providing local industries, then the countryside would no longer be a place out of which youth is anxious to escape. It would return to something like the old ways, when story telling by the fireside was an art, and the "travellin' man" with his news was made welcome. The stories and the news come over the radio to us nowadays, but I doubt if we enjoy them as much.'

He may have been right in his musings on life in general, but he was wrong about the Post Office. Nowadays it is in a different location, but there's no stucco sign, and were he to walk in there to-day he would notice little change.

On a fair day in Foxford the only area where cow dung did not drop was the footpath near the convent; planks were placed on tar barrels to keep the animals away. Everywhere else from the mill to the top of the town, cattle jammed the street from an early hour, and here or there on the pavement a special calf was displayed in a creel or in a crudely made pen. Sows grunted underfoot and squealed disapproval when potential buyers poked them too enthusiastically; many of those dealers chewed tobacco and intermittently launched large streams of brown spittle towards the pavement - small boys down there amongst the merchandise were often the recipients.

Down near the pump the gathering thinned out to herds of sheep and goats and here the latecomers had a last free space where they could gather momentum before plunging into the brown and white mass to buy and sell. Their cattle ran with them and incredibly found a position where none seemed possible. The ritual of bargaining was carried out to the fullest; hand clasps, spits and swears and walking away in postured refusal only to return and negotiate again, until finally the luck penny was argued out.

In the market square were the "Cheap Jacks" standing by the fall-away sides of their canopied lorries. With all the vigour of Arab traders they sold second hand clothes, pots and pans, delph, statues, lamps and glasses, Japanese vases, holy water fonts, brushes, clocks and chow dog mantlepiece ornaments. It was all there and the sing song voices which accompanied it offered a free set of plates with every purchase over a pound.

There were many pubs in Foxford and with them as many businesses. Shops that had long since ceased to sell liquor in any quantity held onto the licence and kept the permit valid. Some had a grocery on one side with the bar on the other, and the "snug" was warm and inviting, with a big turf fire and bags of meal and sides of bacon surrounding the customers. It was a favourite place too for the publican to store his barrels of stout, to being it "into condition," and many a man, who denied to his wife that he had been in a certain hostelry, was revealed for the liar that he was by the red ring from the Guiness porter barrel imprinted upon the seat of his pants.

In the drapery shops the inevitable mahogany counter was tucked away into a corner at the back. Normal business had ceased in many but the nominality of the license was maintained by a few bottles of whiskey or sherry on the dusty shelves. The most famous of all was an establishment where the enterprising proprietor made it possible to order your coffin over a pint; a sign over the door of the premises read: GROCERY AND BAR. FUNERAL REQUISITES SUPPLIED. This same gentleman owned another shop with again the little bar at the rear; prominently on display on the counter was a basketful of spectacles, and the customers tested them for suitability by viewing different articles positioned on the shelves; others brought a few pairs out into the street to assess them in the sunlight.

The Boy's National School which I attended was built over the grounds of an old graveyard, and it never semed to the masters or the pupils to be even mildly sacrilegious, that every time the dry toilets were cleaned out, up came a coffin lid or some such reminder of eternal destiny. The school was old, and the well trodden floorboards had many knot holes in them, which proved to be marvellous urinary targets for the youthful clientele so strategically placed above them. The headmaster was typical of the school system of that time in Ireland, possessing as he did a marvellous love for his boys and a wonderful talent for imparting knowledge to them. Most of those boys were barefooted, and the meagre fuel allowance to heat the building had to be supplemented by the efforts of the children themselves who, each morning brought in a number of sods of turf. On Monday mornings, the headmaster "feeling the weekend" as they say, would have assigned to the class an awesome copy book exercise — calculated to give him an hour's gentle snoring; his snooze always ended the same way — by a wad of inksoaked blotting paper, dispatched at him with unerring accuracy from the catapult of my chum. The master would spring awake and shout, 'I know it's you Gaughan, you little pigeen!'

Our major brush with the church came about during confirmation rehearsal time; we went to the practice via the corner shop, and although we paid for our farthing biscuits, we liberally helped ourselves for free from the sacks of oats stacked outside the store. The crunching of oats was more than the old canon could endure and he threw us all out. Challenge to ecclesiastical rulings was a rare thing then in rural Ireland, and the holding of dances on Sunday was taboo. The local "ballroom of romance", a tumbledown large galvanised shed near the railway station was owned by a dissenter who defiantly advertised and held a dance on a Sunday night; a fellow dissenter waxed eloquent about the event and stated that he admired,' Burke's stand against Rome!'

That corner shop always had a large portion of dried salted ling, hard as a board, hanging on the door jamb. Although Foxford was only sixteen miles from the sea, hardly any fresh sea fish was ever available, and it was only on Fridays that a horse cart arrived in the town with a box of mackerel or herring for sale, and the usual dilisk or carrageen moss — edible seaweeds. Enniscrone was the nearest sea fishing town, and even there the fishermen had a meagre living and could not sustain themselves by it alone. There was no taste for sea fish in the Ireland of those years; people in Foxford who wanted guaranteed delivery for the Fridays, arranged to have a regular supply from McCabes of Dublin — it came down on the night train, all fresh and nicely packed in a small straw bag.

When the dreaded fungus Phytophthora Infestans blighted the potato crop in 1845 and destroyed the staple food of the country, a French diplomat was in Achill, and he described the pitiable condition of the dead and the dying — close by the sea, a sea that he noted was teeming with shoals of fish, but through either apathy or ignorance the people were unable to catch them. It would seem that even then, the inhabitants of the north western seaboard did not eat fish in any quantity.

"Corner boy" was then a disparaging term, but the "corner boy" was not an offensive person; his most heinous crime was to whistle approvingly after every passing girl. Those "boys", some up to seventy years of age, regardless of the weather, assembled after tea at the two main corners in the centre of the town; one corner was more popular than the other but the groups never mixed and always frequented their own side. There was no social stigma attached to being a "corner boy", and most families from time to time had members; a subtle distinction existed between the "regulars" and those who were not permanent attenders, and whose families referred to their presence there as "going up to the corner". The corner was a talk spot — gossip and comment and happenings in the town, and observations on the passersby; it was always necessary to greet the group, particularly from a motor car, because the absence of a courtesy was an indication that the individual would be "getting too big for himself". Not all of the time was spent in conversation, there were often long periods of silence, and on Sunday mornings, with everybody in their best clothes, a game of "pitch and toss" would take place, the coins being thrown into the air from the back of a pocket comb with suitable accompanying invocations from the tosser, which to the ears and eyes of an innocent observer might well be mistaken for an unusual religious practice.

In 1933 I went to a secondary school at the Cistercian Abbey, Roscrea. The country around the monastery was fertile, and it abounded in the past with the estates of the landowners who had acquired plantations during the Elizabethan and Cromwellian rule. Many of our school outings took us to those places; the desmesnes we visited were full of stories, hushed whispers of Cromwell's soldiers and Irish gentry; but they were peopled now by elderly spinsters, retired colonels, eccentrics, and all the left overs of a by-gone age. The mansions had slipped into decay, the ornamental pools were choked with weed, and the large conservatories in need of glass and paint — the once shrub-lined paths had fused quietly back into nature and over it all lay the eerie uncanny twilight air,

52

damp in the winter gloom, and full of ghostly tales of happenings long ago.

The Cistercian monk is a contemplative, but manual labour is part of his daily routine. The abbot would lead the priests and brothers into the fields to dig and weed, no doubt an excellent physical exercise, but it humbled the man and made all equal. The work at the monastery centered on farming, and with it the diverse and allied trades which went to make the community self sufficient; the abbey was the "big house", and all that took place within its walls or on its farmland became guidance or gossip for the local people.

The food for the college was provided by the abbey, and the huge brown and white loaves from the bakery had a fresh, crusty and wholesome flavour, mouth watering even in memory. 'Brown bread! Brown bread!' was the rallying call of the rugby team.

This monastic and scholastic centre was rich in the talent and personalities of its lay and clerical staff, and the most endearing and outstanding character was the president, Father Ailbe Sadlier; but nobody ever called him that. I will always remember "The Boss" as an oil painting: the Cistercian habit fitted him well — he was tall and of moderate build but protruding slightly at the stomach; his sparse and tonsured hair was pure white. He presided firmly but benevolently over his large family of boys; he supervised them at prayer and in the refectory, corresponded with their parents, worried when they were ill, and hooshed them on with a belt of a hurley on the backside when they slowed down going through a doorway. He had a soft place in his heart for the "hard man" — the boy who was always to the fore in devilment or pranks, or the boy who lagged in class.

In keeping with such a character there were so many memorable poses; arms akimbo, feet apart, and chin pushed out, he would fumble for words which would not come because of mounting rage at some rowdy display. Stern faced, with his head bent in confessional concentration, he listened to a small boy ask for an early sleep which would excuse him evening study. Again the hands were on his hips and the feet wide spread, but this time his head was cast upwards and his teeth working as his interest was captivated by a companion's talk. Or hurley in hand at the sideline, his frame fully stretched and arching forward, he would place his hand over his eyes, and pucker his brow in many ridges as he peered intently towards the scrum. I have quite forgotten which pose he held when I told him at the age of eleven that I wanted to be a Canadian mounted policeman.

We were at Roscrea for six years, where we struggled for places on the rugby and hurling teams, sang in the operettas, suffered the bullies and suddenly found ourselves seniors. Before we had realized what happened we were young men sitting our final exams. Secondary school ended for me in June 1939, and by the time of our second college reunion in the autumn, of 1940, some of rny classmates had already died in the war. The sweet days of youth were nearly past and we left Roscrea forever to make our way through a world in turmoil. The choice of a career led me to an engineering school in a Dublin university, but by the time of my first examination in June of 1940, I was in the Irish army.

According to grandfather's notes that war was also starting to effect his woollen mill:

'Our biggest customer during the first year of the Emergency was the Controller of Army Stores. It was simple to deal with his case: he wanted our total output and he got it. History records that an Irish brigade defeated a surprise attack clad only in their nightshirts but thanks to the Irish mills, there was no danger of our army being called on to prove they could do so again. One item in particular that we were called upon to supply about which we feel entitled to boast a bit was the bunting in green, white and orange to make flags. This had never been made in the country before and we feel proud that we were able to make the national flag in the height of the Emergency from Irish wool. Strangely enough we had no trouble in dyeing the correct shade or orange, although we made several attempts before we got a satisfactory green.'

He went on to describe the difficulties which both his mill and all the other Irish woollen mills experienced during the war; shortages of wool, dyes and oils so necessary in the processing. He was a religious man and he placed his trust in the Lord adding a little prayer of his own: 'O Lord, don't send anything my way this day that you and I can't handle — together.'

Chapter
Three

IRELAND AND AVIATION HISTORY

Ireland, land of dreams
But – aviation has not passed you by,
Its wispy trails and wondrous shapes
Daily grace your velvet sky.

The powerful but soft rhythmic whine of the four large engines of an Irish jumbo jet echo down into those places from where many of the brave aeronauts of long ago made their first flights in wicker baskets and cloth balloons. The big metal Boeing, when fully laden, will weigh 710,000 pounds, and all its controls are hydraulically powered by eight separate pumps serving four independent systems. The electronics are routed through many computers, and its two automatic pilots are capable of making a completely blind landing. The air conditioning would rival that of any modern hotel, and emergency equipment is comprehensive: fire protection devices and circuits are distributed throughout the cockpit, the cabin and the engines. The birdproof windows are extremely thick and are heated electrically, demisted by hot air, and provided with washers and rain repellant sprays. The cabin of a jumbo carries over 400 passengers relaxing in armchair comfort in front of four movie screens, with eight track stereo piped to each seat, and as the man said, 'it was the only bloody aeroplane that he could stand up in without bumping his head.' But then, of course, he had never flown in the gondola of Mr. Rosseau's balloon, and listened to the drummer boy beat the grenadier's march........

In his DUBLIN JOURNAL of April 1784, Thomas Todd Faulkner printed an account of a spectacular event in Navan, Co. Meath, which took place on the 15th. of that month. It was on that day, so long ago that Ireland entered the air age. The extract from the paper read as follows:

'Last Thursday, the long expected air balloon was liberated in this town, in the presence of the greatest concourse of people ever assembled here, among whom were many of the first fashion. At half past two, Mr. Rosseau and a drummer boy about ten years old placed themselves in the gallery, which was composed of oziers, and fixed to a net that covered the balloon, and on cutting the cord it rose perpendicular amidst a profound silence, occasioned by the astonishment at so uncommon a phenomenon. After thirty nine minutes progress it became totally invisible but we could distinctly hear the drum beat the grenadier's march for fifteen minutes after. At four o'clock it grounded in a field at Rathoath. Mr. Rosseau and the drummer boy arrived here at six o'clock that evening perfectly well except the drummer, who received a small contusion on his head, through his eagerness in leaping from the gallery. At night a splendid ball was given by the burgesses and freemen of the town, where Mr. Rosseau received the congratulations of a numerous and briliant company.'

An advertisement in the previous edition of that same news paper promised the patrons of the Theatre Royal in Dublin's Smock Alley, 'A Real Air Balloon — invented by the immortal Msr. de Mongolfier, made by Mr. Warrington, and to be filled by Mr. Riddick, under whose direction it will be floated.' It was 'to bear Harlequin on the stage, and take him out of view of the audience.'

Dramatic occurrences were also being reported from Cork during that same month:

'Last Saturday evening at six o'clock, the air balloon which was launched from a field near Mardyke at four the same evening, was seen by two men at Cooper's Hill mountain, near Macromp, distance about eight miles. When first they saw it their amazement was very great; one thought it was the devil appearing in the clouds, taking the tub for the infernal's tail; they made to pursue it but to little purpose, as it fell down between two rocks. Then they brought it home and had a number of villagers to see the wonder, but not having any other light to examine its contents they applied a rush made of bog dale so close that a spark fell on it which discharged the inflammable air with such an explosion as to affright all the spectators, and made them conclude that it really contained the devil. One man was burned in the face in a shocking manner, and a woman slightly.'

Richard Crosbie, a very large man by all accounts, of Crosbie Park, Co. Wicklow, ascended from Ranelagh Gardens by a gas filled balloon on 19 Jan. 1785 and later alighted safely in Clontarf. His ambition was to cross the Irish Sea, and in the summer of that year he made two further unsuccessful attempts, reaching the mid point on his last effort, fortunately to be rescued by a vessel out of Dunlaoghaire. In April 1786 he made a crossing of the river Shannon, near Ennis, in the same balloon. Crosbie was the scion of an Anglo Irish family, whose brother, the liberal Sir Edward Crosbie was hanged at Carlow by the Crown in 1798. Sir Edward's "crime" was the fact that the United Irishmen had assembled before his house on the eve of the rebellion; he was branded by the British as a "leader," courtmartialled and put to death.

Twenty six years were to elapse before another sea crossing was attempted, and then it was an Englishman, James Sadler who soared from the grounds of Belvedere House in Dublin and succeeded in drifting across the Irish Sea; the balloon came down off the coast of North Wales, but Sadler was rescued. In July of 1817, a further attempt was made, but this time by Sadler's son, Windham. He departed from the barrack square at Portobello, and after an uneventful passage landed in a field at Holyhead in Wales.

Ballooning had become a very popular challenge in 18th century Europe and as early as 1786 a technical handbook on the subject extolled its benefits:

'The spirits are raised by the purity of air and rest in a cheerful composure. In an ascent all worries and disturbances disappear as if by magic, due to the change from hot, putrid, and impure, to cool pure air, impregnated with the invigorating aerial acid. 'It seems more than likely, that the euphoric state into which the author — balloonist had transported himself was one of hypoxia — a sickness resulting from a lack of oxygen supply to the body tissues. References in 1800 were nearer to the mark, when they described the condition as "balloon sickness", which, in its milder form would manifest itself in a human being by lack of critical judgement and co-ordination, accompanied by a false sense of well being.

Hypoxia or not the balloonists were still at it in 1817, young Miss Thompson, the first Irish female passenger, went aloft with one of the local gentlemen. By 1844 a Mr. John Hampton was flying his "well known beautiful balloon" ERIN GO BRAGH in Dublin city. The balloon was a monster, having a gas capacity of 26,000 cubic feet, and the local papers waxed eloquent on his ascent from the Rotunda Gardens:

'About half past five o'clock, all the preparations having been completed, the car was attached to the balloon and Mr. Hampton took his seat accompanied by a young lady of pleasing appearance and exceedingly steady nerve, who gave her name as Miss McQuaide of Lurgan Street. A gentleman whose name we do not know also formed one of the party. On the signal being given the band struck up the royal anthem and the balloon ascended in majestic and graceful style amid the plaudits of assembled thousands. Having risen to an unusually great elevation and remained floating over the southern suburbs of the city for more than an hour, a safe and agreeable descent was effected in a field at Kimmage.'

Enthusiasm for the aerostatics varied during the remainder of the century, until in Sept 1889, a Mr. Spencer held his large audience spellbound when he leaped from a balloon, 2,000 feet above Clonturk Park in Drumcondra and floated gracefully down by parachute. Six years later, Professor George Francis Fitzgerald of Trinity College built a glider, and contemporary photographs show him coatless, but wearing his top hat as he ran across College Park in an unsuccessful attempt to get the contraption airborne.

It was not until 15 Feb. 1910 that the next crossing of the Irish Sea was made by a balloon, and it was on that day that Mr. John Dunville, a founder member of the Irish Aero Club, accompanied by a Mr. C.W. Pollock ascended from Dublin in his balloon ST. LOUIS, and five hours later landed safely near Macclesfield in England, having averaged a speed of 34 mph. at an altitude of 10,000 feet.

Harry Ferguson from Belfast, who later became famous as an inventor and innovator in the automotive world, was the first Irishman to design, build and fly his own aeroplane as early as 1909. On 31 December of that year, he took off from Hillsborough Co. Down and flew at a height of ten feet for one hundred yards — no aeroplane had ever flown in Ireland before. On one of his later flights he was accompanied by a Miss Rita Marr of Liverpool who became the first aeroplane passenger in Ireland. Ferguson's monoplane design was influenced by the Frenchman, Antoinette, and had a fuselage of triangular section; the engine was a 35 hp. aircooled JAP — it is still in mint condition in the Irish aviation museum at the Dublin airport. Lilian Bond, a contemporary of Harry's who also hailed from Belfast, was keen on wild bird photography, and the intricate and exquisite movements that she saw through the lens of her camera stimulated an interest in the mechanics of flying. Like Ferguson, she built her own machine and flew it — quite an unusual lady for those days, she manufactured biplane fuselages and sold them through the FLIGHT magazine. In 1912, Mr. Aldritt of Portlaoise constructed a Bleriot type monoplane and installed his own version of a three cylinder engine; unfortunately he died before his aircraft could be flown, but there seems little doubt that it would have been successful.

The first crossing of the Irish Sea by an aeroplane was achieved by a Kilkenny man, Denys Corbett Wilson, who flew a Bleriot monoplane from London to Crane, near Enniscorthy, on 22 April 1912.

The Irish Aero Club had been formed in the premises of the Royal Irish Automobile Club, in Dawson Street in Dublin on 5 November 1909. The annual subscription was set at one guinea and attendants at those early meetings included such well known aviation personalities as John Dunville, J.T.C. Moore-Brabazon, Harry Ferguson, and John Boyd Dunlop inventor of the pneumatic tyre. The club had its first meeting at Leopardstown Racecourse on 29 and 30 August 1910, and it featured Captain Bertram Dickson who gave a demonstration of "circular flying" in his Farman biplane — Armstrong Drexel who demonstrated "high flying" in his Bleriot monoplane, and Cecil Grace flew his Farman biplane.

The next important event to be organised by the club was a Dublin to Belfast and return air race in 1912, and it was scheduled to start from Leopardstown on Saturday 9 September; amongst the fifteen entrants were Lieutenant Porte, Corbett Wilson, Gustave Hamel and Handley Page. The contest turned out to be a dismal failure because of bad weather, and of the few who braved the elements only Astley and Valentine got as far as Newry. These two shared the first prize of £300, Porte received the Shell award of £500 and Desmond Arthur was presented with a special prize of £25; a generous donation of £40 was made to all the contestants to cover their expenses.

At the commencement of the war, the club ceased to function, and it donated the balance of its funds towards Red Cross ambulances. It was to be 1928 before its rebirth.

The years of that first great war of 1914-18, put an end to private flying in Ireland, and very many young Irishmen went to serve with the Royal Flying Corps — the British were not unappreciative, and the following tribute appeared in an aviation journal of that time:

'The first person who ever flew at all in England was an

Irishman — S.F. Cody. The first British subject to fly in this country with the benediction of the Royal Aero Club was also Irish, J.T.C. Moore-Brabazon. The first British service pilot to land in France was Irish — Harvey Kelly, and the first casualty of the RFC was Desmond Arthur from Dublin. The engineer officer who did at least as much as anybody else to build up the Royal Naval Air Service and save the British aircraft industry in 1914-1915 was an Irishman, Gerald Aldwell.'

The attrition of that war was appalling, and particularly so for the fliers of the RFC. In the latter half of 1916, their inexperienced pilots who, because of shortages, had to be posted direct from the flying school to front line squadrons, had a life expectancy of between eleven days and three weeks. When we think of Mr. Spencer and his parachute jump in 1889, and considering that parachutes were issued to the crews of gunnery observation balloons, it is incredible to realize that the British staff believed that, 'Possession of a parachute might impair a pilot's nerve when in difficulties, so that he would make improper use of his parachute.' No parachutes were issued and the stupidity of that decision compelled the airmen, when they were shot down, to jump to their deaths rather than burn alive in their flaming flying coffins; many of them would have survived, even that awful war, if they had been issued with parachutes.

A certain accolade of glory and glamour was given to the air battles by Hollywood scriptwriters and novelists, but nothing was further from the truth: even worse than the battle environment of the second world war, those early fliers died in horrific circumstances. They were also victims of the military propaganda system which lauded them as "Aces", and the longer they survived the more the inevitable statistics preyed upon their minds. Many of the photographs of that time show the aces bedecked with medals and honours, but their bodies are emaciated, with eyes staring far past the photographer into skies that for them were filled with tracer bullets, burning aeroplanes and burning men. The suffering and the wastage of the lives of many young Irish pilots in the RFC is also enriched in that lament, written originally for the "Wild Geese", the Irish soldiers of long ago who fought for every European army:

They fought as they revelled, fast, fiery and true,
And though victors, they left on the field not a few;
And they who survived, fought and drank as of yore,
But the land of their heart's hope they never saw more,
For in far foreign fields from Dunkirk to Belgrade,
Lie the soldiers and chiefs of the Irish Brigade.

*   *   *

The moon hung there in silvery splendour, and the romantic notions of yesteryear saw on its surface an image, the face of a man — the man in the moon; twentieth century technology made a reality of the fantasy, and on 20 July 1969, Neil Alden Armstrong walked on its dusty surface. Almost sixty years before that event, the North Atlantic ocean fired the imagination of embryonic aviation, and the fury of its storms and those same silver moonbeams dancing on its restless surface troubled the dreams of young aeronauts and spurred them towards its conquest. An American, Walter Weller, was the first to try in 1910. His midget airship, hyrdogen filled and driven by two eight horse-power engines with four propellers, was unique in that it was connected by a hawser to equilibrium tanks floating on the ocean surface. This feature proved to be its undoing, as the floating equilibrator transmitted heavy vibrations to the balloon and the flight had to be abandoned.

World War One gave scope to Glenn Curtiss, and he designed and built a huge flying boat — the Navy Curtiss; the four engined boat was superbly planned, and had a hull that was to be the forerunner of all later flying boat shapes. With a capacity of 50, it had been the intention of the War Department to fly the machines to Europe, thus having a psychological effect on the enemy in the progress of the war. With the cessation of hostilities, the United States Navy turned towards a new conquest — the North Atlantic........

Lieutenant Commander Albert Cushing Read ordered the flight engineer of his NC-4 to open up the four throttles to quarter power, as he manoeuvred the big multi-engined Curtiss flying boat in consort with the sister machines of the flight. The three boats had departed the US naval base at Rockaway, Long Island, to taxy out to the open waters of the Atlantic for a formation take-off. This was to be the first sector of a planned flight to Europe, and involved a distance of 1000 miles to Newfoundland. The planes would be in sight of land all along the route. The date was 8 May 1919.

Commander J.H. Towers, the flight commander in NC-3, signalled: "Open up to full power for take-off," and when the engineers advanced the power levers to the stops, the three boats accelerated on the choppy sea, bouncing across the waves until their wingtip floats came free of the water and the powerful propellers pushed the hulls onto the steps. Soon they were free of the ocean and Towers' left hand signalled a climbing turn towards the east.

Although bad luck dogged the NC-4 from the start, it was to be the only flying boat of the formation to successfully make the crossing to Europe. Near Chatham, in Massachusetts, two of the

Liberty engines on Read's machine developed trouble and had to be shut down — he alighted safely and taxied the flying boat for twelve hours to reach the safety of the coast. The weather deteriorated, and whilst the engines were being repaired, his two companions, who had reached Trepassy harbour in Newfoundland, waited patiently for him. Read got off again after a few days' delay, but bad weather forced him down once more at Cape Cod; they eventually made Trepassy on May 15, and left for the Azores the following day with the two other machines.

On primitive instruments and in a wide formation, the flying boats droned on through the night. Beneath on the ocean, a chain of safety destroyers beamed lights which were glimpsed from time to time through patches in the low stratus cloud. Nearing the Azores, NC-3, Commander Towers in charge, ran short of fuel and had to make an unscheduled landing short of destination; the alighting was heavy in difficult weather, and the impact split the hull. The machine remained afloat in appalling conditions, and although badly damaged, Towers was able to taxy it 200 miles to the safety of the island of San Miguel. The fate of NC-1, Lieutenant Commander P.N.L. Bellinger, was similar, a forced landing in a rough sea holed the hull and they were rescued by the SS Iona. Although Read, in NC-4, also had his problems with the weather and a shortage of fuel, he stayed aloft in the hope of a favourable navigation fix. They got a position check from a safety destroyer, and landed successfully near the island of Flores after a crossing of 15 hours.

The two other American machines were totally disabled, and only the NC-4 left the Azores on 27 May and flew on non-stop to Lisbon. Read and his men eventually landed in Plymouth Sound, England on 31 May 1919 — the Atlantic ocean had been conquered by air.

Civil aviation recommended for Ireland in June of that same year, when John Alcock and Arthur Whitten Brown arrived on the soft bog surface near Clifden in their modified Vimy bomber, having made it all the way from Newfoundland. Airships and aeroplanes across the world had made exploratory flights over routes never before attempted, but the long ocean crossing was the major challenge, since navigation was extremely difficult, and an unscheduled landing upon its surface was a prelude to certain doom.

The cairn that marks the exact arrival spot of the Vimy, has proved to be a fascinating place for me, and I have stood near that heap of stone many times and gazed in wonderment at the scene around. The vastness of the bog, the majesty of the Twelve Pins, the colours, the smell and the fresh good winds from the ocean, and then — the memories of the Connemara of the early 19th century where John D'Arcy, the founder of Clifden, had discovered a desolate region, 'inhabited by a rare breed of people, wild like the mountains they inhabited, which were a natural asylum for smugglers, deserters and outlaws.' John D'Arcy was an enlightened man for his day because he undertook the difficult task of improving the land and civilising the people, and for this purpose he commenced building the town of Clifden.

The D'Arcy family was Anglo-Norman and had settled in Galway during the reign of Queen Elizabeth the First; like many of their stock they had married into an Irish family, and as result inherited further vast estates in Partry Co. Mayo. In Connemara itself, the lands were the property of that famous Gaelic clan, the O'Flahertys of Bunowen Castle near Clifden, but by Cromwell's Act of Settlement of 1652, their properties were confiscated and divided by grants amongst certain families — the D'Arcys being one of them. In due course, John D'Arcy who was High Sherrif of Galway in 1811, inherited the family estates and he decided to build a port to service them and to improve the lot of his impoverished tenants. That noble and humane man devoted his life and his monies in the furtherance of that ideal, and the result of his labours is that delightful scenic spot — Clifden in Connemara.

The view from the commemorative mound is splendid on a balmy summer's day, but on that early June morning of 1919 the area was enveloped in a mantle of low stratus cloud and drizzle, but the fortunate protrusion of the wireless masts of Clifden through the overcast gave the Vimy a positive position fix. John Alcock was lured onto the seemingly flat solid surface of one of the late John D'Arcy's bogs — the nose of the aircraft tipped over, but neither of the occupants was injured and the machine itself sustained only superficial damage. No roads traversed that bog surface, only tracks through the heather and it seemed so similar to the conditions in the year of 1831 when John D'Arcy was constantly petitioning Dublin Castle for funds with which to construct roads in Connemara; D'Arcy had written — 'It is impossible for a wheeled carriage to travel during the winter season, and the roads have of late deteriorated to such an extent, that it is also impossible for even a horse to travel any distance on them. Due to this, land communication between Clifden and the rest of Ireland is cut off.'

John D'Arcy's castle in Clifden is now a ruin, with its 200 acres of parkland divided amongst local farmers; the wireless station is gone and the mountains and valleys no longer echo to the exuberant hoot of destroyer's sirens as they escorted the battleships of the British Atlantic fleet to their anchorages in Killary estuary. But the

63

cairn is there, and the granite tailplane monument, and beautiful Clifden, and above them the countless passages of jumbo jets weaving gossamer threads in the summer sky.

* * *

The British rigid airship R 34 — aluminium framework, fabric covered, had a hydrogen capacity of 2,000,000 cubic feet stored in gas bags distributed throughout the structure. Fuel tanks containing 16 tons of petrol ran along the keel inside the hull, and the nose gondola — the command position, carried its wireless and navigation equipment; five Sunbeam 275 hp. engines — two of them in tandem, drove four propellers. By modern standards, what a lethal combination to put one's trust in for so many hours — hydrogen, petroleum and high voltage electricity, all neatly packaged together in a linen bag!

The RAF crew, variously distributed throughout the hull, in working, recreational or sleeping quarters, were separated from the ocean floor only by that same linen fabric, but their accommodation was comfortable, the food good and their work schedule not too demanding.

Airships had to be manhandled, and when the bugle sounded the "All Clear" at East Fortune in Scotland on the early morning of 2 July 1919, the ground crew released the moorings, and the R34 was on her way. After some initial hazardous manoeuverings to gain height, the ship entered the Atlantic, cruising at 55 mph. The progression of the flight to the west was relatively uneventful, with the commander, as the opportunity presented itself, deliberately bringing the R34 down from the clear to a lower level to fly in cloud, so that the resultant drop in temperature across the hull would reduce the gas leakage.

The crews worked a four hour rota, and the only real hazard for the watch was the necessity for the navigators, at set times, to climb up to the "roof" of the blimp for navigational sightings. The airship was in receipt of continuous radio bearings from Clifden and many other wireless stations. The dreaded area of Newfoundland was traversed without difficulty, in sharp contrast to the terrors imposed by it upon other aviators. Sailing gently along over Halifax, R 34 was down at 800 feet and the only intrusion on its serenity was a pleasant one, the fragrance of the pine trees filling the airship. Unfortunately shortly afterwards the weather disimproved, and fuel consumption caused a problem — the difficulties became so acute that Lt. Cdr. Lansdowne, an American naval liaison officer on board, signalled Washington for a destroyer tow in case of dire emergency!

The fuel sorted itself out, and the weather improved steadily as they flew westwards. There destination at New York was Mineola, and when the airship hovered overhead prior to landing, a Major Pritchard, an R 34 officer who was in charge of landing operations, descended by parachute from the blimp and became the first person to land in America from Europe by air. Moments later, in complete contrast to the screaming reversers and shuddering brakes of today, the big airship settled gently down into the arms of the waiting American sailors, and was the first "lighter-than-air" machine to cross the Atlantic.

The return flight to England posed no great difficulty other than the fact that inaccurate meteorological information planned them on a more southerly course, when in effect the actual wind conditions experienced throughout the flight showed that a more northerly route would have saved a considerable amount of time.

At this stage in aviation development, the large hydrogen filled airship had the lifting capacity, reliability and the range to satisfy the demands of the adventurers, and the pioneer crossings of the R-34, and the later R-100 — a dirigible of twice its gas capacity, culminated in the achievements of the helium filled German airship the GRAF ZEPPLIN. On 11 October 1928, and under the command of Dr. Hugo Eckner it carried 20 passengers and 40 crewmen to Lakehurst, New Jersey USA — the flight time was 111 hours. This machine subsequently flew a total of 17,000 hours which included 140 North Atlantic crossings, and it transported 13,000 passengers before being withdrawn from service.

The airship was considered to be, and unquestionably the reasoning appeared to be correct, a more reliable air transport vehicle than the aeroplane in either of its forms: land or seaplane. But, as we would understand all the more today, it was inevitable that that lethal time bomb — millions of cubic feet of explosive hydrogen encapsulated in fabric bags, hovering aloft and tranquilly suspending its mortal occupants in flimsy cabins beneath, was going to be triggered off by either static electricity or ground impact. That flamboyant era of air conquest by "lighter than air machines," ended in the holocaust of the HINDENBURG — forced to inflate with hydrogen because of shortage of helium, as it triggered a massive static discharge from its mooring mast at Lakehurst: and the sophisticated British airship, the R-101, hopelessly overweight on its way to India, erupted in a ball of flame after contact with the ground in France.

The aeroplane in both of its forms proved to be the more reliable vehicle, and the risk factors of crossing the major water surfaces of the world fell evenly between the choice of flying boats or land machines. Already in the United States, an engineer had developed very advanced designs for a seadrome: a 1200 foot long floating aerodrome, to be anchored at an interval distance on ocean crossings of 300 miles. These "islands" would coincide with the normal range, payload capacity and mechanical reliability of the land planes of the time. The designs bear a remarkable resemblance to the oil drilling platforms in the North Sea.

In the end, this invention and many others like it came to nothing, as the aeroplane with wheels and not with floats evolved with a technical reliability and a range potential capable of conquering any large ocean distance. Navigation was, and continued to be a painful difficulty during these development years: sight of the ocean surface to establish wind conditions and drift was not always possible, and most of the machines did not have the capability to climb above the overcast to establish their position in relation to fixes from the heavenly bodies. The increased availability of aid from shore based direction finding stations, primarily established for the navigational aid of shipping, and a massive improvement in engine power and performance — helping them to top the cloud, finally enabled the aeroplanes to proceed safely to their destinations with precise timings, certain knowledge of their positions, and reasonably accurate projections of environmental conditions to be expected up ahead on the route of their flights.

A dual conquest had been made — not just of the skies above the waters, but of the unfriendly ungiving surface of a navigational waste.

*   *   *

Charles Lindberg, pilot of the Ryan monoplane SPIRIT OF ST. LOUIS flew direct to Paris from New York in 1927. On nearing the Irish coast he was unsure of his position, but he saw some fishing boats out from the Kerry shore and he throttled back the engine and glided down near the water, shouting at them through the slipstream and pointing with his hand — 'Is this the way to Ireland?' The fishermen could not hear him, but Lindberg said afterwards, 'I saw the hills of Ireland and I knew that I had hit Europe on the nose — Ireland is one of the four corners of the world.' He may have mixed his metaphors but not his intuition or his prophesy.

The post war flights of the pioneers had triggered off a renewed interest by the Irish in civil aviation, and a start was made in 1928 with the revival of the Irish Aero Club; its two senior executives were Colonel James Fitzmaurice, hero of the BREMEN flight, and Grattan Esmonde, TD. The club had an Avro Avian and a De Havilland Moth, and seventy seven wildly enthusiastic flying members; their tuition was provided by young officers from the Air Corps, and amongst the famous pupils was that distinguished surgeon and man of letters,

Oliver St. Gogarty. Gogarty usually arrived in Baldonnel by Rolls Royce, direct from his operating theatre and enveloped in a cloud of ether, and although his general flying handling was rated as "impeccable" his landings were deemed to be "suspect." Lt. Arthur Russel eventually sent him solo, but he hit a sheep on the aerodrome and wrote off the aircraft.

The lure was on again in the conquest of the Atlantic, and now it was the turn of Kingsford-Smith, an Australian, he planned to take the trimotor SOUTHERN CROSS from Ireland to the United States. The proposed departure date of the flight had been postponed a number of times, as although Kingsford-Smith had realistically accepted a constant headwind of 15 mph, the forecasts kept coming up with mean windspeeds in excess of this figure. Frustrated by successive pessimistic predictions, he initiated plans for an aeroplane to meet him off the coast of Maine to refuel his tanks — he had considered that, by having a large removable plate on the top of the main tank, it would be a simple matter to insert a dangling fuel line! The plan proved to be unnecessary as favourable conditions were forecast for the 24 hour period of the 24 June 1930.

Initially it had been decided to take off from the military airfield at Baldonnel, but the long hard packed sandy beach of Portmarnock proved to be more suitable, and the combined 700 hp. of the Wright Whirlwinds pushed the SOUTHERN CROSS into the air on the morning of 24 June, on the first sector of their planned world flight of 80,000 miles. The pilots were in a separate compartment from their other two crewmen — the huge main fuel tank lay between them. Each man had his own supply of coffee, chocolate and sandwiches and of course, a liberal supply of seven year old Irish whiskey.

The navigator of the flight was Capt. Paddy Saul of Dublin, who was in later years to be the man mainly responsible for the setting up of the Irish air traffic control service, but like others before him he encountered considerable difficulty in the persistent fog banks and subsequent erratic compass indications near the Newfoundland coast. The radio operator received a number of bearings and fixes from ships and shore stations, but the navigational problems experienced near that treacherous coast were more than they could cope with, and the machine drifted well off course; they finally made it to Harbour Grace in Newfoundland after a crossing of 30 hours and 28 minutes. The journey to New York was completed the following day, and they eventually continued across the North American continent to San Francisco to be the first airmen to land there on a flight from Europe.

In Ireland commercial services were not yet available, and what civil flying existed was provided mainly by aircraft not on the Irish register. Speculative companies were floated, but the only solid venture to emerge was Iona National Airways Ltd founded in August 1930 by the late Hugh Cahill, with a share capital of £2,500. The company supplied, as it still does, an air charter taxi service, aerial photography and survey facilities, and provision for private flying and tuition; those were halcyon days when air taxis were always available at one shilling per mile, and the tea rooms were open to visitors at moderate charges.

Cahill commenced his business with a three seater high wing Desoutter monoplane, EI-AAD which was the first commercial aeroplane on the Irish register; he also operated a Gipsy Moth for flying training and aerial photography. The Desoutter was sold after a year and it eventually went to Australia, giving faithful service until 1965 when it was relegated to a museum in Melbourne.

Early operations of Iona were from Baldonnel, but by June of 1931 they had established their own civil aerodrome at Kildonan near Finglas; their little fleet had started to grow and Captain T.L. Young, a veteran of the War of Independence and later our camp commandant at Rathduff in the Divisional Manoeuvres of August 1942, joined them as operations manager. In 1932, with the delivery of a DH 83 Fox Moth, they had plans for a regular route to London and Berlin, with feeder services to Galway and Cork, but the project fell through.

In 1933 they operated regular air mail and newspaper flights between Galway and Dublin, and one of the airmen that flew that service was Captain O.E. Armstrong who was later to be the first pilot employed by Aer Lingus. The original Iona National Airways closed down in November 1933, and the airfield at Kildonan was taken over by a small company, Dublin Air Ferries, run by Lady Nelson and a pilot called Emerson — they went out of business in 1938. By 1961 Iona was back in aviation with adequate aircraft and a well developed hangar and service site at Dublin Airport.

In parallel with the Cahill influence on private and club flying, was the dynamic contribution of Captain P.W. Kennedy, with his own airfield and aeroplanes at Weston near Lucan. "Darby" Kennedy was one of the original pilots of the pre-war Aer Lingus with O.E. Armstrong, Bligh, "Hammy," B.T. O'Reilly and Noel McCauley and they greatly influenced the careers of many young men in Irish post war civil aviation; Kennedy was initially my Chief Pilot, and by an ironic twist of fate, when he left Aer Lingus to rejoin private flying and then returned again in later years, we had changed roles — I was now his Chief Pilot.

A civil service memo of even earlier times outlined, amongst other things, a comprehensive set of proposals made to the government by a private company for the purpose of operating scheduled air services to England:

MEMORANDUM
on
The present position with regard to
Civil Aviation in An Saorstat

As a party to the International Convention for the Regulation of Aerial Navigation, the Irish Free State has certain responsibilities in the matter of civil aviation. The International Convention established a code of International Air Law, by which provision was made, inter alia, for the registration of aircraft, the licensing of personnel, the establishment of International Customs aerodromes, the collection and dissemination of meteorological information for aeronautical purposes, and the preparation of aeronautical maps. Although the Convention does not itself impose any obligations in the matter of the establishment of air services it may be taken that adhesion to it connotes a desire on the part of the Government to co-operate in the development of civil aviation.

Up to the present, the only steps taken to implement the Convention in the Irish Free State have been the adaptation of the British Air Navigation Act 1920, the issue of an Order relating to the registration of aircraft and the establishment of Baldonnel as an International Customs Aerodrome. Regulations to give effect to the Convention with respect to aerial law generally have been prepared and are at present in the hands of the printers. As no allocation of funds has been made for civil aviation from which the necessary expenses could be met, no action has been possible with regard to the collection of meteorological information or the preparation of aeronautical maps.

The remarkable flight of Colonel Fitzmaurice to America and the enthusiasm attending his return had the effect of arousing considerable interest in civil aviation, which was fostered by the visits from time to time of private aircraft to Baldonnel, and in September 1928 the Irish Aero Club was formed. The Club purchased two light aircraft and commenced training pupils for their "A" licences. Owing to the absence of regulations and the consequent impossibility of arranging for the necessary examinations, it was not possible to issue licences to those who qualified, and it is understood that some of these went to England and obtained their licences from the British Air Ministry. In December 1928 a company known as Irish Airways Ltd., was formed for the purpose of establishing a service by air from Dublin to

London. The Company submitted proposals indicating the nature of the service, from which it appeared that the Company guaranteed to provide a capital of £100,000 and operate a daily service each way between Baldonnel and Croydon, provided that a subsidy of £125,000 was given by the Government by the payment of £25,000 per annum for five years.

Following these proposals, an Inter Departmental Air Committee was established, consisting of one representative from the Department of Industry and Commerce (Transport and Marine Branch), one from the Department of Posts and Telegraphs and one from the Department of Defence, under the Chairmanship of Mr. J. Dolan, T.D., Parliamentary Secretary to the Department of Industry and Commerce. The Committee was charged with the examination of the various proposals which had been mooted in connection with the development of civil aviation, and of these the only concrete proposition was the scheme submitted by Irish Airways Ltd. Concerning this the Committee reported that the amount of the subsidy required by the Company had been substantially verified by an examination by the Department of Defence of the requirements of such service as was proposed by Irish Airways Ltd., and suggested that in addition a sum of approximately £5,000 would be required as an initial outlay for the establishment of such wireless and meteorological facilities as would be required by a Dublin-London service. The Committee further reported that while there was no immediate demand for internal air services in An Saorstat, the creation of some such service as Irish Airways proposed was desirable if the Irish Free State were to take its place with other nations in the development of civil aviation.

Following an intimation that no new money would be forthcoming for civil aviation, a discussion took place between representatives of this Department and the Department of Defence in order to find whether any money could be set aside from the Army Air Corps Vote for civil purposes, and whether a scheme could be devised whereby Army Air Corps personnel could be seconded for civil aviation. The Department of Defence representatives indicated that no money could be spared from the Army Air Vote, and further that there was no possibility of releasing personnel, as those who would be suitable for civil work were just those who were most necessary in the Army Air Corps as instructors. The Department of Defence representatives were not greatly impressed with the potential value to them of civil air services — the number of pilots would be so small as to be negligible. They did, however, intimate that, provided certain reorganisation proposals which they had submitted were accepted, they would be prepared to arrange for any

Company using Baldonnel as a base for an air service to obtain free accommodation, with free use of mechanics and workshop equipment. This is estimated as being worth approximately £8,500 per annum.

A further discussion took place with Department of Defence representatives on the question of the financial arrangements necessary between the two Departments in the matter of technical and other work required to be done at Baldonnel in connection with civil aviation. Under this heading are included the despatch of telegrams to Holyhead notifying arrival of aircraft; collection of landing and accommodation fees from visiting aircraft; overhaul and inspection of aircraft for renewal of certificates of airworthiness; examination of applicants for licences, etc. It was agreed that after the end of the current financial year, an accurate account would be kept of all income and expenditure in respect of civil aviation, and that periodical adjustment would be made between the two Departments. It was estimated that allowing for contingencies the annual cost to this Department would not exceed £500.

Other items of expenditure of a non-recurrent type will be the printing of the Air Navigation Regulations, the Air Navigation Directions, and the various licences and log books required under the regulations. While the cost of one single licence or log book will be met by the prescribed charge for issue sufficient will not be issued in the immediate future fully to meet the printing costs, which are estimated at approximately £115.

So far as the establishment of an air service is concerned, the only concrete proposal which has been received is that from Irish Airways Ltd. A short time ago a Mr. Kennedy called at this office representing the Air Express Company of Croydon, and discussed a tentative scheme which appeared to have much to recommend it. His idea was to operate a Dublin-London service with an extension from Dublin to Belfast and arrangements for meeting trans-Atlantic liners at Galway. He did not require any subsidy, but proposed to ask for permission to carry mails, his suggestion being that an extra air mail charge of one halfpenny per ounce could be made and paid to him. He also proposed seeking accommodation at Baldonnel at greatly reduced fees. His main object in seeking an interview is to submit his whole scheme in writing. Up to the present nothing more has been heard from him although he was written to some time ago reminding him of his promise.

Irish Airways proposal has the advantage of being a national enterprise, but in this connection it may be remarked that there may be difficulty in raising the £100,000 capital in Ireland. Further, it is somewhat difficult to see where the necessary trained personnel are to be found here. Omitting details, the estimated cost of the service and the estimated revenue over three years are shown in the following summary:-

Estimated Cost of Dublin-London Service:
6 trips per week each way.

Capital Charges	£50,000	
Running Charges	14,300)	
	)	Operating Cost £40,300
Standing Charges	26,000)	

Estimate and Revenue
and Subsidy required.

First Year.

Average of 4 passengers per trip	£5.	£12,000
Subsidy 3/- per mile flown		28,800
		40,800
Total operating cost		40,300
Leaving Profit on year's working of		£500

Second Year.

Average of 6 passengers per trip	£4: 10: 0d.	£16,200
Subsidy 3/- per mile flown		£28,800
		£45,000
Total Operating Cost		£40,300
		£4,700
Required to bring interest on capital to 10%		2,000
		2,700
Two thirds returned to Government		1,800
Balance to improvement and development		900
Subsidy actually paid by Government .		£27,000

72

Third Year.

Average of 7 passengers £4: 10: 0d. per trip	£18,900
Subsidy of 2/6 per mile flown	£24,000
	£42,900
Total operating cost	£40,300
Required to bring interest on capital to 10%	£2,600
	£600
Two thirds returned to Government	£400
Balance to improvement and development	£200
Subsidy actually paid by Government	£23,600

It will be observed that for the first two years the annual subsidy necessary would appear to exceed the amount required by the Company (£25,000), but the passenger receipts are conservative, and no allowance has been made for possible freight receipts.

If it were decided to acquire the amount necessary for a subsidy, and to give it to Irish Airways rather than explore the possibilities of obtaining the services of some company with a long experience of operating air services, it would be necessary to prepare a detailed working agreement setting out the conditions on which the subsidy would be payable, and to pay the strictest attention to the qualifications of the personnel and the type of machines to be used. Nothing could be left to chance in such a matter, where a single accident in the initial stages would do irreparable harm to the cause which the service is designed to promote.

Summarising the estimated expenditure on civil aviation the following figures appear:

Annual subsidy	£28,800	
less services free at Baldonnel	£8,500	£20,300 approx.
Cost of technical & o. work at Baldonnel		£500
Cost of printing		£115
Cost of meteorological and wireless services		£5,000

The foregoing figures are of course estimates, and so far as the anticipated number of passengers is concerned are merely guesswork. Perhaps a more reliable estimate of the amount of government subsidy that would be required to foster and develop Civil Aviation in the Saorstat can be obtained from the following table showing the amount contributed by the Governments of the Countries mentioned to Civil Aviation services established by Companies in their territories:-

Gt. Britain	£250,000	Holland	£49,500
Belgium	36,000	Italy	521,200
Denmark	13,750	Poland	138,800
France	927,200	Sweden	27,500
Germany	988,400	Switzerland	10,400

It will be observed that the subsidies vary from £10,400 to £988,400 per annum, and it would appear from these figures that some existing non-national Company could be induced to establish a service say between Dublin and London for a subsidy considerably less than that which the Irish Airways Ltd. ask for.

There would, of course, be objections to introducing foreign Companies into this branch of our transport, and it would certainly be more desirable that an Irish and not a foreign Company should be assisted, although it is anticipated that Irish Airways Ltd. would be forced to raise the capital necessary for the establishment of a service outside the Saorstat, and that in fact the Company would be Irish in name only.

Assuming, therefore, that the Government policy is to encourage an Irish Company, or at least a Company with its head office in the Saorstat, it is thought that before any reliable estimate can be put forward as to the minimum subsidy required, the Directors or those interested in Irish Airways Ltd. should be interviewed and the whole matter of the necessary financial aid gone into thoroughly. It is believed that the scheme put forward by Irish Airways Ltd. is too elaborate for a beginning; that an experimental service could be established at a much lower figure taking into account the facilities to be provided free at Baldonnel. At such an interview the details in regard to lights, wireless and meteorological services could be discussed and probably a much less ambitious scheme evolved.

The idea would be to put to the Irish Airways Ltd. what service they are prepared to give for a subsidy of say £10,000 per annum. A further sum of £1,000 per annum would probably be required for administration and other expenses so that if a sum of £12,000 can be obtained from either the General Army Vote or from the special vote for Army Aviation probably a beginning could be made.

The proposals came to nothing, and Irish Airways Ltd faded away, but the discussions in the memorandum provide an interesting resumé of the status of Irish civil aviation in March of 1930.

In England, the major airline and flag carrier of that time was Imperial Airways, but the four main British railway companies had been casting envious eyes at the air scene, and already by 1929 they had obtained government permission to operate air services; the Southern Railway had also bought heavily into Imperial Airway's stock. It was not however until 1932 that their four internal British services emerged, variously under the aegis of Imperial Airways and some of the large railway companies. Sir Eric Geddes, chairman of Imperial Airways was concerned about railway involvement in matters of the air, and in order to establish affairs on a more regular footing he approached the London Midland and Scottish Railway with a concrete proposal to establish air services linking Dublin and Belfast with Glasgow, Birmingham and London. The LMSR response was sluggish, and a Scottish bus operator was the first to introduce a Glasgow-Belfast service in June of 1933, followed in August of the same year by a short lived London-Dublin schedule.

The two Irish railway companies now evinced interest, having obtained air licences from the government; this was a direct response by Sean Lemass, minister of Industry and Commerce, in an endeavour to ensure Irish participation in any projected air links between the two countries. The culmination of negotiations and discussions between the railway companies of Ireland — the GSR and GNR, and their British counterparts, and both of the governments resulted in the establishment of RAS — Railway Air Services, but the Irish finally decided that the scheme was not acceptable, and London-Belfast-Glasgow was the only Irish route operated by the new company in 1934. A previous operator on the Belfast run was Midland and Scottish Air Ferries, and now Hilman's Airways Ltd, commenced flying in direct competition with RAS.

The RAS service to Belfast was to continue right up to 1939, and in 1938 alone it carried over 7,000 passengers, but the cost to the railways of their airline venture in its five years of operation was £201,694 — a considerable amount of money in those days.

In 1935, Sean Lemass in consort with Dr. John Leyden who was the head of Industry and Commerce, took part in discussions with the representatives of the British and Canadian governments; they had for their purpose the establishment of a joint operating company specifically for North American operations, and again,

75

Imperial Airways was chosen by them to commence the service. In return for landing facilities to be granted to the joint company by the United States government, Pan American were to be given similar assistance by the United Kingdom, Irish, Canadian and Newfoundland governments. As a result of these talks, and the realisation by the Irish that Ireland would be an important focal point in the long ocean crossings, the facilities contributed towards the joint venture were the flying boat base at Foynes on the Shannon, and the airfield at Rineanna on the opposite bank in Co. Clare.

Survey flights immediately commenced and were carried out by Pan American and Imperial Airways on behalf of the joint company, but Deutsche Lufthansa and Air France also operated proving flights during that year. Range problems still bedevilled the pioneers, and the route via the Azores was contemplated, but in the end technology triumphed and all the efforts were concentrated on the direct routing.

After the fruitless negotiations with RAS and the railways a few years before, Lemass decided to proceed independently and to promote domestic aviation development at home, and in 1936 he gave encouraging support to the founding of a national airline with an authorised capital of £100,000. Aer Lingus was initially associated with Blackpool and West Coast Air Services, a company in the west of England that advanced further monies for the purchase of an aircraft to operate their joint venture — Irish Sea Airways. The machine chosen by them was a De Havilland Dragon, a twin engined biplane called IOLAR; with Dublin-man Captain O.E. Armstrong in command, it operated their first commerical air service from Baldonnel on 27 May 1936. Five passengers travelled on that inaugural to Bristol; and after years of faithful flying, through icing, turbulence or limpid skies, that linen covered zipped-up plane is still safe and sound, gently suspended from the ceiling of the aero museum at Dublin airport. That air service proved to be a success and was extended to London, with seasonal flights to Liverpool and the Isle of Man, but the onset of the second war restricted further development, and although a spanking new DC-3 was delivered in 1940, the company was restricted by wartime security to a single route to Liverpool with Manchester as a diversionary airfield.

Side by side with the progress of local aviation, the base at Foynes continued to develop, and although the flying boats of those early years had a very good range, the carriage of such large quantities of fuel to make it possible meant that payload was extremely limited. Major Mayo of Imperial Airways developed a piggy back combination, whereby a heavily laden seaplane was carried into the air on the back of a large flying boat, and then released at a safe speed. After takeoff from Foynes in July of 1938, the composite seaplane MERCURY, separated from its lower component, and flew a playload of 1,000 pounds, nonstop to Montreal. As an unusual and innovative experiment in achieving a good range with a reasonable payload, it was a success, but it proved to be impractical insofar as normal commerical operations were concerned.

By late 1939, Pan American was operating the Boeing 314, a very large flying boat, into Foynes — the machine was unique in that it did not possess wing tip floats but was equipped with "sponsons", a sort of stub wing down at the water line that gave the machine practically the same type of stability on the water — almost. It had a distressing habit when anchored in fluctuating wind conditions of heeling over on one of its sponsons and remaining there, allowing the wingtip to dip beneath the surface, which, when the boat subsequently righted itself decanted a fair amount of sea water down through the wing and into the cabin furnishings. Operationally, it was almost as good a stabiliser as the wing tip floats on the takeoff run, and airborne it was aerodynamically more efficient; they imparted drag but, the sponsons imparted lift. This boat was in the grand manner of the latter day Boeing jumbo jets, it had an all up weight of 82,500 pounds, with a range of 4275 miles at 150 mph. Seventy four passengers could be accommodated in cabins, or 40 in sleepers — the upper deck was carpeted and comprised the crew section, from which a tunnel in each wing gave access to the engines. The lower deck contained five main passenger compartments, with a dining room and a private suite at the rear.

In a further attempt to increase the range and payload of its Short class flying boats, Imperial Airways devised a system of inflight refuelling by means of tanker aircraft which were stationed at Gander in Newfoundland, and Rineanna on the Shannon estuary. The onset of the second world war reduced the development of the new route, but the Allies derived immense benefits from its establishment, and throughout that conflict a continuous lifeline was maintained with the United States through the flying boat base at Foynes. Nevertheless, during the early stages of the war, some of the staff of BOAC at the station were considered to be a security risk by army intelligence; with the exception of one or two senior representative personnel, they were all returned to England and total control of the base given to the Irish.

The Anglo-Irish agreement signed after the war gave Aer Lingus the sole right to operate and develop services between the two countries, and by 1956 the agreement had been amended to allow British companies to participate. Route expansion continued with more DC-3's, acquired cheaply from war surplus and modified to civilian standard, until by 1948 the Irish company was serving London, Liverpool, Manchester, the Isle of Man, Paris and Amsterdam.

In 1947 an affiliated company, Aerlinte Eireann was formed for the purpose of operating transatlantic aeroplanes. Three Lockheed Constellations of the most advanced type had been purchased, and proving flights carried out on the route, but because of political pique or calculated economic necessity, the operations were suspended, the company demolished except in name and the aircraft sold at considerable loss to British Overseas Airways. That government decision was a serious mistake, which the previous administration, Fianna Fail would not have made, because Europe was resettling itself after the war and commerce was flowing across the North Atlantic: Marshall Aid, troop contracts, displaced personnel, business people, diplomatic representatives — everybody and everything was on the wing and Ireland was in a prime position to obtain its share of that lucrative traffic and establish Aerlinte as an international carrier, years before some of the large nations had contemplated such an air service.

The shut down of the company in 1948, took with it some of the most experienced pilots of Aer Lingus of that time. It had seemed then that this curtailment of Irish aviation was a bitter blow to young ambitious men, and like the mercenaries of yesteryear, Irish pilots left for foreign service — one to die in the futility of the Berlin airlift, and another amongst the hills of Prestwick through the miscalculation of his Dutch captain. Others — their fortunes varied in regular airline companies or in tenuous charter setups that spawned in profusion after the war and as quickly disappeared, when the harsh and tragic reality was, that had they remained where they were, in a relatively short few years they would have been able to participate in the successful re-establishment of the Irish transatlantic route. Three Boeing 720's went into service in Dec. 1960, to be rapidly followed by 707's and then in 1971 — the wide bodied 747's — the jumbos.

Meanwhile Aer Lingus itself continued to prosper and expand, and in 1954 the first of the successful Vickers Viscounts were delivered. The triumph of this aeroplane was totally due to the brilliant turboprop engine of Rolls Royce, an economic rugged wonder still years ahead of its time in radical design and dependability. The Viscount was easy to fly, and as far as its handling characteristics were concerned, it was devoid of vices, but it was a single spar aircraft and had a number of primitive engineering design faults in the early models. The Viscounts were soon augmented by twin engined Fokker Friendships, an eminently suitable aircraft for the Aer Lingus routes, although slightly short in range. In later years the machines were disposed of, for a relatively low price, as a result of a disastrous commerical decision which decided that further secondhand Viscounts were needed to provide increased capacity on some of the routes — the routes did not develop, and had the Friendships been retained they would have provided adequate economic route capacity even to this day.

Whilst the Viscount was a winner for Vickers, with almost 500 of the series being built, their immediate post war commerical venture was not — the Vickers Viking, based to some degree on wartime design concepts. A midwing metal monoplane with two Bristol Hercules engines, seven of them were bought in 1947 and after a year's operation, Aer Lingus was more than relieved to find a purchaser for them.

Another aircraft which did not enhance the reputation of the airline or endear itself to its passengers was the Carvair. This was a bulbous nosed modification of a standard DC-4, front loading for cars and bulk freight items; the design idea was good and the airframe had been modernised, but the year was 1963 and the Pratt and Whitney R 2000-D5 piston engines with which it was equipped were a product of World War Two, and were at that stage, highly suspect and mechanically unreliable. The Carvairs were withdrawn from service and disposed of within three years.

In 1952 the airline received delivery of four Bristol Wayfarer 170s; they were used either as purely freighter aircraft or in a mixed version of passengers and cargo; the aircraft had a poor performance but it was rather pleasant to fly. To provide deicing protection for the wings, a thin strip of crushed ballbearings ran the length of their leading edges, and the idea was that fluid was slowly exuded across the wing surface from the matrix; I'm not too sure as to how well it did its job, but I do know that the operating switch was placed by Bristols in the exact spot that it could be accidentally turned on by the pilot, catching his foot on it as he clambered out of his seat — in ten minutes the sight was farcical, as the big ungainly thing stood weeping on the tarmac. It had one unusual feature — when the hostess climbed up the small ladder to gain access to the cockpit from the cabin beneath, if the captain timed it correctly by opening his side window at the precise moment that the co-pilot opened the floor hatch, the result was spectacular, because the lady's clothes were instantly sucked right up over her head.

Aer Lingus had been instrumental in developing interest in the small Lourdes airport of Tarbes, and in 1954 a full scheduled service was opened, with the company rapidly attaining worldwide acclaim for the care and attention which it gave to invalids and pilgrims. We flew many of those flights with that same Bristol Wayfarer, that ugly looking machine with its large box section fuselage, thick high wings and fixed undercarriage. It was noisy and unpressurised, but its very large cabin was ideally suited for the carriage of stretchers.

Because the aeroplane was unpressurised we had to fly at low levels where most of the bad weather existed, but on this day we cruised uneventfully along at 5,500 feet, down the Wicklow coast and across the mouth of the Bristol Channel, until we approached Dartmoor. Here great heaps of white cumulus and bulky grey cumulonimbus storm clouds were inextricably mixed. The thunderclouds fanned outwards and upwards until, at 30,000 feet, some of them were pressed against the heavens as a great solid head with fibrous texture at their upper edges — they blocked our way to the south. McKeown who was flying it, said, 'Tell air traffic control I am climbing to see if we can get through visually; I'm not going through that lot in this yoke with all those invalids.'

Down below in Devon the day had been oppressive, and the echoing distant thunder rolling over the fields had driven the cattle together and bunched them close to the shelter near their pasture. On the ground the silence in the countryside became uncanny; even the low swooping and the shrill cry of the swallow had ceased. A bee was still in search of honey and the noise of his coming and going was accentuated by the growing absence of other sounds; in time his workings stopped as he sensed the impending downpour and flew hastily back to the safety of his bower, with his tiny wing beat labouring from the weight of the pollen attached to his body. There was an oppressive silence, a silence that you could hear, and the grey low quiet skies were pressing their weight towards the ground. Near the little church at Ashburton, the chestnut leaves gathered the first warm, heavy, slow raindrops to drip them down, singly at first — until the tempo increased and the drops hopped back up their silver stems with a light echoing rhythmic patter, as the pools expanded beneath the trees to receive them.

The thunderstorm rained and flashed itself out, finally moving away to the south, permitting the familiar sounds and sights to return. The bee was first, next the swallow, and then a drone which grew more compelling and resonated in an expanding way. It was the sound of the two Pegasus engines of a Bristol Wayfarer, carrying thirty invalids, two doctors, two voluntary staff helpers, two hostesses and two pilots. The aeroplane became visible under the billowing grey cloud of the receding storm and it seemed to hang there — a helpless thing against the challenging sky, moments later it turned slowly away towards Plymouth, where there was a tiny patch of blue the size of a sailor's breeches. Into this gap sped the aeroplane and the storm broke in fury over Plymouth — but the Wayfarer was gone.

McKeown put it down nicely on the uneven paved surface at the enroute stop, Dinard in France. The invalids were carried by Red Cross helpers to the wooden building which also housed the small restaurant.

There were two notables at Dinard: the customs officer and the bulldozer driver, and they had two things in common: girth and laughter. The customs officer was as formal in his finery as his figure would allow, but the driver wore dark glasses on a suntanned chubby face, an open khaki shirt barely met around a great hairy barrel chest, and the smallest pair of shorts in all of France clung tightly to his big arse.

Wooden tables, red and white squared cloth, crusty bread, a trace of garlic, somebody else's half-corked bottle of vin ordinaire, persistent flies, and the odours of cognac, oil and vinegar and French cigarettes merged to remind me of what I had seen disembarking from a collection of French aeroplanes on the day of a rugby international in Dublin. There were mini-skirted girls with tight short hair, busty sweaters and big bottoms; mini-skirted girls with long hair, flat sweaters and footballer's legs, and girls with cluster necklaces and vivid gashes of lipstick. The men were as varied, with crew cuts and formal lapelless striped suits, fringe haircuts and Napoleonic faces, multicoloured jerseys and blue jeans. The smell of Gauloise tobacco filled that Irish customs hall, and gesticulating hands, expressive faces, and animated conversation was everywhere.

I said to McKeown, 'Can you just imagine the impact that collection must have had on the boys of Killala when the French landed there in 1798?' to which he borrowed from a learned Irishman and replied, 'Killala yawned and went back to sleep.' I turned the Wayfarer onto the runway and opened up the power.

From Dinard to Bordeaux the countryside slid slowly by beneath, with only the white puffy clouds born of the glorious day dotting the brownish tint of the earth. There were no radio aids between Bordeaux and the Lourdes airport, and the only way to get there was by map reading; we read the signs like Indians: a railway there, a white tower here, now a valley, soon we were steady on the inbound bearing of the beacon to the airport at Tarbes, and the swathe in the heavy grass which was the runway loomed ahead.

One did not have to be a believer to find peace or see it in others in this extraordinary place. Undoubtedly the natural surroundings in themselves are conducive to tranquillity of mind; indeed the landscaping and the architecture when combined with the simplicity and contrast of the cave where the apparition took place, produced an intense spiritual feeling. The Gave de Pau flowed turbulently by the wall of the grotto to carry away the glacial waters of the Pyrenees, who, in their ravined and jagged glory raise themselves up to peaks 11,000 feet high to divide France from Spain. Those mountain peaks have echoed down the years to the voices of the countless thousands, singing in their own language the Lourdes hymn, and the pilgrims wind their snakelike way in procession at night along the walks of the shrine, holding lighted candles that sputter and then glow and then flicker, and sometimes extinguish — almost like the passage of a life.

Moslem, Hindu, Christian, atheist — all sworn enemies even within themselves; I thought many times in Lourdes, that in the few seconds it takes the Gave de Pau to flow thousands of gallons of water past that place of peace, thousands of those enemies are laid to decay — side by side. Perhaps they would have been better, if at some stage in their lives they were hand in hand, admiring the majesty of the Pyreneean thunderstorms, drinking wine or mint tea and listening to the countless voices just singing — singing.

In my dreams at Lourdes, I used to fill that amphitheatre-like grotto with all the great military and political leaders of the world, together with their awesome weaponry: atomic bombs, nerve gas, supersonic planes and vast naval fleets, and when they were all comfortably installed with their reassuring arsenals, the following psalm would flash on a vast panoramic screen — but the "you" in the psalm would not be them, it would be the cosmic Christ, or whoever or whatever is the architect of the universe, and the words would be compulsory viewing every day for several years:

You turn men back into dust
and say, 'Go back, sons of men.'
To your eyes a thousand years
are like yesterday, come and gone,
no more than a watch in the night.

You sweep men away like a dream,
like grass which springs up in the morning.
In the morning it springs up and flowers:
by evening it withers and fades.

*   *   *

Six biplanes of No. 2 Squadron, Royal Flying Corps flew to Ireland in 1913 to exercise with the British army — this was the first operation of military aircraft in this country, and then there was practically no further activity until the German submarine fleet increased its operations in the Irish Sea during the first of the great wars. By 1917 the Admiralty had established two airship bases, one at Malahide Castle in Dublin, and the other at Johnstown Castle in Co Wexford.

British military engineers had already surveyed possible sites for the location of aerodromes and a young officer, Sholto Douglas, later to be a Marshal of the RAF in World War Two, flew over the areas and selected as suitable Aldergrove at Belfast, Gormanston in Co. Meath, Collinstown — now Dublin Airport, Tallaght, Oranmore in Galway, Baldonnel outside Dublin city, and Fermoy near Cork; a landing strip was also deemed essential at that centre of British military power in Ireland — the Curragh. Work commenced on the bases in 1917, and the layout was to a standard plan; Tallaght was the first to be completed, and aircraft from it soon joined the airships in the antisubmarine patrols. American flying boats were located at Cobh, Lough Foyle, Whiddy Island and Wexford during 1918; their shore based aircraft operated from Bangor in Co. Down. The US Naval Air Station situated on the river Slaney commanded the strategic area of the south western approaches — a favourite hunting ground for the U boats of the German navy. The flying boat patrols were extremely effective and the base was a comprehensive military establishment manned by 20 officers and 406 men. These planes had excellent radio communication with their headquarters, but the back up was provided by carrier pigeons stowed on board and used quite frequently!

With the ending of the war most of the bases were closed; flying ceased at Gormanston and it became an internment camp during the War of Independence — it also doubled up as the Transport Division of the Black and Tans. Baldonnel had become the headquarters of the Irish Wing, Royal Air Force.

*   *   *

In the autumn of 1921 Commandant Sean McKeon was a prisoner in Mountjoy gaol, and, after examining the various possibilities and the risks involved, Michael Collins decided to attempt a rescue. The plan required the capture of a British armoured car, and envisaged its use in obtaining entrance to the prison in the hope of effecting the escape. The armoured car he was after was a Peerles double turreted vehicle equipped with twin Hotchkiss, a type of machine gun principally used by the British cavalry during World War One.

Emmet Dalton, who was then Director of Training of the IRA had discussions with Collins, and Dalton undertook to search amongst the volunteers of the Dublin area to try to locate at least two men who would be capable of operating the machine gun. By chance also, Dalton knew a Jack McSweeney who had been a pilot in the RAF, and having approached him he found out that he still had a good knowledge of the gun; McSweeney accompanied Dalton to a rendezvous with the two volunteers, where he outlined the details of the weapon by means of blackboard diagrams. The plan in the end came to nothing, but it was to have important repercussions because of Dalton's meeting with McSweeney.

When the Truce was declared and Dail Eireann nominated Michael Collins as one of the plenipotentaries to the negotiations in England, the General Headquarters Staff became gravely concerned about his safety, because he was at that time Director of Intelligence with a price of £10,000 on his head. The fears of the army centred around the fact that if the treaty negotiations broke down, then one of the most important Irish figures involved in the war could be trapped in London and the entire position of the Irish forces jeopardised. General Dalton voiced these fears to Collins during the negotiations, and together they devised a plan which they placed before the General Staff. The suggestion was that the Irish should purchase an aeroplane in London, and have it standing by in readiness should Collins or members of the negotiating party decide to return to Dublin, in the event that the talks broke down. The scheme appealed to GHQ and Dalton made the arrangements accordingly.

The idea had come to Dalton as a result of his previous contacts with McSweeney relative to the Hotchkiss machine gun, and in consequence of further enquiries amongst the Dublin Brigade, a Commandant Dowling of the 4th. Battalion was able to put him in touch with yet another ex-RAF officer, Charlie Russel, who had spent some time in Canada. Russel was to pretend that he was seeking a suitable machine for the Canadian Forestry Department; in the event the two pilots encountered little difficulty in the purchase of a Martinsyde Type A Mark 2 biplane. The aircraft was new and had never flown, but on the orders of the two Irishmen it was taken out of storage and test flown at Brooklands on 24 Nov. 1921 — meanwhile Russel was acquainting GHQ of the preparations necessary should they have to fly the machine to Dublin:

London
21 October 1921.

To: Chief of Staff.

We have succeeded in purchasing a Martinsyde aeroplane

which can carry ten passengers or 1,600 pounds weight of munitions. We intend that this shall serve several purposes — it can be used if necessary, in the event of a break in the present negotiations. I have the pilot over here and the machine will be ready for flight within two weeks. In the event of this necessity arising we will take the following course: London-Reading-Bristol-Greenore and then follow the DSE railway as far as Leopardstown Racecourse.

The following arrangements would be necessary to be made on your side, and for this purpose I have also a first class air pilot in Dublin with whom I can put you in touch, and who would understand and look after the following arrangements:

As the flight would probably take place in daytime it would be necessary first to have six men on the approved landing place i.e. a flat part of the race course. It would also be necessary to have two motor cars convenient, 60 gallons of first grade aero petrol (this can be purchased from Lemass of LSE Motor Company) and 2ft. square of chamois cloth, five gallons of water, and a white cloth signal which would correspond to the attached diagram.

It should be possible to obtain in Dublin one air mechanic who would understand the Rolls Royce aero engine; also a man understanding the rigging of aeroplanes would be necessary — they are known as riggers. The other four men need not necessarily have aero qualifications. McSweeney would be able to give all instructions for the landing, but it must be clearly understood that the two men who are to catch the wings and rear struts make sure not to catch the edges of the wings. If it so happens that they misjudge the distance it must be impressed upon them to fall flat to the ground and let the aeroplane pass over.

In the event of having to cross at night it would be necessary for our people over there to mark out an "L" shaped figure on the landing ground — this should be done by means of four petrol tin fires or flares at intervals of sixty yards — see diagram. The fourth flare would be placed in order to indicate the direction of the wind — the remaining placed accordingly. The cloth signal to be used by daylight is also a wind signal. The triangular piece would be placed indicating the direction in which the wind is blowing.

I will be able to notify fully the time at which departure would take place, and the journey is calculated to take $3\frac{1}{2}$ to $4\frac{1}{2}$ hours, this I think, would be sufficient notice to get things moving.

Yours respectfully,

C. Russel

His letter was accompanied by some suggestions relative to the establishment of an air force for the newly emerging state:

WHAT IS REQUIRED:

The establishment of an Air Service Department, separate and distinct from any other department. The chief executive of the Air Service being a member of the General Staff and having equal rank to the heads of the other departments.

REASONS FOR THIS ARRANGEMENT:

1. In order that the General Staff may have first hand information on aerial matters.

2. In order that the Officer in command of the Air Service may work his department on the correct lines, he must be in possession of all the facts in connection with the military situation as a whole.

3. In order that the Air Service may have the status which is its due.

4. In order that the combined intellectual strength of GHQ may be used to the best advantage for the Air Service.

As a result of these events, the Army Air Service was formed, and in Feb. of 1922 a lieutenant of the newly established Irish army journeyed to Baldonnel and formally took over the aerodrome from Group Captain Bonham-Carter in command of No. 2 Squadron Irish Wing RAF. An Irish volunteer was driven each day to Baldonnel to obtain tools which he stored in an empty hangar; he recalled that most of the unserviceable aircraft were burnt by Bonham-Carter's men, who also drove their lorries over equipment and fittings to prevent them being used again. The British vacated the camp shortly afterwards, but they left it derelict and with all the main gates wide open.

That original Irish volunteer was Sergeant Johnny Curran who had started his long career as a mechanic in the RAF. In a statement to Colonel W.J. Keane in 1944 he recalled his experiences — Keane was a member of the first Air Corps cadet class of 1926:

'I came to Baldonnel about May of 1922 with a Pte. Hughes and reported to Capt. Stapleton. There were no Air Service people in Baldonnel at that time, neither officers or other ranks. There were no aircraft other than a couple of old machines left behind by the British. We eventually rebuilt one of them which was an Avro 504 K with a Le Rhone rotary engine; none of the others was ever rebuilt. Apart from the few machines that were here, the first aircraft to arrive was a Bristol F2B Fighter which was flown from Collinstown by Colonel Russel , who was, when flying it, wearing a hard hat and carried a bag of stones in the back seat as ballast. That was July 1922. About two weeks later another Bristol was flown here from England, piloted by Major General McSweeney with Lt. Nolan as observer.'

Early in 1922 the two ex-RAF pilots had been assigned an office in the old Beggars Bush barracks near Ballsbridge; both were now major generals with McSweeney commanding the Air Service and Director of Military Aviation, and Russel as his second in command and Director of Civil Aviation with the Provisional Government. Colonel Keane, who later commanded the Air Corps, typified in a remark the instant ranking system of those days when he said, 'both were volunteers one day, and suddenly found themselves major generals the next. A formidable challenge for any man!'

A further ten ex-RAF pilots, Irishmen and mostly highly decorated, were recruited by GHQ, but, after the Civil War the government decided that they did not want the newly formed corps to be officered entirely by ex-members of the RAF, and a transfer of twelve selected officers of the regular army, who had seen service in the IRA, was initiated. This was further augmented by a direct intake of nine cadets — by 1927 the "other rank" strength of the Air Corps had reached a total of 126 NCO's and men.

Second Lieutenant D.V. Horgan — "Vinnie" to his friends, was one of those transferred officers; too young to join the IRA he had enlisted in Fianna Eireann and as a boy in Cork city had helped the rebels in the fight against the Black and Tans; his older brother, Ned, was an active member of the 1st Cork Brigade. Vinnie recalls that he owes his life to an RIC sergeant, a friend of his father's, who, when he was arrested in mistake for his brother, recognised him and pushed him out of the Tan lorry; the two other prisoners who were with him were shot. The Horgans were typical of the many Irish families of the time, finding themselves on opposite sides of the fence during the ensuing civil war — D.V. to become an officer in the newly established Free State army, and his brother Ned, to go on the run with the anti-treaty faction. To Horgan's unenviable lot fell the task of escorting his captive brother to gaol, but Ned responded magnificently to his plight by saying, 'You'll have no trouble from me Vinnie,' and neither did he.

The saddest recollection by this distinguished Air Corps officer of those early years, was of the grief of the Irish mothers, who had first seen their sons involved in the Black and Tan campaign and then, in the culminating anguish of the civil war. His more humorous reminiscences are of the local situation unique to Cork city, which had:

An anti-Sinn Fein Society
Excommunication – and
Four o'clock curfew.

That young officer turned out to be one of the finest sportsmen in the army, excelling in every variety of the art throughout his long career, culminating in his service to Irish boxing both as a referee and an administrator of international repute.

Horgan's first encounter with the panache of a flying unit came one morning with Fitzmaurice. The commandant strolled up to the line of aircraft readied for the day, and said to the second lieutenant, 'Horgan, have you ever flown this kite?' indicating the rotary engined Avro 504K. 'No sir,' the young officer replied, 'neither have I, but hop in' said Fitzmaurice, and they took off and beat the hell out of the Dunlaoghaire mail boat, departing for England with a friend of Fitz's on board.

Kingsford-Smith of SOUTHERN CROSS fame was in Baldonnel in early 1930, and flew a number of practice runs prior to his celebrated departure from Portmarnock Strand on 24 June; Horgan was aloft with him on many of those trips. Kingsford-Smith was at that time practically bankrupt, because of the previous costs involved in his long Pacific flights of 1928, and the funding of the Irish venture had exhausted his finance.

It was partially in this context, that on the eve of the historic flight he gave one of his shoes to Vinnie as a souvenir, with the quip that 'if he didn't make the crossing, he wouldn't need it anyway.' The Horgans still have the shoe.

Reverting to the initial acquisition of aircraft and spares by the newly formed Air Service: the Treaty with Britain had been signed on 6 Dec 1921, and a few days later the Martinsyde was delivered to Croydon aerodrome and stored — the necessity that motivated its purchase had fortunately not arisen: it was to arrive in Baldonnel by sea and road in June of 1922; meanwhile it had appropriately been named THE BIG FELLA, because of the association with Michael Collins.

Although vast stocks of every variety of aircraft were available for years after the first world war, when a gunner of the newly formed army of the Irish Free State pulled the lanyard of one of the two eighteen pounder field guns facing the Four Courts and its occupants — the "Irregulars," at the precise time of 0407 hours on the morning of Wednesday 28 June 1922, and the civil war had begun, Major General McSweeney at Baldonnel had no aircraft except THE BIG FELLA, and it was still in its crate. On the 4 July 1922, a Bristol F2B Fighter was delivered from Shotwich in England — the machine had already flown a total of 113 hours; the following day General Russel collected another F2B from the RAF, still in occupation of Collinstown — now Dublin Airport; this aircraft was manufactured in 1919 and had accumulated a time of 174 hours.

McSweeney was airborne in the Collinstown machine on 16th July 1922 on a routine reconnaissance patrol, but things did not go too well, and he subsequently wrote to the Adjutant General, Lt. General Gearoid O'Sullivan:

At 3.45 p.m. on Sunday the 16th. inst. I left here, (he was writing from Baldonnel,) with Lt. T. Nolan as observer, to make a reconnaissance of Tullow, Baltinglass and Newtownbarry. I flew over all the roads between Naas to Tullow at a height of 600 feet, looking for road obstructions and movements of troops. On arriving at Baltinglass I remained over the town for about ten minutes and noticed nothing unusual. I then proceeded to Tullow and remained over it for about fifteen minutes. The town was full of men and they were only standing around and there appeared to be no activity of a military nature. Each entrance to the town at about 200 yards distance was blocked by a stone barrier half way across the road with sufficient space to allow cars to pass. There were no sentries on these barriers. There is a barracks in the centre of the town but there was no activity in or around it. I then started out for Newtownbarry, but after flying for about ten miles my air pressure started to fail. I immediately turned back, using my handpump to keep up the pressure. The engine was running perfectly when I reached Naas and without any warning it completely cut out. As I was fairly low at the time observing the roads, I had to land in the nearest field. In the centre of the field was a ditch, four feet deep and unfortunately covered with grass, and the machine ran into this and turned over. Lt. Nolan was pinned underneath, and after I had pulled him out he lost consciousness. At present he cannot move, but the doctor informs me that he will be alright in a day or two. I have not been able to obtain his reconnaissance report.

It is absolutely essential that I should, as soon as possible, have two more machines, and if these are handed over by the British a demand should be made for new material and not the oldest machines in their establishment. Both machines handed over last week are old. One has crashed and the other is giving trouble. It will take about two weeks to repair the damaged machine.......

By late autumn of 1922 the deficiency had been remedied and the strength had risen to six Bristol fighters, four Avro 504K trainers, four Martinsyde F4 Buzzard Scouts, one SE 5A fighter and the original passenger Martinsyde of Michael Collins.

The Avro 504 was a multi role British made biplane; serving mainly as a trainer, almost 12,000 were produced in various engine forms before manufacture ceased in 1933. Many variants saw service with the RFC, the RAF and numerous countries before, during and after World War One. Powered for the Air Corps by a 100 hp. Gnome Monosoupape rotary single valve motor to which the propeller was attached, the entire engine revolved around the crankshaft. Many of these rotary engines were in their earlier versions lubricated by castor oil, and because the engine was poorly sealed the pilot was deluged with castor oil droplets — a purgative of some potency. There was little throttle adjustment, and the procedure when coming in to land was to interrupt the ignition by means of a push button on top of the control column.

The SE 5A had played a major role in reversing the fortunes of the Allies in the air battles of the Western Front from mid 1917 until the end of the war. It was a fast rugged fighter and proved to be one of the best gun platforms of that war, although, very stupidly, equipped with only one belt fed Vickers machine gun firing through the arc of the propeller: the drum fed Lewis gun, rail mounted over the top of the mainplane had to be aimed and fired by the pilot, as he flew his machine with his other hand; changing the magazine entailed gripping the joystick between the pilots knees, to allow freedom to both his hands. Unfortunately, this fine aeroplane suffered an engine failure during a patrol from Fermoy — it forced landed in a field near Mallow and was burnt by the Irregulars; the pilot escaped without injury. The first fatal flying accident of the corps occurred on 25 June 1923; a DH 9 piloted by Lt. McCulloch crashed 30 minutes after take off, the observer, Lt. McDonagh was killed.

On 7 March 1924, after the Civil War had finished, a small bloodless mutiny broke out in the army amongst members of the officer corps. Dorothy Macardle, in her book THE IRISH REPUBLIC, describes the events that led up to that mutiny:

The trend of the government's policy was alienating many who had supported the Treaty and especially those who, adherents of Michael Collins, had trusted his promise that the Treaty would be used as stepping stone to Independence. Certain disaffected army officers, members of the Irish Republican Brotherhood, formed an organisation within the Free State army to which they gave the name of "The Old IRA." This was countered by the group of IRB members led by General Mulcahy and, in March 1924, a crisis developed which involved the resignation of Mulcahy from the Ministry of Defence and of other members of the army council.

A total of 115 officers absented themselves, on 7 March 1924 "in such a manner as to show wilful defiance of authority," and a further 92 officers "resigned without having been absent since the crisis began." In the conclusion of the affair, the majority of the absconding officers were allowed to resign, but a small number had their commissions withdrawn by the government. Major General W. J. McSweeney, OC Air Services was one of those absconding, together with another 12 officers from Baldonnel and Gormanston. Not a lot of materiel was taken from the various army commands, but from the Air Service alone, defecting junior officers stole 4 Lewis machine guns, 27 rifles and 7,500 rounds of ammunition. The mutiny fizzled out in a few days and all of the arms were returned through the good graces of influential friends; the late Mr Joseph McGrath T.D. handed in the guns and ammunition on behalf of the Air Services officers involved. McSweeney eventually resigned and was succeeded by a Major Maloney, another RFC veteran, but he was unfortunately killed in a crash in 1925; Colonel Russel was now appointed to the command.

The delivery of eight De Havilland Mk.9 bombers to Baldonnel had begun on 1 Jan 1923; they were the most advanced machines of their type with an unprecedented range of 450 miles at a cruising speed of 90 mph. Eight further Bristol Fighters were acquired, and in 1926 the first of the truly postwar trainers, the delightful De Havilland Moth. One Fairey 3F was purchased, but now followed eight Vickers Vespa army co-operation machines plus a plethora of training aircraft from the Avro stable — 621's, 626's, 631's — the Cadet, and then in 1935, a very interesting and graceful machine, the Avro 636. Four of this type were built by A.V. Roe especially for the Air Corps, and they were designed around the Armstrong Siddley Jaguar engines taken from the Vespas which had experienced a high attrition rate and were no longer serviceable. Although the 636 had tandem open cockpits, its performance was reputed to be better than that of the famous Gloster delight — the Gladiator biplane fighter.

Meanwhile, those nine young men had been recruited in 1926 for training as pilots in the service; this was the very first class of cadets to be selected by the Irish army. Colonel W.J. Keane was one of those cadets and again he recalls the nostalgia and the devil-may-care attitude of those early days, an inheritance of course from the harrowing memories of the flying losses of World War One:

'At this time, all of the aircraft in the corps were of World War One vintage — open cockpits, no parachutes, no brakes, and no refinements of any kind. Engine failures were common, and they used to say in bravado that the other greatest hazard in flying was being strangled by your scarf getting caught in the tailplane. We always believed that the good pilot was the fellow who did most aerobatics, aerobatics good or bad and the nearer the ground the better........'

'There was a Commanding Officer's dinner every Thursday night, a kind of RAF pattern prevailed,' — Billy Keane remembered every detail — 'Dinner jacket was compulsory. The cadets resplendent in their new unpaid-for dinner jackets dined at a separate table at the bottom end of the dining room. One fine summer evening in 1926, I was sitting with the other cadets, the "You may smoke, gentlemen," stage had passed, and the bored and subdued cadets sat watching the fresh cigar smoke wafting its way gently towards the rafters. Coffee and liqueurs had been served and the customary after dinner banter filled the room. I sat facing out of the window, at the neat but deserted tennis court, then suddenly, literally out of the blue, shot a Martinsyde Scout — grazed the tennis court and zoomed up out of my picture window view, I was rooted to the chair. Nobody moved for the five to ten minutes that the beat up continued, but the sight, the sound and the sensation of that moment was there and then deeply implanted in the mind and body of a very young and immature cadet.'

Those early years of service flying had taken its toll of officers and cadets alike. A particularly tragic accident occurred in 1934, when the only Fairey 3F, flown by Lt. Arthur Russel crashed into some trees in Rathgar; the pilot and one of the two crewmen died instantly, and the only survivor was very badly burned. Oliver St. J. Gogarty was a friend of the dead officer and he mourned his death:

He had the kind and langorous air
Of gentle knights detached from fear:
And he was quiet in his ways,
He who could set the heavens ablaze
And overtake the setting sun
With speed and soar into his throne.
If modesty clothes bravery,
If gentleness activity;
If earth has ever been the pen
Of heaven-aspiring denizen,
Then Arthur comes into his own,
From lowly things released and flown,
And stands for that haut chivalry
Which scorns the world and scales the sky;
So Death, which no brave spirit harms,
Let him pass out retaining arms.

*   *   *

92

Earlier in 1932 the Air Corps had assisted Jim Mollison, husband of the famous Amy Johnson, in his preparations for the first successful solo crossing of the North Atlantic from east to west. Mollison departed from Portmarnock Strand in a De Havilland Puss Moth on 20 August and flew 3000 miles non stop to Roosevelt Field, New York. Two years later, the Italians, Pont and Sabelli arrived unscheduled in Lahinch, County Clare, after a crossing of the ocean in the LEONARO DA VINCI; the machine was brought to Baldonnel and repaired and continued on its way to Italy. The year 1935 saw a government survey of the Shannon area by the army, and in '37 Baldonnel was scheduled as a fuelling stop in the King's Cup Air Race. One day in the summer of 1938, a small single engined aircraft landed at the corps headquarters and its young pilot enquired as to where he was. On being informed that he was in Ireland he expressed amazement, and explained that he had left New York 30 hours previously intending to fly to California — that was "Wrong Way Corrigan."

With the commencement of the war in 1939, "Central Control," a new unit of the Air Corps was established in a secluded monastery in Clondalkin, County Dublin; this unit was a fundamental part of the Air Defence System. Reporting centres throughout the country, and particularly the LOP's (Look Out Posts) dotted along the coastline provided each of the area military commands with instant information on the movements of belligerent aircraft, shipping, drifting barrage balloons, mines, and personnel or equipment washed in or brought ashore. The data was filtered and sorted out at Command level and then passed on to Central Control who correlated the information and informed GHQ. The data processed was prodigious; for example during the month of May 1941, a total of 2721 aircraft were reported to have been seen or heard over or near our territory; overall aircraft movements for that year came to 19,540 and by 1944 the figure had risen to 30,000.

Central Control records show that at least 162 barrage balloons drifted across Ireland during those years, but only four of them were shot down by Air Corps fighters. Shooting down of barrage balloons was a dangerous business because some carried an explosive pack suspended beneath them, with the charge set to detonate upon the slightest contact — those that were shot down fortunately carried no explosive devices and had to be got rid of because they had been drifting very low and causing damage with their trailing cables to the electricity grids; power line damage from barrage balloons was to plague the ESB during the war.

The officers who established Central Control was a Major W.P. Delamer, who later commanded the corps from 1943-1946. At the

Colonel Charles Lindberg prepares to take Mr. E. DeValera aloft for his first flight in 1936. The aircraft is a Miles Mohawk. Major P.A. Mulcahy, officer commanding the Air Corps, is on the right.

Photo – Irish Press

commencement of hostilities he had been sent to England by the government to gather knowledge of the British Air Defence system. The military there, polite and formal, readily supplied him with what he already knew — data on the workings of the Observer Corps; their telephoning in to a central bureau of the estimated altitudes, speeds, direction and type and the numbers of enemy aircraft etc. etc. He realised, that; although involved in several meetings, he was not obtaining any really relevant information, and he despaired of the success of his mission — the one big answer that eluded him was the British use of radar.

At a final conference with the Air Ministry, and on the eve of his return to Ireland he noticed that one of the senior RAF officers kept glancing at him and smiling during the discussions. When the tedious business was over the officer came across to him and invited him to a drink in the quite corner of the mess bar; he said to the major, 'Remember, Del, the day we met Richthofen's Circus, and you looked across at me to see what I was doing — and my tail was pointing skywards.' Major Delamer of the Irish Army Air Corps was talking with his former flight commander of World War One, who then discreetly said to him, 'Del, what do you want to know?'

In 1917 W.P. Delamer transferred to the RFC from a London house infantry regiment. His "training" was completed in just over 8 hours, but prior to his departure for France, one of the flying instructors at the school was killed, and the CO asked Delamer to stay on as a replacement. This meant that when he was posted to the front in the autumn of 1917 he was a veteran of eighty hours flying experience. His machine was a Spad fighter, a French aircraft of which the RFC had only a few squadrons; the biplane had a 220 hp. in line Hispano Suiza engine which gave it the fastest speed of any aircraft on the western Front — flat out at 10,000 feet it was capable of 120 mph. It proved to be one of the war's outstanding aircraft.

Because of his eighty hours experience, Delamer recalled, 'I could fly that Spad through the eye of a needle.' And that he did, because he survived in the battle area until the spring of 1918 when he was shot down by anti-aircraft fire.

Capt. Manfred von Richthofen, the "Red Baron" was the leading German ace of the war — he commanded Jagdeschwader 1, dubbed "Richthofen's Circus" and equipped with 76 Albatros D5 fighters. At this period in the battles the Germans had obtained total air superiority, and they flaunted their success by decorating their aircraft with garish colour schemes — greens, purples, gold, grotesque figures and ancient symbols; the ace fliers had their names in large lurid lettering painted on the upper wing surfaces, placed there to strike terror into the inexperienced pilots of the RFC, who were pitted against them straight from the flying school, but Delamer and his companions dived home to fight another day.

The brief encounter with the "Circus" came about during a dawn patrol when the flight of three Spads met, head on, a huge formation of multi coloured German aircraft. Delamer's flight commander realized that they had no chance in combat and they made for home — vertically; the Spad could out dive any German fighter.

*   *   *

Coincidentally with the establishment of Delamer's Air Defence Command, and before the dissidents and the IRA had realised what was happening, the government implemented a major decision and the army and the police force went into action and had rounded up by April 1943 almost 600 men who were destined to spend those long years in internment in the Curragh, or in the military detention barracks at Arbour Hill, Dublin. They were considered a danger to the sovereign state that had declared a policy of neutrality; Europe was in turmoil, embroiled in yet another conflict, a war in which Ireland felt that it had no part to play, and yet a war for which there was a fair measure of support for the German side, not based on the rights or wrongs of the confrontation but simply because it was fighting against England — a sympathy which was to rapidly evaporate as the knowledge slowly percolated as to what the Nazis were all about.

In Berlin, an imposing building on the Tirpitz Ufer was the headquarters of the Amt Ausland Abwehr, a sub division of the secret intelligence organisation in the power structure of the Third Reich. The Abwehr, headed by Admiral Wilhelm Canaris was responsible for providing espionage and counterespionage service to the armed forces, and was also involved in sabotage and the collection of foreign intelligence. The activities of the admiral and his large staff were bedevilled from time to time by the SS through the personage of Reinhard Heydrich, a social friend but a technical enemy, who also controlled another unpleasant and interfering agency — the Gestapo. The web of German intelligence was complex and laced with personal animosities, with the work of different groups overlapping and often contradicting in the pursuit of the same information; somebody, somewhere in that web totally mismanaged and miscalculated Irish affairs.

Procurement of information relative to the military strength and armament potential of foreign powers, the agents' network, dropping points and radio and courier links abroad, was the responsibility of Sub-section One under the command of Oberst Piekenbrock, Irish affairs were dealt with by Hauptmann Veesnmayer, whose tenuous contacts with Ireland had led him, and the Abwehr into the false assumption that if Britain went to war, Ireland would automatically take the other side. During World War One, German intelligence had endeavoured to foment trouble amongst the peoples of the colonies of the Allied powers, but the strategy was not very successful, yet it was only when the IRA bombing campaign started in England in 1939 that Canaris took notice, because he then realised that Irish affairs had all but been ignored. He pinned his hopes on Sean Russell, Chief of Staff of the IRA, and their explosives expert, Jim Donovan who had been Director of Chemicals in the anti-treaty IRA of 1922 — they were both in Berlin at the time, but Russell was later to die on board the U boat bringing him to Ireland. German military intelligence had hoplessly miscalculated the potential of the IRA; their maps were forty years out of date, and finally their efforts were totally eclipsed by an Irish colonel, and his dapper assistant who was to master mind Irish intelligence through most of the World War Two — Major Dan Bryan. Colonel Liam Archer was the Director of G2 — the intelligence section of the army, until his appointment as Assistant Chief of Staff in June 1941, Bryan now succeeded to the command with the rank of colonel. In total contrast to its German counterpart, G2 existed in a modest building in army headquarters on Parkgate Street, Dublin, and its personnel had no grandiose titles; the Abwehr even got this location wrong, their out of date maps showed GHQ as a hospital.

Irish Military Intelligence during the crucial years of 1939 - 1945 was organised along the following lines:

FIELD AND COMBAT INTELLIGENCE.

Information obtained by observation, reconnaissance patrols, captured documents, prisoners, aerial photography. Data obtained from actual combat.

FOREIGN ARMIES.

Knowledge of the enemy, allies or potential allies.

AIR AND MARINE.

External air forces and naval forces over and in Ireland and Irish waters. Coast watching.

CENSORSHIP AND CONTROL OF COMMUNICATIONS.

Censorship — prevention of leakages and collection of information from censorship.

Communications with Europe and Great Britain — cables, shipping and radio.

SIGNAL DETACHMENT.

Illicit and other radio detection of clandestine transmitters.

MILITARY AND SECURITY PROBLEMS WITH VARIOUS
COUNTRIES.
Great Britain, Germany, USA, Spain, Portugal, Italy, Japan and
the Vatican.
PUBLICITY AND PRESS RELATIONS.
Public and press relations, and involvement in censorship
activities.

Despite the declared neutrality of the state, close ties existed
between the Irish and British military forces, although these
relationships waxed or waned in direct proportion to the success or
otherwise of the allies. At the commencement of the war Churchill
was deeply concerned about the possibility of German submarines
receiving supplies in Irish harbours, and Archer went to London to
confer with the British, and to assure them that no such succour was
being given. His opposite number was Rear Admiral Godfrey — Chief
of British Naval Intelligence; the admiral amongst other things, was
seeking information on the effectiveness of the Irish LOP's - look out
posts, established around the coast to feed constant data to army
intelligence. Archer gave him the details and further assurances
relative to the submarines: the colonel was telling the truth — no
sustenance had been given to U boats in Irish waters either then, or
at any other time up to the end of the war. Later the British were to
broach the subject again, when Irish cigarettes were found on a
captured German sailor, but the explanation was relatively simple —
a sub surfaced near a trawler and the fisherman gave the Germans
some fish and a few packets of cigarettes. At the conference,
Admiral Godfrey conveniently omitted to inform Archer but the
colonel already knew, that the navy was paying for information from
pro British Irish residents, and that they had also sent in a former
officer of the Indian police who contacted people with Indian colonial
backgrounds, and offered to supply them with radio sets to transmit
intelligence information on activities in Ireland.
At this particular meeting in London, and indeed at many others
the British continually expressed worry about the possible leakage of
Allied military matters to the Germans from Irish sources, but they
were to find out that Archer and Bryan's people had done their work
very thoroughly – there were no leaks, andthis fact was borne out by
their own paid agents who never had anything to report. G2 had tabs
on each of those agents, but left them alone unless they became too
inquisitive about Irish military affairs, in which case they were
quietly rounded up.
The chief concern to the Irish and also to the British, was the
high powered transmitter in the German embassy; although silent in

the latter years, this equipment was not removed until late 1943, and then only after intense diplomatic pressure. Herr Hempel, the ambassador, was a true diplomat, but as Colonel Bryan discovered relatively early, the ambassador's clandestine capability was limited and highly suspect, as the embassy tapped out to Berlin in 1940, that the Air Corps had just received delivery of 170 fighters and 12 seaplanes! Berlin itself was interested in the mobilisation plans of the Irish army.

From captured German documents passed on to the Irish, there seems little doubt that the Nazis had planned to invade Ireland when the opportunity presented itself; this would have been after the defeat of Russia when they intended to turn their military might to the west. Like the French and the Spanish before them, they had realised that militarily, Ireland was the back door to England, and therefore side by side with their preparations to invade Britain after the fall of Dunkirk, Operation "SEALION" was to be paralleled by Operation "GREEN", the invasion force for Ireland. Hitler had already stated at a naval conference, 'if we could seize Ireland, we would end the war.' Their planned scheme of attack was to be an assault landing at Wexford, followed by an advance up the Nore valley; whether or not they knew it, this was a very heavily defended area known as the "BOX," and manned by troops of Major General Costelloe's First Division; Cork harbour was regarded as too tough to take from the sea, and the plan was to capture the port by parachute troops dropped to the north. These preparations were augmented by a folksy run down on the people, their culture and past history; a tourist type Irish dictionary was also supplied together with two cardboard covered tabloids of photographs, one for Northern Ireland and the other for the South. The photographs were like the old black and white picture postcards of long ago and gave views of every harbour, estuary, lough, mountain range, river mouth and major beach, interspersed with shots of thatched cottages, pigs, cows, hens, small towns, farmers and townspeople — a collection of photographs undoubtedly copied from every picture postcard collection in Ireland, supplemented by the camera shots of innumerable German "tourists" during the years before; whilst the photographs might have been quaint, there was no mistaking the sinister intent of the detailed survey notes. There was even a warning about the unhygenic habits of the natives!

*　　*　　*

It was the dawn of 22 June 1940 and Oberleutnant Max Gruen was becoming exceedingly impatient: three times had he flown his Heinkel 111 bomber in a slow 360 degree turn over County Meath;

beneath him in the bomb aimers' position was a big man with his face glued up against the perspex — Hermann Goertz; the spy was desperately endeavouring to locate the recognition signal supposedly to come from the area below. Fifty three year old Dr. Hermann Goertz, veteran of World War One — alias Heinz Kruse, was wearing the uniform of a major in the SS unit of the Luftwaffe, but he was also in the employ of the SD Abwehr; his uniform was a ploy to cover up the true nature of his mission and to avoid being executed as a spy if dropped in enemy territory. It was a tradition of past wars that only agents wearing civilian clothes were truly regarded as "spies;" being captured wearing regulation uniform usually afforded protection against the firing squad; Goertz would destroy his uniform after the drop was safely completed.

The pilot's impatience was not stemming from the fear of interception by Irish fighters — he had flown many times over Ireland without interference, but the sky to the east was changing colour, and Goertz or no Goertz, he was not going to be caught in daylight on the return flight to France. His enthusiastic passenger finally spotted the light and Gruen brought the Heinkel down for a low pass, but they lost the beam of the torch on the run in and he had to go around again. Gruen shouted through his larynx microphone, 'For God's sake Goertz, will you get the hell out of here before somebody shoots the arse off us.' The signal showed up clearly on the next approach and the spy parachuted down upon the target; the Heinkel had already turned for home when the crewman remembered the second parachute containing the precious radio transmitter — it was to have gone out immediately after Goertz; the airman pushed it out anyway as the bomber climbed away towards France.

Goertz was free for almost eighteen months — he was arrested by the Garda in a house in Clontarf on 27 November 1941. Without his radio — it had probably drifted into the sea during the drop, he had only modest success in his activities; some of his IRA associates, whom he had sent across the border to spy on the British, were gathering information which was useless: the numbers of troops stationed at various locations, but without the provision of regimental identification, equipment, transport status etc. — worthless stuff which Goertz endeavoured to dispatch to Germany by any means possible, including via the cook of an Irish ship bound for Portugal, who was later detained in Lisbon by English agents in the act of passing on this information to another German spy. The message was in code, but Colonel Archer was able to facilitate the British; thanks to his cryptologist, the cipher was passed to London. There is some evidence to substantiate the claim that, thanks to Irish army intelligence, the Allies were in possession of one of the German cryptograms used during the Battle of the Bulge — the Ardennes: Goertz's code. That battle cost the Allies 76,980 casualties, but it destroyed the last of the German reserves with incurred losses of 70,000 men and 50,000 prisoners, together with the destruction of 550 tanks and 1600 aircraft.

Long before that battle, German invasion plans for Ireland had been seized in a house in Terenure in May of 1940, and G2 associated Goertz's presence and activity with such plans. Imprisoned in Arbour Hill and subsequently in No. 3 Internment Camp in Athlone, he proved himself to be an extremely difficult detainee — although always courteous and correct. He flatly denied that he was involved with any such invasion plans and went on hunger strike a number of times to assert his innocence; he denied that his involvement with the IRA was to cause trouble in Eire, but rather to direct Irish national activities against the British in the North; he also claimed that he missed his true landing point in Co. Tyrone.

Goertz was the only German spy to remain at liberty for such a lengthy period; the other eleven, who had either parachuted in or come ashore from U boats, were apprehended within twenty four hours. Typical of the Abwehr's mishandling of their Irish affairs was the fate of Karl Anderson — fresh out of his submarine in the Dingle Peninsula, and speaking English with a perfect Irish accent — only to enquire from a postman as to when the next train was due to leave for Tralee, not knowing because of his maps and his briefing that the last train out of Dingle had left twenty years before; twenty minutes later for him, he was in the Garda barracks in the town.

Colonel Bryan and his staff at G2 had everything under control: the German spies were in prison, the British informers had nothing to pass on, cable and radio worries were sealed and constantly monitored, and Britain had finally realised that the presence of a neutral and friendly nation on their flank was a worthwhile possession. Everything was quiet and totally co-operative, until the insensitive United States ambassador, David Gray, stirred it all up again. Gray, through family relationships with the Roosevelts was able to bypass diplomatic channels and had direct access to the president. United States policy at that time was appreciative and supportive of a "neutral" and friendly Ireland, but the ambassador's avowed mission was to drag the country into the war. Newspapers in the States had carried lurid stories of Germans, and even of Japanese, supposedly wandering freely around Ireland, and then Gray brought up the old chestnut — leakage of information from Ireland. Gray's approach to Irish affairs was so sour that a press correspondent for an English newspaper, Bertie Rosse — Lord Rosse from Kerry, wrote of him that he was 'like a cushion — his face bore the imprint of the last man that sat on him.'

The conferences and the assurances started all over, and eventually it was the British who convinced their ally of the integrity and the quality of the measures taken by Irish military intelligence — achievements which contributed considerably to the maintenance of Irish neutrality during the years of World War Two.

Military and "security" problems with the Vatican arose in a most unusual way. Allied intelligence had been aware of the fact, that after Dunkirk the Germans had segregated a number of British soldiers of Irish nationality, and were indoctrinating them with propaganda, and giving them special training to prepare them to commit acts of sabotage against the Allies after their surreptitious release. A captured officer, Major McGrath, was placed in charge, and a request was made to the Vatican for the services of a Catholic chaplain. An Irish priest duly arrived, and he was later to report to his superiors in Rome, who informed G2 of the Irish army through clerical sources in Dublin, who then informed the British, that Major McGrath, a loyal officer, had advised the soldiers to "co-operate" and when the opportunity presented itself, to escape. Thirty of the saboteurs arrived in Sweden to "blow up the British legation" — as soon as they crossed the border, they surrendered to the Swedish army — that was the end of the indoctrination exercise.

After the war was over Goertz was still in custody, but he had been sentenced in absentia by the British to four years hard labour. He was extremely agitated by the Nuremberg Trials because the SS and the SD Abwehr had been categorised as criminal organisations and he was a member of both. He now campaigned anxiously with letters to the Department of Justice to be allowed to remain in Ireland; as his home was in Potsdam which was occupied by the Red Army, if he was repatriated he argued, he was a marked man, having been an active anti-Bolshevik in the German "Free Corps" long before Hitler came to power. By August of 1945 he was willing to trade with the government for his freedom by telling all, although he still maintained that his activities were misunderstood. General Freiher von Lahausen, his immediate superior, had testified at Nuremberg that, before the war three separate Irish groups had approached the German government for support for a revolutionary rising in Ireland with a view to unity; Lahausen was in favour of the idea and Goertz was part of that help. He, Goertz, was "unhappy" about his assigned mission to friendly Ireland and he quietly approached Admiral Canaris who advised him to cause no such trouble, but to direct Irish energies towards the Six Counties and await developments in Eire. His story was not convincing and his health was poor; he was discharged from custody by an order dated 26 August 1946 signed by the Minister for Justice, Mr. G. Boland — further difficulties evolved before he was finally released on parole on 19 October 1946.

Of all of those spies, Major Dr. Hermann Goertz's ending was the most tragic: after being released he had decided to remain in Ireland, but he was suspected by the Allies of being an ardent Nazi and pressure from them forced the Irish government to prepare to hand him over — in the presence of his sympathetic apprehenders on 23 May 1947 he crushed the deadly cyanide capsule between his teeth. He rests with many of his countrymen in the glen of Glencree, County Wicklow.

*   *   *

One hundred and sixty three foreign military aircraft crashed or forced landed in Ireland from the date of the British declaration of war on 3 September 1939 until the surrender of Germany on 8 May 1945........

Oberleutnant Kurt Mollenhauer received his first command at Abbeville, France, in the summer of 1940; a pilot in the maritime patrol group KG 40 equipped with Focke Wulf 200's, his squadron was, according to Churchill, "the scourge of the Atlantic". Their aircraft, the Condor, was a sophisticated four engined machine, powered by nine cylinder 800 hp. BMW radials with fuel injection; it had first flown in 1937 as a civil airliner with an immense endurance: with fuel for 48 hours, combined with a cruising speed of 200 mph. — an almost unbelievable capability by the standards of today. To the Luftwaffe it was an ideal long range reconnaissance and anti-shipping aircraft, and when war broke out, the remaining six aircraft of the initial series were drafted into military service and equipped with machine guns and bomb racks.

Mollenhauer took off into the dawn of Tuesday, 20 August 1940, from Abbeville and headed SW across France to enter the Bay of Biscay over the German direction finding station at Nantes — well to the south of the range of British aircraft from Fighter Command. The routine reconnaissance anti-shipping mission of KG 40 aircraft was twelve hours with a standard crew, but quite frequently the radius of action was increased by doubling the crew complement, with the result that these aircraft could patrol up to a thousand miles from the Irish coast. Mollenhauer's flight had a single crew but its function was important: all long range Luftwaffe aircraft were fitted with automatic recording equipment which traced out a continuous reading of temperature, pressure and humidity — these observations were of prime importance to the air force and they were supplied either by patrolling aircraft, or by radio transmissions at set times from low profile anchored buoys; U boats rarely broadcast weather information because of the risk of their signals being picked up by the enemy which would disclose the position of the submarine; Mollenhauer had on board a Luftwaffe meteorologist, Dr. Eric Kruger, who was on a fact finding task calculated to up date the techniques of the air patrols.

The outbound route posed no difficulty — it was a beautiful morning, and once the patrol had made the hazardous Bay of Biscay crossing and entered the North Atlantic well to the south of Ireland, the danger of attack from RAF aircraft disappeared and the crew were able to concentrate their attention on the secondary purpose of their detail — the interception and destruction of Allied shipping. The pilot eased the Condor down lower and lower to maintain sight of the ocean, as visibility and ceiling had diminished with increasing stratus cloud, but Kruger and himself had come to the same conclusion — a warm front was approaching Ireland from the Atlantic, five hundred miles of stratified cloud and drizzle — ideal for meteorological observation but useless for an anti-shipping strike. He stood down the crew from their action stations — Beumer, Kyck, Bell and Wochner, but Wochner was the navigator and he kept the plot going on his chart, the others watched the met. man. Climbs, descents, to port for 30 minutes, to starboard for 40 — they penetrated the front at different speeds as Kruger made endless notes and observations and compared the readouts of the automatic recorder with his own instruments and with the standard instruments fitted to the aeroplane; Kurt had had enough after three hours and he asked Feldwebel Ludwig Wochner for a course for home — Wochner gave him the heading and said: 'Herr Leutnant — any height you like until I tell you to climb; we will be well to the south of the mountains of SW Ireland — but just in case.'

At 1300 hours the navigator called for the climb and Mollenhauer took the Condor up to 4000 metres just to be sure; Wochner requested the level to be maintained for 30 minutes, a distance of about 100 miles at their cruising speed; at 1330 hrs the Condor descended in an endeavour to resume its patrol on the homeward leg, but at a height of less than 1000 metres it was seen from the ground to be proceeding west along the northern edge of the Dingle Peninsula. Fifteen minutes later, in full level flight the four engined aircraft graunched to a halt along the slopes of Bealnaleacon Hill near Mount Brandon, Co. Kerry — two of the crew were injured, but the others were safe, and all were eventually escorted down the mountain by about sixty local people with whom they shared two bottles of brandy and innumerable bars of chocolate.

They were the first German airmen of World War Two to land here, and they were interned in the Curragh for the duration — to be followed in the next few years by forty six of their Luftwaffe compatriots. Fifteen of their aircraft later came to grief in various parts of the country, and twenty four crew members were killed. No German machines were flown out — most of them had been wrecked anyway, either in the crash or subsequently by their crews.

*   *   *

Four hundred and seventy eight RAF personnel were crewmen in a total of 106 incidents and accidents involving their aircraft in Ireland — 182 were killed, with 12 missing; 45 were interned and 239 handed over at the border, the interned were to be returned later. The circumstances of their tragic deaths varied, but as with the other belligerents in many of the crashes, little was left of either the aircraft or its occupants. The dead were gathered with reverence by the army and afforded full military honours; the records of the time contain ample tribute from the representatives of the warring nations to the respect and consideration which was given to their downed airmen. Flying Officer B.J. Sawiak was one of the casualties.

At 0756 hours on Monday, 23 August 1942, the observer at the LOP on Carnsore Point entered in his daily log: "Aircraft out to sea moving north." — that was Hauptmann Gottfried Berndt and his three crewmen in their JU-88, serial number 1688 from squadron 4U-KH: they carried no mines or depth charges and were on a patrol reconnaissance of the Irish Sea and the eastern coastline of Ireland. The JU-88 continued flying parallel to the coastline and was next reported from Clogher Head, but this time when spotted it was inland and was flying south with three RAF Spitfires in full pursuit — a running battle was in progress and the lookout heard the chatter of the machine guns.

Flying Officer Boleslaw J. Sawiak was stationed at Kilkeel in Northern Ireland; he was a pilot in 315 Squadron RAF — a Polish unit equipped with Spitfire VB's, a superb fighter aircraft powered by a Rolls Royce Merlin engine of 1440 hp. and carrying the powerful armament of two cannon and four machine guns. His flight was on standby that morning, and when British radar picked up the enemy plane Boleslaw was the first to scramble, and within minutes of his takeoff had intercepted the German who was hugging the surface of the sea in Dundrum Bay — Unteroffizier Josef Reiser on the upper guns shouted the warning on the intercom, 'Achtung Spitfire!' but Sawiak had caught the JU-88 with his first burst and wounded Oberfeldwebel Karl Hund in the hand; pieces of aluminium flew from the top of the port wing. Hauptmann Berndt turned inland and hugged the contours of the ground on a southwesterly course for the safety of Eire; Boleslaw was joined by the two other Spitfires from his flight and they commenced a series of beam and stern attacks on the Junkers — soon there was a telltale wisp of smoke streaming back from its starboard engine, but it did not diminish speed. Boleslaw Sawiak, who was the flight commander, now realised that they were over neutral territory and he ordered the others to break off the action to the east. Since they possessed a speed superiority of 100 mph. over the Luftwaffe aeroplane he calculated that they would be able to intercept again off the south coast of Eire, when the enemy flew out to sea on its way back to France — he pulled up into a steep left climbing turn, but a single bullet from the MG 81 of the ventral gunner of the JU-88 penetrated the side of the cockpit and entered his chest. He got the Spitfire down in a field near Rathoath, Co. Meath, but died from his wounds later that evening in St. Bricins Military Hospital, Dublin.

His two companions intercepted the JU-88 near Tramore and gave it the coup de grâce; Gottfried Berndt crash landed in one of M. Eugene Power's fields in Tourgare near the town, with no further injuries to his crew. They were interned.

*   *   *

In 41 crashes or forced landings, 275 American airmen or soldiers came down on Irish soil — 15 were killed, and the remainder were handed back at the border, none were interned. The most noteworthy of all those war crashes was the unscheduled arrival, in the grounds of Athenry Agricultural College, of an American lieutenant general and his staff ....

Jacob Loucks Devers was born in Pennsylvania in 1887, and was educated in a very popular type of school in the America of those years — the military academy. Commissioned in 1909 as a second lieutenant in the field artillery, his career became routine in the army and he went to war in France as a captain with his regiment. Seventeen years of his subsequent service was to be administrative with most of it spent in the United States Military Academy at West Point; his credentials were impressive. That day, at 1150 hours on 15 January 1943, when he arrived with his Flying Fortress, TENNESSE BELLE, in the grounds of the Agricultural College in Athenry, Co. Galway, he was a lieutenant general in charge of all the

US armoured units, and was later destined to command the US 6th Army Group in its advance from Marseilles to Strasbourg — included in that advance was one of the most successful airborne operations of the war........

General George C. Marshall, head of the Joint Chiefs of Staff of the American forces required first hand information from a trustworthy source on the various theatres of war to which American troops had been committed; Marshall selected an impressive team: in addition to the lieutenant general there was Major General E.H. Brooks, Brigadier General G.N. Barns, Brigadier General W.B. Palmer together with a staff colonel and a major. Devers' mission was to be extensive and demanding: a comprehensive report from the Far and Near East, the Mediterranean and the European battlefronts. The task was so important that nothing was left to chance: a special crew was assigned from the Fifteenth Air Force with a brand new Flying Fortress, a B-17G, service number 19045, promptly christened TENNESSEE BELLE by the crew, and emblazoned upon each side of the nose by the ground crew chief with the name, and a bathing beauty of astounding mammalion proportions; the three stars denoting the personal transport of a lieutenant general were discreetly painted just beneath the lady's feet.

This Boeing Flying Fortress, the B-17G was the late 1942 variant of a four engined bomber that was a classic machine of its time, and although lighter in bombload capacity than many other contemporary aircraft, it had an awesome defensive armament and an ability to absorb almost catastrophic battle damage together with an altitude capability and performance far in excess of the other heavy aircraft of World War Two. Devers' machine was powered by four Wright Cyclone 1200 hp. radial engines giving it a maximum speed of 300 mph. and a service ceiling of 35,000 feet with an impressive range; 13 Browning large calibre machine guns provided the defensive armament. They left the United States on 14 December and flew direct to Marrakech in Morocco, North Africa — then to Cairo, Bombay, Calcutta; the final leg of the fact finding tour was to have been from Gibraltar to a bomber base in Scotland.

At 0600 hours GMT. — 0700 hours local Gibraltar time, Capt. T.M. Nullings opened up the power levers of the TENNESSEE BELLE — destination Scotland; Nullings flew west for 300 miles to get well clear of the Spanish coast before turning NNE on his course for Scotland. As the bomber climbed, Lt. J.K. McLaughlin, the co-pilot, vacated his seat to allow the lieutenant general to view the splendid dawn and the coast of Cadiz; Nullings continued his climb to the west. At the navigation station, Lt. B.G. Collins had laid out his charts, his plotting was precise as always and he utilised the last fading glimpse of the stars to confirm his position and work out a speed, and from it an estimated time of arrival at the point at which Nullings was to head north for home.

At precisely the same time as Devers was airborne from the Rock, Oberst Horst Ludwigshap, commander of Jagdeschwader 32 at Bordeaux, equipped with the Jabo-Rei, the long distance fighter bomber version of the deadly Luftwaffe FW-190, was awakened by his servant; he took coffee and bread rolls, washed, shaved and donned his leather flying suit and for one hour attended to the paper work in the squadron office. Fuel was short and he was going to fly the only mission scheduled for that morning — a sweep of 400 miles into the Bay of Biscay, he was airborne at 0800 hrs. GMT. Meanwhile, Devers, back in the belly of the bomber had his breakfast: fresh Moroccan orange juice, coffee and crisp bread rolls uplifted at Gib. during the stopover.

The Boeing 17-G featured a new chin turret which was manned by Sergeant Louis Harris, the twin Brownings occupied the turret, but the sight and the traversing and firing mechanism was in the nose dome — Devers was anxious to see the new installation and he moved up to the nose dome to look at the setup — Harris politely moved aside, offered the general his bone dome and explained the mechanism of the guns; Devers fired a burst — it was 0920 hours GMT. Oberst Ludwigshap saw the red points of the chatter from the bomber's guns against the cloud background and he manoeuvred into position to attack from above at the front, the vulnerable spot of the Fortress; his first burst of 13 mm. armour piercing penetrated the bomber in the nose but did no further damage, no ricochets and the rounds exited the other side. 'Let him have it General,' said Harris, Devers had Ludwigshap approaching the outer ring of the electrical sight on his second pass; he waited until the Focke Wulf touched the edge of the red circle and then he pressed the triggers and held them — the 190 disintegrated. The bomber continued north.

Cloud cover increased as they flew over the Bay of Biscay; Collins became increasingly disturbed when Nullings refused him permission to ask for radio bearings — Nullings was afraid of a further interception and he was also conscious of Collins' capacity as a navigator — 'keep the dead reckoning plot going Gerry — we're right into wind and all you have to worry about is the estimated time of arrival — if you are worried about the wind I'll come down to ocean level for a drift, but that depression is stationary and we are running solidly up along its west side — that forecast is deadly accurate and it was confirmed by a Liberator coming the other way this morning.'

At 1110 hours Collins decided that they must be in Scotland, since for the preceding 19 minutes they had been flying over land — mountain, bog and loch but yet no aerodrome; after 30 minutes of circling and frantic work now by his radio man, he had to admit to Nullings that they were lost and fuel was dangerously low.

Above the radio operator's position were pasted the following instructions:

1. Do not land in EIRE except in an emergency.

2. How to tell you are over neutral Ireland (EIRE): The word EIRE has been spelled out in six foot block letters at 83 places along the EIRE coastline and along the border.

3. Shortly after aircraft are observed over EIRE, Irish authorities broadcast same on Irish radio giving location so, if unsure of position standby on the listed frequencies and intercept message.

The radio man had checked out the listed frequencies but to no avail; after further speculation Nullings fell into the trap: he read the green sward beneath him as solid ground and he lowered the wheels for a landing — the Fortress skidded to a halt, badly damaged but in one piece on the grounds of Athenry Agricultural College.

The LDF was first to the scene, and in accordance with the custom of the Defence Forces, the crew were treated with every courtesy — their property was guarded, but of necessity their personal weapons were seized. Because of the importance of the passengers of the TENNESSEE BELLE, senior officers were quickly on the scene and the party escorted to lunch at the Railway Hotel in Athenry — Devers returned the courtesy and paid for the meal.

Once the general realised that they were not going to be interned he spoke quite freely to his escorts about his mission and his idea about the conduct of the war. He was greatly surprised that Ireland was still able to get petroleum from the British, as according to him, the U boat onslaught on the tankers in the Atlantic had increased in ferocity and had caused an alarming number of sinkings. Surprisingly, he knew very little about the war in Russia, other than the massive losses incurred by American shipping, not in the delivery of supplies to the Soviets when they were heavily guarded and in convoy, but on the return sailings, empty and without escorts. He was angry with the Red Army who had accepted any help that the Americans could give — massive supplies of every variety, but who in turn steadfastly refused to give the Americans any information on the progress of their war. He blamed American government policy for bungling in the Philippines, where during the preceding years the American army had been advising their government to give them their freedom; if this had been done, according to Devers, the Philippines would not have fallen into Japanese hands. Major General Brooks was most impressed with the discipline dress and behaviour of the Irish soldiers, and he confided to one of the Irish officers that he considered that Ireland's policy of neutrality was the correct one.

By Midnight of Friday 15 January 1943, Lt. General Devers and his party were safely in Northern Ireland through the courtesy of the army and the permission of the government. His B-17G, the Flying Fortress, suitably dismantled, followed sometime later.

*   *   *

Civil aircraft did not escape the tragedies of that war........

At 2215 hours on 27 July 1943, G-AGES, a BOAC S.25 Short Sunderland type four engined flying boat departed Lisbon on a scheduled flight to the base at Foynes Co. Limerick; Captain Tom Allitt was in command, and on board were 6 other crewmen and 18 passengers of different nationalities, some of whom were civilians, others were military. The flying boat carried a very important cargo — 30,000 letters to relatives in England from British servicemen in Japanese POW camps.

The flight was routine, but it arrived at Foynes thirty minutes ahead of schedule and the base was closed in low stratus. Allitt proceeded to orbit above the cloud at a position they believed to be Loop Head at the mouth of the Shannon, but apparently, "night effect," a phenomenon which intensifies at sunset or sunrise and induces errors into the accuracy of bearings obtained by the aircraft's own antenna, together with a wind change, led the crew into the mistake.

A decision was made to break cloud in the vicinity of Loop Head and to fly up the river to Foynes; tragically the actual position of the flying boat was twenty miles further south and the descent was taking the aircraft on a parallel course into Brandon Bay. Unknowingly, it was letting down into a valley which was sloping upwards towards them; Allitt finally glimpsed the wall of rock approaching ahead and he frantically endeavoured to make a tight turn; twenty feet would have cleared the rocky outcrop, but at 0430 hours on 28 July 1943 the wingtip impacted the surface of Slieveglass, Mount Brandon, at a height of 1550 feet, and in the dreadful crash eleven of the occupants were killed including the captain. Only 2570 of the precious letters were salvaged.

That deadly mountain was to collect yet another aeroplane within a month, when an RAF Search and Rescue Sunderland, from Castlearchdale in Northern Ireland, crashed with the loss of all on board.

*   *   *

The Air Corps had to salvage every one of the crashes, and most of the aircraft involved were of the heavy type; they came down in the mountains, upon the islands and in the sea. Many of them landed on the bogs, as the treacherous green surface seemed flat and inviting from the air; a recovery crew from Baldonnel discovered an American fighter, intact but lying over on its back on the soggy moss. The pilot was dead, but ironically received no injuries in the forced landing; he had survived the impact, only to break his neck against the canopy top when he released his harness straps as he hung upside down.

My assigned duty for one of those recovery missions concerned a balloon, not an aeroplane. A forestry worker heard its cable thrashing through the trees, and looking skywards saw what it was attached to. With the help of his companions he wound the cable around a tree trunk, effectively anchoring the balloon; the head forester telephoned the army. We got there in an armoured car and immediately saw the danger — the deadly explosive device was hanging some few hundred feet down the cable; we released the balloon and it drifted out towards the Atlantic.

The armoured car driver brought us back to the barracks by way of one of the completed runways, and there — jogging along in the opposite direction was our man with his cart and the two large barrels. Some of the dry toilet facilities at the camp required the very necessary chore of being cleaned out a number of times each week, and that was the job of our friend, and there he was moving into action with the horse and cart and the two honey barrels. He augmented his pay by selling homemade butter, which was called "shitman's butter" by everybody except those who bought it.

The State listed its activities relative to the war participants in the following categories:

ALLIED AIRCRAFT PERMITTED TO LEAVE AFTER LANDING (FLOWN AWAY.)

ALLIED AIRCRAFT SALVAGED AND RETURNED TO BELLIGERENTS CONCERNED.

ALLIED AIRCRAFT NOT SALVAGED AND BROUGHT TO AIR CORPS STORES.

BRITISH AIRCRAFT WHICH FORCED LANDED AND WERE SUBSEQUENTLY PURCHASED FOR THE AIR CORPS.

GERMAN AIRCRAFT WHICH CRASHED OR FORCED LANDED IN THIS COUNTRY.

The corps had three fulltime salvage crews in action, and right from the beginning of the war it had been discreet government policy to hand back to the Allies at the border, their forced landed or damaged aircraft, or what was salvageable from the crashes;

machines that could be flown out were allowed to do so and were usually taken away by the crews that flew them in.

British aircraft permitted to depart:

Flying boats ·	9
Twin engined	9
Fighters	6
Training	4
Four engined	1

Seventeen other machines were salvaged and returned together with fifty other aircraft partially salvaged.

American aircraft permitted to depart:

Four engined	8
Twin engined	7
Training and co-op	3

A further 21 part or fully salvaged were handed over.

The main problem on the crash sites was the presence of explosive materiel such as cannon shells, bombs, mines or even flares, and because of the location of these places it was extremely difficult to gain access to the area of the crash. Because of the nature of their missions, many of the machines were blown up on impact by their own ordnance and horrific scenes of carnage were commonplace. It is to the credit of the Defence Forces and the LDF and the local Irish people that in every instance remains were gathered and identified and given full military honours.

Captain Basil Peterson was an Air Corps officer in charge of one of those salvage teams, and he recalls this story:

The American airmen had more than their share of amusing characters, and the most interesting one I encountered met me at the border.

A Lockheed bomber had landed safely on a beach in County Meath and, while I was getting my men and vehicles together at Baldonnel to go and dismantle it, I received an order to take a car and go immediately to the scene of the landing; there I was to report to a senior officer from GHQ. On arrival, I found that officer supervising the loading, into a turf lorry, of a number of guns and equipment taken from the plane. In addition there were the personal kits belonging to the crew, who had already been taken away and were probably over the border by now.

The senior officer listed all the equipment, and then had it covered with a tarpaulin over which turf was piled; I couldn't understand this, as the transfer of American crews and aircraft was an open secret along the border. The senior officer impressed on me that this was all very hush-hush, and that we would be met at the border by some senior US officers. As he was senior to me I couldn't argue with him, but I did ask him did the concealed equipment contain the new Norden bombsight — the one they claimed could drop a bomb in a pickle barrel from 20,000 feet. He refused to answer, and we went on our way; we were in a car and the turf lorry following at a distance behind.

When we reached the Irish customs post, the customs man came over to the car and, recognising me, said, "Hello Captain, what are you running over today?" I got a nudge from the other officer, and so replied nonchalantly, "Nothing really, we are just here to meet someone."

"If it's the Yanks you are looking for they are down at the bridge," the customs man replied. I thanked him and drove on to where a large Chevrolet truck was stationary — our turf lorry having been parked discreetly behind us. By this time the senior officer was looking somewhat nonplussed — I think he had expected to be met by a staff car. As soon as we stopped, the cab door of the truck opened and a very unusually dressed soldier appeared. He was wearing a sort of a baseball cap with the peak pushed up, below that he wore a lumberjacket marked with a corporal's stripes. The rest of his clothes were more or less standard army gear; he had at least a three day growth of beard.

The senior officer exclaimed, "My God, see what he wants," I got out and moved up to the front of the car. The corporal came up to me, eyed me up and down and then asked, "You're an officer?" I replied "Yes, I'm a captain." At that he drew himself up, gave me a smart salute and said, "Corporal Joe Wilkins, United States 8th. Air Force reporting, sir."

Then we got down to business. I said, "Look Joe, there's a side road just up there. I'll put my lorry into it and if you back your truck up, we'll hand over the goods." This we did, and the senior officer, now speechless because he was acutely aware of the veil of secrecy surrounding the Norden bombsight, and the extraordinary precautions taken by the Americans to prevent it falling into German hands, finally produced the list of the equipment — including the bombsight. Each item was ticked off as it was handed over, but Corporal Joe was becoming restless. He turned to me and said, "Look Cap, all I want is the Lootenant's pants — he's going to a dance tonight. Just dump in the rest!" '

*   *   *

The fortunes of war for some Allied and German airmen and their navy personnel brought them, either to their deaths in Ireland

113

from crashes or as a result of combat with the enemy and from wounds received in action, to two internment camps in the Curragh on the plains of County Kildare. The British and Allied Camp was opened on 17 October 1940 and was subsequently transferred to Gormanston aerodrome County Meath; at its peak it contained a total of forty five airmen — British, Canadian, Polish, French and New Zealanders, together with an American in RAF service; eleven escaped and the remainder were quietly released from Gormanston in late October 1943. This group of internees was distinct from the many other RAF personnel who on arrival here were either allowed to "fly out" in what they brought in, or were "handed over" at the border.

The German Camp at the Curragh, established on 31 August 1940, eventually contained fifty two Luftwaffe fliers and two hundred and ten sailors. One internee escaped, Oberleutnant Konrad Neymeyr, only to be recaptured by the British at sea, and Oberfeldwebel Max Hohaus was returned home because of injuries received in a Condor crash at Durrus, Co. Cork. The German internees were repatriated on 13 August 1945, leaving Alexandria Basin on the steam ship St. Andrew — a number elected to remain in Ireland; their release from the Curragh was accompanied by a signed statement from the Camp Commandant to each man which read:

1. I am to inform you that you are leaving for Germany in a week or two. I have been so informed by my authorities officially.
2. No one to be interned, to be treated as honourable demobilised soldiers.
3. To be sent to the British or American zone of occupation. Will not be transferred to any other zone, only with own free will and consent.
4. No bicycles to be taken.

Their repatriation proceeded smoothly, but one of the Internment Camp senior supervisory officers had subsequently to report to his superiors, that never in his long service as an officer, had he seen such filth and disarray left behind on that day to a man, by the German officers, NCO's and ratings.

The situations under which those German navy sailors came to be interned in Ireland is quite interesting. A major sea battle erupted in the Bay of Biscay on 27 December 1943 between eleven German destroyers and torpedo boats escorting a blockade runner and some British warships — the convoy was attacked at long range by HMS ENTERPRISE, a Royal Navy cruiser of 9435 tons displacement and the more modern 11,350 ton cruiser

GLASGOW; the action lasted for two days with the Germans incurring losses of one destroyer and two MTB's. The tiny Irish ship, the SS KERLOGUE of 330 tons was 360 miles out from the Fastnet when it was intercepted by two Focke Wulf Condors, both of whom signalled by Aldis lamp requesting assistance for their stricken comrades — the KERLOGUE proceeded to the position given and picked up 164 men, and although its gunwales were awash from the extra load, it landed the survivors safely at Cobh — two had died.

During the early hours of Sunday morning, 11 March 1945, belligerent air activity was intense over the south coast, and the observation posts were unusually busy passing along the information to the main centres. At 0200 hours, a low flying RAF Coastal Command Sunderland passed over the LOP at Galley Head on the Cork coast and shortly afterwards loud explosions were heard out to sea.......

The U-266, Kapitanleutnant Klaus Becher, a standard German submarine of the VIIC Class — submerged displacement 870 tons with a range of 7000 nautical miles, had schnorkled its way underneath the waters of the Bay of Biscay for twenty days and had now reached a submerged position 40 miles SW of Galley Head; it was a moonless night and the sea was calm. Becher decided to surface and give his sailors a few hours of real fresh air — at periscope depth he searched in the darkness for telltale lights. Everything seemed tranquil and the boat surfaced gently; Becher was first out on the conning tower and he quickly scanned the horizon with his night glasses — all was calm and peaceful and he ordered the diesels shut down, and half of his crew — 24 men, up on deck for an hour of fresh air. Two hours later he was preparing to submerge and the last of the sailors were clambering down into the boat, when the bow lookout shouted 'Achtung Sunderland!' but it was too late. The Coastal Command aircraft was twenty feet above the water and approaching fast from the direction of the Irish coast; fitted with the latest radar, an ASV Mk. III operating on a ten centimetre wave which the U boat could not detect, the Sunderland had picked up the surfaced submarine at a distance of thirty miles. At half a mile the U-266 was instantly silhouetted by the powerful beam from the Leigh searchlight of the aircraft; the switching on of the intense light was immediately followed by the release of three bombs which straddled the target.

The klaxon was hooting, the diesels were running and all his men, unscathed, were safely back in the boat; Becher crash dived and was fully submerged before the Sunderland came back for the second run, but the kapitanleutnant knew they were finished: the hull was leaking like a sieve. He took as much water as was prudent

115

to give them underwater time and then ordered the submarine to the surface — the flying boat was gone and the surface was still calm; they opened the sea cocks to scuttle the U boat, and five minutes after they had pulled away in the rubber dinghies the U-266 was on the bottom.

The LOP at Galley Head observed red signal flares out to sea at 0306 hours on Tuesday morning, and at 0511 hours eleven German seamen came ashore near the post. In a few words of halting English they expressed concern for 37 of their comrades still at sea. The lifeboat from Courtmacsherry was launched, the naval base at Haulbowline alerted and later that morning Lt. Thompson in command of a motor torpedo boat escorted the lifeboat, and the German crewmen whom they had rescued, into harbour. They joined their compatriots in the internment camp at the Curragh.

Kapitanleutnant Becher did not do such a thorough job on the disposal of the ship's documents, and a few days later two fishermen found a metal container bobbing up and down in the sea near Glandore, Co. Cork. The canister was brought to Collins Barracks in Cork and was subsequently conveyed to Dublin by Lt. Douglas Gageby of the army intelligence service. It was found to contain the signal codes and ciphers, maps, charts, technical documents and the war orders of the German submarine arm. An unusual aspect of the documentation was the collection of reports and messages from other U boat commanders, citing their experiences of various battle situations — what action they took to meet various contingencies, and the success or otherwise of the measures and lessons learned. These reports were transmitted at regular intervals from Bremerhaven so that other U boats might benefit from the experiences without delay.

It was very interesting to army intelligence to read the war orders of the German navy as they applied to Irish ships. Grand Admiral Dönitz had decreed in his "Special Neutrality Instructions of Jan. 1942:"

Ireland forbids the entry of warships into its territorial waters under penalty of internment. This prohibition must be strictly observed in order to maintain her neutrality.

In April of 1943, the admiral was emphasising that "Irish ships were not to be brought in or sunk." Supplement 3 to Standing War Order No. 105 of Aug. 1944 stated that:

All Irish ships, including those crossing the North Atlantic are marked on both sides with the national colours and with the word EIRE, and are manned by Irish crews. The ships on the Atlantic and continental traffic are lit up at night. The voyages to Lisbon, Cadiz, and Vigo and transatlantic are mostly made with ballast. On the return journey they usually put into Dublin but sometimes Waterford, Cork, Limerick and Galway.

Appendix 3 to the same war order read:

Irish ships and the occasional Irish convoys should not be attacked inside the blockade area for political reasons, if recognised as such. There is no special obligation however to establish the neutrality of ships inside the blockade area.

The war orders listed the tonnage, name and description of 19 merchant vessels in the Irish fleet, but the satisfying fact from the point of view of army intelligence and Irish neutrality was, that there were no war orders outlining any procedure for succour in Irish waters, and as the government well knew, none had been given.

The interrogation of the U boat crew by an officer of G2 was revealing: they spoke freely of the progress of the war but knew little if anything about Ireland. The French were dismissed as a "morally decadent race, treacherous and quarrelsome," and they had an equally biased view of the Russians, particularly of the "poor quality of their weapons." There was no reply to the Irish officer's question, as to whether war expendable materiel should be made to last for ever; little did they know that in many aspects the Russians were way ahead of them, particularly in the standardisation of the calibre of small arms ammunition.

The G2 officer was very impressed with the calibre of the U boat crew — young, intelligent, under twenty five and totally different from the usual German soldier. He rated them as the "cream of the German forces": tragically, as with all the deaths of young men at war, that cream had gone to the bottom of the oceans in 785 U boats, but they in turn had sunk 2,828 Allied and neutral merchant ships, which, despite Grand Admiral Dönitz's strictures and similar orders to the Luftwaffe, included 16 Irish vessels.

One of those naval internees was Petty Officer Guenther Klaar and he wrote gratefully to his mother in Germany:

'We could not complain, we are getting on very well we do not feel the war at all. The first day I could not stand the fat food but now it is alright. Mother, the meat I eat here and the lovely white bread with it would make you open your eyes. The Irish behave towards us in a very respectful way. They look after us as if we were invalids — we will never let anything happen to Irishmen........'

Undoubtedly Klaar's sentiments echoed the feelings of many of the internees in both camps, but they also suffered from the frustration of being forcibly removed from the events which were affecting both of their countries — helpless onlookers as history was being decided without them.

In the compounds the circumstances of their confinement had been relatively comfortable and the internees were allowed out on weekend parole, many attended university schooling in Dublin or worked locally. They frequented their own special hostelries in the Naas area and considering their plight they got along quite well together.

On the eve of an escape, the Germans refused an offer of a case of whiskey from the British, who wanted them to make a racket to cover up the departure of two of the RAF internees. The Luftwaffe pilots refused on the grounds that they would be aiding an enemy to escape; the British got away — one to die on his next operational sortie and the other to survive the war. A new Allied arrival, not too au fait with the parole arrangement, made his exit to Belfast just a short time after he was interned — the British promptly sent him back and the Irish at the Curragh promptly removed privileges and the right of parole; when the hapless escapee had returned, the military police had to intervene to prevent him being lynched by Germans and English alike.

Incredibly bizarre situations arose from the internments; a relative of mine, who was a captain in an infantry battalion of the First Division — the 27th. based at Ballincollig, County Cork, and known as "Dev's Secret Weapon," was in the officers' mess of the divisional headquarters in Cork city — whilst waiting to use the phone he realised that the occupant of the booth was a Luftwaffe officer, in full uniform, talking to the German legation in Dublin.

Two of the German aircrew were invited to Christmas dinner at the home of an Irish officer in Dublin but, when their host met them at the bus he appeared to be ill at ease. It transpired that he had received a telephone call from a relative who was an officer in the Royal Navy — the cousin had just escorted a convoy into Belfast harbour and had invited himself to Christmas dinner in Dublin. The evening proved to be most pleasant, including a description by the navy man of a U boat attack on his convoy, and a farewell greeting to him at the end of the evening from his two fellow guests — 'lookout how you go, and mind those U boats!'

The German dead from Irish skies and Irish seas of two world wars are buried in a small cemetery in the mountain pass of Glencree, County Wicklow — the graveyard lies in the shadow of an old British barracks built to aid in the suppression of the Irish rebellion of 1798. From that barracks of old, troops of English cavalry went out into the mountains to search for that gallant Irish rebel, Michael O'Dwyer, and many times the whole troop would disappear even to the accoutrements of the horses. Those enemies are now with God, and Stan O'Brien the poet has incised on a granite plinth in that lonely place these haunting words:

> *It was for me to die*
> *Under an Irish sky*
> *There finding berth*
> *In good Irish earth.*
> *What I had dreamed and planned*
> *Bound me to my fatherland.*
> *But war sent me to sleep in Glencree.*
> *Passion and pain*
> *Were my loss – my gain;*
> *Pray, as you pass*
> *To make good my loss.*

* * *

In terms of aeroplanes and equipment, the years of the "Emergency" — World War Two, were lean for the Air Corps. Three Gladiators remained of the original four delivered, and a further twelve which were ordered never arrived, as understandably they were diverted to RAF usage. There was a Lysander army co-op unit, the Walrus amphibians and a squadron of Avro Ansons for patrolling coastal waters. Seven further Ansons, which already had been painted in Irish colours for delivery, were also retained by the RAF due to the outbreak of war. There were only two fighter squadrons of Hurricanes, and one of these at half strength, but the training side was more than adequately equipped with the best in primary and advanced trainers in generous numbers. Looking back at the shortage of equipment during those years, it seems extraordinary, in view of the benevolence of Irish neutrality towards the British, that out of a total production series of 14,231 Hawker Hurricane fighters, "Eire" was only able to acquire eighteen secondhand machines from them.

In simple terms of battle assessment, if an invasion by either the British or the Germans had taken place, this tiny force would have been destroyed in a matter of hours. Since the range of all fighters was limited, it is more than likely that it would have inflicted losses out of all proportion to its size on unescorted German troop transports — slow flying JU-52's and bombers. The result would still have been the same — the few airfields smothered with bombs, if the whole force had not already been put out of action by parachute troops before it got off the ground.

An assault by the British in terms of survival would probably

Photo – Army

That seductive Gloster Gladiator.

Presentation of Trophy to No. 1 Fighter Squadron, Baldonnel 1944. The Minister for Defence, Mr Oscar Traynor T.D. is making the presentation. Colonel W.P. Delamer, OC Air Corps, is the officer behind Mr. Traynor.

Photo - Army

Baldonnel 1943, Sergeant Pilots with their flying instructors. Capt. M.P. Quinlan is fourth from the right, front row.

Photo – Army

Operation Sarsfield, Baldonnel 1960. An Taoiseach, Mr. Sean Lemass T.D. reviews the 33rd. Infantry Battalion of the U.N. Force to the Congo. The aircraft is a Douglas Globemaster 2 of the United States Air Force.

Photo – Army.

have caused a swifter elimination — fighter escorted bombers — Spitfires against a handful of Hurricanes. The army co-op side of Lysanders and Hectors would probably have gone on for some time longer, operating from suitable dispersed sites, until enemy action, lack of fuel, spares and ammunition produced the inevitable result.

The role of the Corps during the war was mainly one of defence, but that force was only token, and even if there were six or ten squadrons of Gladiators before that war, they were obsolescent by 1940; the same number of Hurricanes would have made their presence felt if they were obtainable, but they were not. The story of the ground forces was totally different — although lightly armed, there were 40,000 regular troops organised in two divisions, augmented by the LDF, a force in itself of about 104,000 trained men; there is no doubt that this Irish army was a major deterrent to an Allied or German invasion.

The reality of Irish neutrality during those years as far as it relates directly to England was, that some bases on the Irish western and southern Atlantic seaboard were denied to the British navy, and that some airfields which were closer to the scene of maritime operations were also unavailable. The fact of Britain possessing these facilities through either allegiance, coercion or force would have permanently required the presence of large numbers of British troops and equipment, aircraft and ships, precious commodities which could be ill afforded during the crucial years of the war. As events transpired, in return for a limited amount of petroleum products, minimal war supplies and a plethora of post war criticism, Ireland had given: a benevolent neutrality, hundreds and thousands of men to the British armed forces, and an abundance of foodstuffs to feed them.

In the light of today's defence debates in the context of modern Europe and the posturing of the NATO powers and the forces of the Warsaw Pact, it is interesting to record the attitude of a major NATO power relative to the traditional stance of successive Irish governments on Irish neutrality, and the continued reference by that power of the 'inability of the Irish to defend themselves, and their tendency to shelter under the umbrella of NATO........' when the ironic fact is, that the only protection that Ireland ever needed, and was unable to provide, was a defence against the rapacious capacity, down through eight hundred years, of that neighbouring NATO power, England.

Modern Ireland is well served by its Defence Forces, and although the army and navy are small by world standards, they possess the finest equipment, purchased internationally to suit Irish needs, with the navy's ships built in an Irish dockyard.

The Air Corps is a compact but expanding service, adequately provided with new aircraft — trainers, search and rescue and troop helicopters, jet transports, fighters and reconnaissance planes. The multiple functions of Dalton's original Air Service now include air support for the ground forces, troop transportation, fishery protection duties, patrols from naval vessels, carriage of government officials to Europe, photographic survey, and aid to the civil power. There is a coninuous programme of training for pilots, technicians, apprentices and recruit personnel, and Baldonnel has been provided with modernised runways, approach light systems and electronic landing aids; Gormanston in Co. Meath is the headquarters of No. 2 Support Wing. All a very long way from May of 1922 and that fine old soldier, Volunteer Johnny Curran.

Chapter Four

ATLANTIC CROSSING - 1928

Ocean waves toss in endless array,
Wild winds are flecking the waters in spray,
But hugging the surface on course to the west,
A small plane is flying on resolute quest.

Technical progress in aviation had advanced considerably as a result of World War One, and by the time that the conflict had ended, as we know there were many airships and large aeroplanes capable of flying very long distances. The speeds at which these machines flew were modest by today's standards: relatively none of the larger planes being able to exceed 100 miles per hour, nevertheless, the engines were reliable and the carriage of large quantities of fuel was rarely a difficulty. The inadequacies of the flight instrumentation was the major problem, together with an inability to navigate accurately in all types of weather.

The standard instrumentation for aircraft then was: a simple compass, an altimeter which read the height, an airspeed indicator, and a primitive slip indicator akin to a carpenter's spirit level, the central position of the little bubble indicating that the aircraft was steady on course and not skidding to one side or the other; a revolution counter indicated the speed at which the engine was turning.

Aerial nagivation was usually a matter of "dead reckoning," in which the path flown by the craft over the earth's surface was regulated by allowing for the effect of the probable wind, and thus, its speed and position could be determined with reasonable accuracy. On flights of any significant distance, these observations were plotted on a chart, and an accurate record kept of any changes of course; hence the progress of the aeroplane could be monitored constantly, provided the magnetic variation of the compass was always known, and the speed and direction of the wind. It was essential then to have a very accurate and continuous knowledge of the velocity of that whimsical element, the wind. Over land, when it was possible to fly within sight of the ground, then the absence of totally accurate wind information would not be so critical, since the pilot could obtain his position by the observation of towns and cities and other well known landmarks. Allowance could also be made for the observed wind drift.

Dead reckoning navigation over the sea was a totally different matter, and unless the aerial navigator was able to regularly scan the wind effect on the ocean, or drop smoke floats on its surface and observe the smoke direction, and traverse the float to take readings, the accuracy of his progress would be seriously impaired. Wind effect or "drift" was assessed through a drift sight — a viewing device which the observer aligned, so that objects beneath him appeared to move steadily down the sight; this gave the angular effect the wind was having on the path of the aeroplane, and hence the pilot made a correction for it.

Although radio direction finding equipment was available in the 1920's, it was cumbersome and heavy, and therefore involved a weight penalty in carrying it. The very basic wind driven generators which were used to power it were not very reliable either.

Celestial navigation, observation of the heavenly bodies by sextant, and the use of special tables to enable the information obtained to be transferred to plotting charts, was the ideal method, but the sun was really the only aid during the day and might be totally obscured by cloud. At night the aviators were concerned in maintaining an even keel on crude instruments; and because of cloud conditions, and an inability to climb above the formations, the precious vision of the stars was more often then not denied them, and too frequently "deduced" or dead reckoning navigation became a mocking reality — hopelessly lost and low on fuel, the ocean claimed another victim.

By the end of the year 1927, the North Atlantic had been conquered nine times by flying boats, landplanes and hydrogen filled airships. Eight of those flights were west to east — from the North American continent to Europe; the difficult east to west crossing was achieved only once, and then by that British airship R 34.

The dramatic difference in these timings highlights one of the difficulties of the east-west crossing; it was of course the effect of our whimsical friend, the wind: westerly winds generally dominate the North Atlantic, and if they were missing in one sector they could be found in another. But, for the aviators attempting to fly the other way, those who dared to fly from Europe to North America in the slow flying planes of the '20's, they had to wait and plan until favourable weather and wind conditions were forecast to be forming over the ocean.

Their point of departure was from a continent running north south; a land mass difficult to miss if proceeding in the opposite direction. The first point of their landfall was on a continent whose coastline roughly paralleled their course. Tactically, 50% of the certain land contact was already in jeopardy if they missed the inhospitable ground of Newfoundland, or the more northerly icy wastes of Labrador. These areas are cursed with recurring low cloud and fog, and I have often looked down from the comfortable cockpit of a Boeing 747 at 37,000 feet and watched a thousand miles or more of ocean and land go by, shrouded in layers of icy grey fog, all along this very region. We flew with automatic navigation computers and excellent reliable compasses, but their devices ran riot in the magnetic disturbances of Newfoundland and Labrador.

*   *   *

James Christopher Fitzmaurice was born in Dublin on 6 January 1898. His parents came from Limerick farming stock, and his father was in the Prison Service of Mountjoy jail. Shortly after the birth of their son, the family moved to the Midlands, as the father had been transferred to duties in Maryborough — now known as Portlaoise.

Young James attended a Christian Brothers' school until he was 16 years of age; his formal education terminated with a short spell in a business college in Waterford. Education in the Ireland of those days tended to be classical rather than practical: emphasis on languages, prose and poetry, took precedence over physics and chemistry and the modern subjects of today's curriculum. The Brothers have won a deserving and endearing place in the history of

129

Irish education, and their tutelage has extended to lands far away from Ireland; they specialised then in imparting "the three R's" — Reading, Writing and Arithmetic, and they were certainly implanted in James C. Fitzmaurice. In researching his later army records and his writings, I was deeply impressed by the incisive bite, and the eloquent style of his English. The letters in his file evidence a clear orderly mind, and an intelligence that was above average.

In 1912 when the Home Rule Bill for Ireland was introduced in the British House of Commons, it was opposed by militant elements in Ulster, and as a counterpoise in the south of Ireland, the nationalist politician, John Redmond had established the Irish National Volunteers; Fitzmaurice joined the City of Waterford Battalion. The onset of the war caused Redmond to subjugate his national feelings to a concern for the plight of Europe, and 100,000 Irishmen joined the British army to fight the Germans. Fitzmaurice entered the cadet company of the 7th. Leinsters in 1914, but when his true age was discovered he was sent home.

In 1916 at 18 years of age, he again enlisted, but this time in a cavalry regiment, the 17th. Lancers; later wounded and transferred to the 7th. Battalion Queen's Royal West Surrey Regiment, he was on the Somme as a sergeant in 1917 during the German retreat. In May of 1917 he again entered the line to take part in the battle of Arras; the attack took place at 0345 hours — 'a colossal chaotic failure, with battalions of 700 men reduced to 30 by evening.'

Commissioned as a second lieutenant into the King's 8th. Irish Liverpool Regiment in November of '17, he was again wounded in action. All during those terrible months he yearned to fly, knowing full well that the life expectancy on the western front in the Royal Flying Corps was even less than it was in the trenches. His transfer to the RAF, as it had become, came in 1918 and he spent two months at a school of military aeronautics at Reading checking out on Camel fighters, powered by a rotary engine and very difficult to fly. He was due to go to France on 11 November, the very day the war ended.

The capabilities of this man, even then, were becoming very evident to his superiors, because at a time when vast demobilisation was taking place, he was offered commissioned service in the RAF which would have brought him up to the year 1925. He qualified as a navigator at the British Admiralty Compass Observatory and was posted to 120 Squadron, a unit specialising in experimental night air mail flights to Germany with DH 10's — a large machine fitted with two 440 hp. Liberty engines. By now he was a very experienced pilot having amassed considerable flight time on 11 aircraft types including heavy bombers.

Destiny was pointing the 23 year old Irish RAF officer, first in the direction of another veteran war flier, Captain R.H. McIntosh — "All Weather Mac", and then towards his meeting with two erstwhile enemies of the western front: the jovial Bavarian, Captain Hermann Koehl, and his aristocratic sponsor — Baron Guenther von Huenefeld, the monocled Prussian.

Resigning from the RAF in 1921, he offered his services to the newly formed army of the Irish Free State. Major General McSweeney commissioned him in the Army Air Service, and the last paragraph on his commission scroll read: "I hope you will be spared many long and honourable years in the service of your country." He was to give honourable years.

Appointed to the command of the air station at Fermoy, he flew on numerous sorties during the civil war: reconnaissance, observation, train escort duty and army co-operation; a day in October 1922 found him over the Kerry mountains in a Martinsyde Scout. He was dropping amnesty leaflets on the areas held by the Irregulars when, with a few ominous backfires the 300 hp. Hispano Suiza engine went dead, and he put the Martinsyde down in a field near Killarney. The local regular army garrison rendered aid, and he was airborne early the following Sunday morning, but in a semi stalled condition in an endeavour to surmount a belt of trees. He cleared the wood, only to mush down the far side into a hail of republican bullets. They riddled the plane but he escaped injury, having only to force land again near Mallow; this time the engine was finished. On his way on foot to seek help, he was ambushed at Castletownroche bridge by a large force, and again escaped a fusillade of rifle fire without injury.

The neighbourhood proved to be decidedly unfriendly, and he had to steal a ploughhorse, and ride it bareback a considerable distance to the nearest military garrison. Despite the fact that he answered the sentry's challenge correctly, and 'advanced to be recognised' — the sentry loosed off three shots, which missed; what the soldier saw advancing towards him was a horseman dressed in a flying suit, helmet and goggles, and with a service rifle strapped to the animal's side. The next air patrol took him over west Cork, in an endeavour to locate and bomb a Rolls Royce armoured car which had been acquired by the Irregulars; he had to force land once more, close to their headquarters in Cork city.

Promotion was rapid, and by October of 1926 he was officer commanding the Irish Air Corps, with the rank of commandant. Again, his army files reveal his initiative and capabilities, and the clarity of his thought; a contemporary newspaper reporter stated:

'I was much impressed by the air of efficiency which pervades the aerodrome, Baldonnel. The Free State Air Service is small but it is remarkably up to date, and Comdt. Fitzmaurice is to be congratulated on the way in which it is run. At present he has only 300 men on the aerodrome staff, and when one remembers that this number includes the garrison, one is struck by the way in which a compact small establishment keeps the aerodrome in such excellent order. Everything is spick and span........'

Much of the equipment which the corps possessed was purchased from an English war surplus firm, Aircraft Disposals, and they supplied the DH 9's and Bristol Fighters. Captain W.H. McIntosh flew them in, and he was impressed by the desire of the young commandant, who wanted to conquer the North Atlantic from east to west for the first time for the honour of Ireland. Fitzmaurice told him how the ambition had haunted him from the moment that he had set eyes upon General Michael Collins' five seater Martinsyde A MK 2, he had intended to modify the Martinsyde with extra tankage, floatation gear and navigation equipment. Official approval was not forthcoming and his schemes came to nothing.

McIntosh returned to Baldonnel in 1927 with the PRINCESS XENIA, a Fokker F7 monoplane with a Bristol Jupiter engine. Fitzmaurice and himself set out upon an Atlantic venture on 16 September but 300 miles out from the Irish coast, the engine began to give trouble and the weather worsened in a deep depression. They were lucky to make it back to land, and McIntosh put the machine down on Beale Strand, near Ballybunion in County Kerry, in complete darkness and in a deluge of rain.

As he sat in the warmth of a hotel lounge in Ballybunion, Fitzmaurice reflected on the fate of the others before him who had not succeeded: appalling weather, no radio, no flight instruments of any value, finally culminating in engine failure from fuel starvation, and then quick oblivion on the dark sea. Many lives had been sacrificed in an effort to fly that ocean from east to west, and all to no avail. The French airmen, Nungesser and Coli were lost in early 1927 in an east west attempt by a Lavasseur landplane. Later that year an experienced Imperial Airways pilot, Colonel Minchin with an air-woman, Princess Lowenstein Wertheim, and Leslie Hamilton apparently made it as far as Newfoundland, but perished in the treacherous coastal conditions. A second Imperial Airways pilot, Captain Hinchliffe with Miss Elsie Mackay, daughter of an English earl, disappeared in a Stinson monoplane in a further futile attempt.

Fate was again pointing at Commandant James C. Fitzmaurice, officer commanding the Irish Army Air Corps at Baldonnel, County Dublin. In April of 1928, a German Junkers W33 monoplane arrived there under the command of Captain Hermann Koehl, an ex-

Lufthansa pilot. The BREMEN, registration D-1167, was compact and rugged; an all metal aeroplane, originally designed as a freight carrying seaplane it had been specially modified for an Atlantic crossing. The engine, a 6 cylinder in line water cooled Junkers LV of 300 hp. was simple and reliable, and had already proved itself in many test flights, including an endurance test in the previous year, in which the aircraft flew 1800 miles. Now the two Germans planned a non-stop flight to New York.

James C. Fitzmaurice was invited to be co-pilot for this east-west attempt on the North Atlantic. The die was cast........

* * *

Hermann Koehl was born in Bavarian Swabia, in April 1886. His father was a captain in an artillery regiment, and the son followed his parent into the army, to be finally commissioned in the Muenchen Cadet Corps in 1910. He entered World War One as a sapper officer — an army engineer, only to be wounded at the outset. This early hospitalisation was fortuitous, because it availed him of an opportunity to realize a cherished ambition: he obtained a transfer to the Air Service, and trained as an observer at Aldershaf Flying Reserve Detachment at the Johannisthal aerodrome. Here the set up was similar to early training in the RFC; there was no system, and once the instructor had introduced the observer to the flying machine in a matter of an hour or so, the rest was a "do-it-yourself" affair.

Posted to the front with his Fokker unit, at Ghent, he was the only one to arrive, the others got lost and he earned the nickname of "Beobachter Kanone" — observer gun. Although he subsequently qualified as a fighter pilot, he preferred to command a unit in the air, rather than actually fly the machine. The German air force used the system then, whereby a highly qualified observer officer commanded and directed the tactics of a squadron in the air, Koehl fought over the Somme as an echelon leader in a combat squadron, and went on to a night bombing unit. Shot down and wounded again in 1916, he recovered and later commanded a night bombing squadron in 1918.

In May of that year he was downed again, but this time behind enemy lines and captured, but not before his crewman and himself had blown the bomber up with an "aeroplane destroyer". A tactic which the Germans used again in World War Two; when some of their planes landed virtually intact in neutral Ireland, they destroyed them either by explosives or fire.

When hostilities ended, Koehl got back into aviation at Boeblingen, flying many types; he had rejoined the army aviation corps, but the terms of the Versailles Treaty forced its disbandment and by 1922 he was in Berlin as an infantry officer in the Wacht Regiment. The army gave him permission to co-operate with Junkers Luftverkehrs AG, in establishing the first German night flight route from Berlin to Waremuende, and by 1925 he was a full member of that company and had extended the route to Sweden, flying seaplanes on day and night flights.

On the formation of Lufthansa, he joined the airline and was placed in charge of the Night Flying Department, but his interests kept returning to the North Atlantic, and he studied the world pioneering flights in an endeavour to gain valuable knowledge from the experiences of others. Many had ended in tragedy, but Koehl had made up his mind in what he wanted to achieve: the conquest of the North Atlantic from east to west: Europe to North America. The Junkers works was interested in the possibility and he flew many machines, finally selecting a modified JU W33 as the ideal aeroplane for the purpose. In this heady environment he met Baron Guenther von Huenefeld.

Von Huenefeld, a monocled Prussian from Koenigsberg was a classical scholar and a writer in philosophy. A romantic, his life stlye and that of his companions reflected all the nostalgia of early 20th. century student Europe. The very self expression of the man's own disability, highlights the strength and personality that was inbred into his caste: 'The one eyed was given a full share, although he never obtained, and will never receive a pilot's licence. He was called Huenefeld, and from his birth had only been able to see with his short sighted right eye. That accounts for the inseparable monocle........'

A friend of the crown prince, the leisure time of his university days found him either fencing, or as an inveterate frequenter of the cafes in Berlin where the young men were obsessed with the new wonder — aviation. A flying day at nearby Johannisthal was nectar to the baron and his companions, but the war engulfed his dreams and himself — almost. An officer of marines, he was crippled by a shell outside Antwerp in early 1914; shrapnel ripped his body and his legs, and he underwent 11 operations before he was able to walk again. In 1927 he met Koehl at the Junkers works at Dessau, and here he discovered a companion who was as totally dedicated as he was, to achieve for Germany the honour of that elusive prize — the first North Atlantic crossing from east to west. Professor Junkers supplied them with the type that Koehl had favoured and the two low wing metal monoplanes, the BREMEN and the EUROPA set out from Dessau in August of 1927 to make the flight.

EUROPA developed engine trouble and had to turn back, but the

BREMEN with Captain Hermann Koehl, Herr Loose and von Huenefeld flew a round trip of 1800 miles, bad weather having forced them to return to Dessau; they had been in the air for 22 hours. Still determined in their purpose despite the failure, the flight of the PRINCESS XENIA from Baldonnel the following month caught their attention and drew their interest towards Ireland; never before had they considered the possibility of a start from a position further west.

The baron got together with some eleven financiers from Bremen and they now purchased the aeroplane which proudly bore the name of their city. He set about planning another ocean flight with Koehl, who had left Lufthansa: they first considered using the Irish military aerodrome at Renmore in County Galwy, but decided against it as further expense would have been involved in lengthening the available take-off run.

Baldonnel was finally decided upon, and Koehl and von Huenefeld flew the BREMEN there on March 26 1928. They were impressed by Fitzmaurice's background which was similar to Koehl's, and his earlier endeavour with McIntosh in the PRINCESS XENIA; these factors combined with his enthusiasm and obviously high intelligence led to the almost immediate invitation to crew the aeroplane as co-pilot; Fitzmaurice accepted. As von Huenefeld put it: 'In this Irish aerodrome, the composition of the BREMEN crew was definitely decided upon. Their Irish comrades accorded us one of the nicest receptions we had ever experienced........'

*   *   *

When Fitzmaurice saw the BREMEN he was tremendously impressed: the Junkers aeroplane was of all metal construction, unusual for those days; the water cooled engine developed 350 horse-power at 1500 revolutions per minute. The design allup weight was 5,512 lbs, but for the Atlantic crossing the BREMEN would gross 8,140 lbs, which included the three aviators, 20 gallons of oil, and 500 gallons of gasoline mixed with benzol, an additive which improved the power rating of the fuel. The gasoline tanks were in the wing roots, with four extra tanks in the cabin; the two pilots were seated side by side in an enclosed cockpit.

The BREMEN, was designed by Professor Hugo Junkers, a man who had made his living by manufacturing water heating appliances at Dessau, but who had in 1910, added an aviation research centre to the factory. In December of 1915 he produced his first aeroplane — a Junkers JU-1, with metal cantilever wings, and by 1918, in

135

association with Anthony Fokker, they had built 400 military aircraft. After the war, Junkers developed the first all metal low wing monoplane; this machine had four seats in an enclosed passenger cabin. By 1925 his aircraft had carried 100,000 people over 3,000,000 miles, with the later W-33 being particularly successful and holding several long distance and endurance records. Junkers eventually built 800 of these aircraft and they featured, for the first time, the now familiar corrugated sheet metal skin of the Junkers' design.

Commandant Fitzmaurice had already applied to his superiors at army headquarters 'for leave of absence for the purpose of undertaking a trans atlantic flight.' The reply, from the adjutant general, arrived on the 10th of April 1928:

'Leave of absence granted, but you undertake the flight at your sole risk — any loss of life, injury or disablement arising out of, or consequent on the said flight will not be considered to have been caused in the course of duty, or be a ground for any claim against the State or the military authorities.'

There is an accompanying note attached to this memo in his file at General Headquarters, and it was penned by a staff officer to the records officer: 'You might as well put the attached away in Col. Fitz's file. It was considered likely at the time, that Col. Fitz and his companions were going to "go west" instead of succeeding in flying west.'

The army later repented for their lack of support and James C. Fitzmaurice was promoted major on 13 April 1928, and colonel on 24 July 1928 'in consideration of distinguished services rendered.'

Whilst awaiting a favourable weather report for the crossing, preparations continued at Baldonnel for the take-off. The grass strip was lengthened to 1300 yards, and tyres were placed at intervals to outline its edges; a special red marker identified a spot by which, it had been calculated, the aircraft would have to have reached a certain speed if it was to become safely airborne in the remaining distance available.

Huenefeld and Koehl readily took to Fitzmaurice's charm, and enjoyed the hospitality of his brother officers. He confided to the baron that the flight was to be the realization of his dearly cherished hopes for his country: 'That Irishmen, under their own flag and with all the distinctiveness of their nationality, unhampered by any ties, can participate in the conquest of the air.' Huenefeld saw to it that the Irish tricolour was carried beside the old German imperial colours on the side of the BREMEN. The weather reports from the atlantic continued to improve.

On 11 April the long awaited forecast arrived from the British

Air Ministry; it was ideal for the initial route of the flight, although there was increasing cloudiness further to the west, but with diminishing winds. Fitzmaurice burst into the anteroom of the officers mess with the good news: 'Crack goes the whip, off go the horses, and round go the wheels at 5 o'clock in the morning' he sang out. Whilst his fellow officers celebrated the coming event, the three fliers continued to study the weather charts and complete their flight plot — planning the courses in each sector to allow for wind and calculating the time and the fuel consumption. The tanks carried 500 gallons which would give an estimated endurance of 40 hours.

To minimise the risk of ice accretion in flight, the plane had been swabbed down with a liberal quantity of kerosene; now the benzol fuel was pumped aboard, and the wing stubs propped up to prevent sagging whilst waiting for the take-off. Weller and Lingrich, the German engineers, with the help of their Air Corps colleagues, checked every item on the machine minutely. The BREMEN was ready.

At 0400 hours fifty soldiers pushed the aeroplane from its hangar to the take-off point. They lifted the tail up onto a small trolley, which would have the effect of placing the machine in its normal flying attitude from the very commencement of the take-off roll. The dolly would discard itself half way down the runway.

Soon the debonair Commandant James Fitzmaurice appeared with the jovial Captain Koehl; then the monocled Baron von Huenefeld. They were dressed in flying clothing, and Fitz was wearing his Irish army uniform beneath the heavy suit; it was the same uniform that he had worn during his previous atlantic attempt in the PRINCESS XENIA, and his lucky charm, a gold four leafed clover was still in his tunic pocket. He gave it to the baron, who in return presented him with a tiny silver doll that he had carried during the war. Huenefeld was to travel in the passenger cabin, and well wishers had added to it some typewritten prayers and a little gold cross.

Koehl was pilot in command, with Fitzmaurice as co-pilot. The baron, as the aircraft owner, acted as both flight manager and cabin attendant, and for this latter purpose had stocked his little cabin with thermos flasks of tea, beef-tea, chicken and beef sandwiches and bars of chocolate.

Warmly accepting the well wishes and farewells of the many officials present at Baldonnel, the trio boarded their plane, and as Hermann Koehl described it: 'At 0510 hours Weller and Lingrich turned the propeller with sinewy arms. Upon the third "Frei" it started, not to stop again until it broke the thin crust of ice on Greenly Island after our long relentless struggle with the elements.' They allowed the motor to warm up before signalling for the chocks to be removed from the wheels — they looked at each other and bowed, and at 0538 hours Captain Koehl pushed the power lever fully open, and the BREMEN commenced a sluggish roll into its hazardous take-off run.

The grassy runway was bumpy and muddy and despite the railway sleepers that had been laid to smoothen part of its surface, the wheels were sinking deep into the moist ground and it almost looked as if the feeble engine would fail to drag the four tons behind it up the slope. The crew were quite certain at this stage that they were not getting the essential increase in speed — the morning was quite calm, and the red warning marker had gone by on the left side. At 68 mph. Fitzmaurice grabbed the control column from Koehl and pulled back hard — a stray sheep had walked from the right straight onto the runway.

The BREMEN left the ground momentarily and cleared the sheep, but it stalled back on again, and as Koehl recalled: 'Ahead of us the exhaust pipe was red hot and spewing flames — behind us almost 500 gallons of fuel was stored. If a spark brought the two of them together, we were done for.' 'He deliberated whether or not to abondon the take off by switching off the ignition, but decided to keep going as there was approximately 1,300 feet of runway left.

With 300 yards to go the machine had not yet accelerated to the magical 75 mph. required to give it lift, and then with literally feet between them and the boundary, Koehl got it off, only to mush through the tops of some small trees and then go into a partial stall. They had to make an immediate slow flat turn to the right to avoid a hill and the wing brushed a hedge, but the snarling 6 cylinder in line Junkers engine was getting a grip on the cool morning air, and the BREMEN climbed slowly west towards the ocean and silence; the radio had been sacrificed in favour of additional fuel. The machine was so overloaded that they had to use practically full throttle for the first three hours; a lone army bomber escorted them to the coast.

Fitzmauric described how 'low lying fog blanketed the whole countryside, through which hilltops and the spires of village churches pushed their way up into the crystal clear atmosphere above. The majestic dignity of those church spires brought us close to the God of Hosts who had stood so quietly at our elbows during this most critical moment at the end of the runway, and lifted us clear of the obstacles which were such a terrifying menace. Silently we muttered a simple prayer of thanks, and resolved to tackle with everything in us, the dangers that lay ahead.'

Hermann Koehl had already muttered several pater nosters during the critical stages, and the brave baron, in his small compartment, trapped behind those huge fuel tanks, although an unbeliever gained some consolation from the little gold cross and the posted prayers.

They entered the ocean sector over Slyne Head in Galway, and with a waggling of wings from the departing army bomber and a wave of farewell from the lighthouse keeper. They had already passed over the spot at Clifden, where nine years before Alcock and Brown had landed after the first non stop crossing of the North Atlantic by an aeroplane.

Initially the weather was excellent, and as the fuel burned off the BREMEN settled down to an airspeed of 130 miles per hour at 1250 revolutions from the motor. They flew visually at heights from 50 to 1,000 feet above the ocean surface, and at intervals dropped their smoke floats on the water, and doubled back over them to check the wind; when they detected an easterly they climbed up to 3,000 feet to take advantage of it, and they constantly checked their compass course against the sun.

The baron kept them supplied with food, whilst the pilots alternated on the controls in three hour shifts. He also ran the navigation plot and advised the necessary changes of course.

Hugging the surface of the ocean as they flew towards the west, Fitzmaurice later described the huge shower clouds in mid ocean: 'Here and there ahead and to the left and right of us, local downpours of rain gave the appearance of vast solid columns reaching up from the ocean surface to support the enormous banks of dark clouds reclining in the sky. Several isolated snow storms looked like giant marble pillars fulfilling the same purpose. It all presented the appearance of a high vaulted, domed and arched cathedral of colossal proportions, the dome and arches being supported by gigantic vari-coloured columns and pillars, the whole illuminated by sunshafts flooding through great windows and apertures in the sides and ceilings. The lights and shadows were awe inspiring and deeply majestic. It looked so completely unearthly it brought us close to God.'

Soon the dreaded fog banks of Newfoundland engulfed them and they climbed to 6,000 feet in the darkness to be at a safe altitude approaching land. The weather grew progressively worse with strong winds and sleet, and the air pressure line to the simple blind flying instrument iced up; so Fitzmaurice opened the cockpit hatch and fitted a spare venturi close to the heat of the exhaust stacks. He dropped his maps on the cockpit floor and when he picked them up, he found to his horror that they were covered with oil. An oil leak!

Again he opened the roof hatch in an endeavour to locate the source of the leak at the rear of the engine — he could not find it; the

139

oil supply tank was well depleted, and they pumped it full — only to discover some time later, that it was still slowly seeping out. Aware of the great differences in magnetic variation over relatively short distances in the vicinity of Newfoundland they laboured the BREMEN up and up to surmount the cloud bank, in the hope of checking their compass against one of the celestial bodies — but to no avail.

They flew on through the overcast in icing conditions, and now with the added complication of failed instrument lighting, but the BREMEN handled well and the engine never faltered. Their navigation became totally dead reckoning: an estimated wind, an estimated variation — and the realization that they were flying over the graves of their predecessors. Fitz checked the oil level once more, and it was dangerously low; they might not have sufficient oil to complete the flight to New York. A decision was made to alter course to the north to make sure of an earlier landfall, and they battled on through the night with only an occasional glimpse of the Pole Star.

A blood red sun came over the horizon heralding more storms, and now they were flying over deserted wastes and endless snow clad forests, jagged peaks and huge rivers and the antics of their compass made proper course keeping impossible. They estimated that they were well inland in Labrador and decided to turn back and head south east to make contact with the coast.

By now the fuel was getting low, and they knew that all hope of making New York was gone; their pressing need was to get the plane down close to some human habitation. They flew along a wide river at a height of about ten feet for two hours in the hope of identifying a landmark — they estimated that there was about three hours fuel remaining. The strain of the flight was beginning to tell, and with it came fatigue. They were troubled with mirages and imagined that they saw in front of them large towns complete with church spires; at other times the illusion took the form of airfields complete with hangars and living accommodation.

Fitzmaurice kept scanning the horizon with binoculars and suddenly he shouted: 'A ship.' The ship turned out to be a lighthouse on the coast, and they skimmed low over it to see men and dogs moving on the ground beneath them. Huenefeld tossed out a smoke bomb to assess the wind direction, and Koehl put the BREMEN down on the frozen surface of a small lake in Greenly Island, in the Strait of Belle Isle on the Gulf of St. Laurence. The plane was in the air for 36 hours and two minutes. Eighty gallons of fuel remained, and the date was Friday, 13 April 1928.

Regrettably, no log was kept of the flight progress and only the few notes made by Koehl remain, reflecting in their latter stages the fatigue which had almost overcome them:

'Continental climate as in Russia ... the winds, winter, snow then again areas of storms. Japan the same — check the temperatures during cyclones; the theory of cyclones is correct but the meteorology on large continents is not. Germans cannot perceive such conditions at all. Russia has also got a lot of fog at certain times; the start of bad weather should be calculated more in advance. There are always low pressure areas starting from the continents. Trans ocean calculation is easier than others. When an airship enters such a hurricane it is lost.

Over the sea, storm is only conspicuous ... also at night. Temperatures over Labrador in higher altitudes were increasingly cold, but on land it was warmer at the top.

On landfall northerly gales below but warm southerly airstream above. Fog over the Gulf of St. Lawrence....

Man is the biggest and most important factor. Continuous flying is too difficult, you need special training for it. You have to get some sleep in between, then your decisions will not be influenced by over tiredness. Ability is decisive for such a performance — to begin with you have to have nerves of steel as for everything else.

Trans ocean traffic is feasible, but you need the best horse from the stable and this one has to be trained.

Aircraft worked perfectly as predicted, it is simply marvellous. Engine good-excellent. Arrangement of tanks excellent — oil pressure was not tested and the full viewing glass showed empty very quickly which influenced the course, and wind velocity increased. In addition there was a bit of a leak from the meter, and yet it looked OK.

Guenther told me we are now flying over land — also near Labrador. All are confident to ... on land ... lighthouse. There should be weather stations in the forests of Labrador. Air traffic control should be directed by men and not cowards. Our lives should be staked for high values and air traffic is worth it... So easy to make accessible by aircraft. Beautiful countryside, meteorologists need this — exquisite in fog. Everything becomes difficult in the end — nerves — the best remedy is prayer, it brings serenity. The will of a Higher Being gives peace, nerves unrest — such a simple remedy — you can float.'

The North Atlantic had been conquered for the first time from east to west by an aeroplane, and the victors were two Germans and an Irishman........

Colonel Fitzmaurice left the army shortly afterwards, but there is a fitting tribute to his military career in the last entry on his army

Photo – New York Times

President Calvin Coolidge with Koehl, von Huenefeld and Fitzmaurice at the White House.

file. It reads: 'Recommended for higher appointment because of ability, zeal, initiative and faculties for leadership.'

Those three brave aviators are dead now, but I found in Fitzmaurice's writings a verse of Tennyson which is a fitting epitaph to them, and to those who went before them on pioneering flights:

For I dipt into the future, far as the human eye could see,
Saw the vision of the world, and all the wonders that could be;
Saw the heavens filled with commerce argosies of magic sails,
Pilots of the purple twilight dropping down with costly bales.

Chapter Five

LOGBOOK

*Chronicle of tales
– old and new.*

The most important chronicle of a civil or military pilot is called a "logbook;" this was an ongoing narrative of dates, types of aircraft, registrations, journeys airfields, hours flown, departure and arrival times, category of pilot, night flying, day flying, instrument time, number of passengers flown etc. etc. The tabulations were endless dependent on which type of log book was used: that of an oil company and usually supplied free, or the purchased "approved" type. The military logbooks were even more detailed and had to be compiled with great attention to neatness and accuracy — finding their way each month through precise orderly room sergeants, to flight commanders, and then on to squadron commanders for final approval — in air forces from Ireland to China.

My first hardback logbook carried the designator FORM 414 ROYAL AIR FORCE PILOT'S FLYING LOGBOOK. The "ROYAL AIR FORCE" bit was deleted by the Irish military, who had also typed the following caveat inside the cover:

1. This book is an official document and is the property of the Minister for Defence.

2. An accurate and detailed record is to be kept in the log of all flights undertaken in military aircraft by the individual to whom it relates.

3. On the last Saturday of each month, the log will be ruled off, and the total of each type of flying inserted immediately under the ruled line.

4. The log stamp will be inserted on the left hand page appropriately aligned with the ruling.

5. The first entry for the following month will be made immediately under the space occupied by the official stamp.

6. Accuracy, care and neatness must be displayed in entering up the log book.

Miles Magisters and two variants of Masters, Avro Cadet's, Avro 626's, Hawker Hinds and the "Squadron Hind," Hawker Hectors, Gloster Gladiators, Westland Lysanders, Hurricanes with either eight machine guns or four cannon, occupied those memorable pages of aviation youth, spelt out in the detail of the military employment involved — the missions, and when in exercise, the quantity of ammunition expended or bombs dropped. I note that with a total flight time of 120 hours in Sept. of 1941, I delivered, on behalf of the State, to the cliff targets at Gormanston, 100 rounds of ball and tracer 303 ammunition from the single synchronised Vickers machine gun of Hawker Hector 78. In this context, I recently came across a man in a Dublin pub, who had wanted to meet me, because, years before he had stood as an infantry soldier on the railway bridge at Gormanston near those same targets, watching the diving aircraft, and the expelled empty cartridge cases from the eight guns of my Hurricane peppered him as he dived for cover in the belief that he was being fired upon.

Hector 78 was no different from the twelve others purchased "part worn" from the RAF, where they had proved to be unsuitable in their design role of army co-operation machines; it also has to be said that they were slightly elderly. The Air Corps used them as advanced trainers and they were ideal for this purpose, except for one snag — the power plant; a 24 cylinder H block air cooled in line Napier Dagger engine of 806 hp. Each clyinder of this monstrosity was fired by two plugs — 48 in all, but in addition to propelling the Hector, the engine had a continuous history of cooking the ignition harness. Earlier that year, Hector 78 and I nearly came to grief.

The main fuel tank of this aeroplane was equipped with a rearward facing static vent, located on top of the centre section; understandably when the aeroplane was upside down, the vent was pressurized with the full volume of the fuel in the tank. "78" and I were flying inverted across Baldonnel, and the detail was being carried out for the benefit of my instructor viewing the exercise from the comfort of his office way down below; I hung upside down from the straps with the Napier Dagger grunting and growling and objecting to the intermittent flow of fuel. Meanwhile the static vent commenced to discharge a flow of high octane gasolene across its pilot, which was unpleasant but normal, until, in my case, the engine backfired and ignited the fuel, and me, and the aeroplane. I had enough sense to roll right way up, and the fire burnt itself out, leaving little damage, except superficial skin burns to my face.

On 29 October. 1941, I note that I was posted to No 1 Fighter Squadron with a total flying time of 149 hours; Lt. W.P. Delamer, who later commanded the Irish Air Corps, went to France in 1917 in his Spad biplane fighter as an "experienced" pilot of 80 hours.

The cosseting, given by instructors to their pupils during elementary and advanced military flying training, ended on posting to a fighter squadron. Training aircraft were fitted with dual controls, either the side by side type or in tandem, and the fledgling was not released for solo until the tutor was satisfied with his performance; the introduction to a heavy fighter was totally different. Details as to the machine's peculiarities were spelt out by the flight commander — its required speeds and techniques, and skimpy technical notes were supplied by the manufacturer; the hapless one finally signed an entry in his logbook which read, 'I understand the fuel and oil systems of this aircraft,' — and away he roared.

Simple pre-flight cockpit drills evolved out of military necessity for readiness and quick getaways, and an almost universal form was as follows:

T	— Trim adjustment of the tailplane.
M	— Mixture Control Position.
P	— The pitch setting on the propeller for take off.
Fuel	— Fuel tank selection.
Flaps	— Flaps fully retracted for take off.
Gills	— Engine cooling flaps.

A friend of mine, not even still renowned for his piety, decided not to take any chances as the big day arrived for him and he was faced with his first solo in an awesome fighter. In error he had left his radio transmit button switched on, and his voice was heard coming through the speaker in the control hut, enumerating the details of the drill that he knew so well. As he opened up the Hurricane's throttle and the roar of its Rolls Royce Merlin drifted across the airfield, the youthful voice continued — now slightly quavery, 'In the name of the Father, and of the Son........'

*　　*　　*

Rathduff, in Co. Tipperary, was the site of our temporary landing strip during the Divisional Manoeuvres of August 1942; a mixed unit of Lysanders and Hectors provided the reconnaissance information for our division. One of the Hectors crashed, running out of fuel because of its over enthusiastic pilot who had miscalculated and remained over the exercise area in excess of his endurance. He made it to Rathduff but the engine quit on the approach; the Hector crashed on the field, with the top wing of the biplane and its centre section, ripping back from the fuselage and pinning the pilot and his observer underneath. The observer escaped injury, but the pilot, who survived to become Chief of Irish Air Traffic Control, left his moustache on the windshield.

The lands on which this temporary airfield was located were the property of the widow of a major of the British army, a most charmingg and genteel lady who not alone welcomed us, but entertained us royally. Our adjutant, who was a captain, a most precise and loveable man, and who had been a commandant general in the army until the demobilization of 1929, kept his young officers in line at the lady's table, and I thought to myself many times in that house — what a wonderful cross section of all that goes to make us Irish: a decorated hero of the War of Independence whose eyes were yellowed and sight diminished from his job of manufacturing explosives for use against the enemy, and our hostess, the gracious Irish widow of a British army officer.

Amongst the many reconnaissance flights that I made from that airstrip, I logged an "air test" of one hour and ten minutes flown on 9 Sept. 1942 in Lysander 64; the "observer" was Fr. W. O'Riordan — "05 Riordan" as he was more commonly known, the numerical designator being the last two figures of his army number. The air test duty was just a cover up for the fact that our chaplain wanted to fly over Lismore, the place where he was born. A shy gentle person, drafted by his clerical superiors into the newly formed Irish army in 1922, he would have been more suitable to the chaplaincy of a convent, but though they were tough times and tough soldiers, he remained at his post until assigned to a parish in the 1960's. Beloved by the soldiery for his understanding, he had his problems from time to time and his reaction was always direct. The female staff of a local hospital were receiving excessive attention from Fr. Bill's parishoners, and the matron had lodged a complaint with the commanding officer. The barracks was located near a "T" junction on the road, with the centre piece of the "T" being occupied by a newsagency run by a retired soldier — the left junction led to the hospital, the right to a small town. Fr. Bill thundered from the pulpit that next Sunday, an ominous warning,' 'Any man that turns left at Johnny Cleary's paper shop has ALREADY committed mortal sin.'

*   *   *

My logbook does not recall the details, nor indeed the trepidation of twenty Air Corps cadets who were aroused from their billets on a cold winter's night of Dec. 1940, and whom minutes later found themselves with rifles and machine guns manning their sector of the defence perimeter of Baldonnel. The camp had been called to stand-to, and the night air was alive with the staccato bellow and stabbing flashes of protesting cold engines as the ground crews and the pilots opened then up to taxi our aircraft to the safety of their dispersal areas. We lay in fear in the ditches, bayonets fixed awaiting German paratroopers; the chaplain visited the lines by truck and gave general absolution to Catholic, Protestant and Jew alike, all in the firing line. As the night wore on the tension eased and the only exciting occurrence in our sector was a nervous cadet putting "one up the spout" without the order to do so; this was the bolt action of arming the Lee Enfield rifle by inserting a round into the firing breech — regarded as a heinous crime in army drill.

About two o'clock in the morning the alert was called off, but speculation was rife as to the cause of the alarm. It had evidently started with some redeployments of British troops north of the border, and the Irish soldiers facing them misinterpreted the moves and called General Headquarters for orders. The border alert coincided with the real cause of the emergency: the German minister had just then made a formal request to the Irish government to open the airfield at Rineanna to allow a German military aircraft to land, with an army and navy attache on board who were to be accredited to the Irish state. In consultation with "G 2," army intelligence, the government construed the request as a German ruse and a prelude to invasion and therefore refused the application of Herr Hempel. The army was immediately placed on stand-to, and the base at Rineanna ordered to shoot down any German aircraft that attempted to land; the manoeuvres of the British along the northern side of the border were in reality the direct result of the alert being passed on to them by the Irish authorities.

That stand-to was in 1940, and writing about it now I am

reminded in contrast, of another stand-to that took place in earlier years in Dublin. That description was written by Lt. Sir Jonah Barrington, an officer in a cavalry unit of the Lawyers' Corps of the Irish Volunteers, circa 1798, and that alert had been called by the British because of the presence of Irish rebels in the Swords area:

'Actual hostilities now commenced by skirmishes around the city of Dublin, and several simultaneous attacks were made by the insurgents upon various posts and garrisons, with surprising pertinacity. They had neither officers, regular arms or discipline; their plans therefore, though acutely devised, could have no certainty of regular or punctual execution; yet a masterly system of tactics, of combinations and of offensive warfare had been originally determined upon. Though these, in great measure, had been frustrated by the death of Lord Edward Fitzgerald, and the arrest of the Directory, they were executed sufficiently to prove that there had been a plan of effectual resistance to the government.

The number of the insurgents is impossible to state with accuracy. There then existed in Ireland at least 125,000 effective men at arms, who, from the smallness of the island, could be collected and marshalled in a week throughout the entire kingdom.

The insurgents were unpaid — many of them nearly unclothed, few of them well armed, all of them undisciplined, with scarcely any artillery; no cavalry, their powder and ammunition mostly prepared by themselves, no tents or covering, no money, no certainty of provisions; obedience to their chiefs, and adherence to their cause, were altogether voluntary. Under these circumstances, their condition must have been precarious, and their numbers variable. No one leader amongst them had sufficient power to control or counteract their propensities, yet they fought with wonderful perseverence, address, and intrepidity.

A night attack on the metropolis had long been meditated by the United Irishmen, but its early execution had not been anticipated by the government. The Lord Lieutenant ascertained that such an attempt was to be made on the 23 May 1798, by a large body of insurgents then collecting on the north of Swords and Santry, and on the south, under the Rathfarnham mountains, five miles from the city. Of their numbers, leaders, arms or tactics, everybody was ignorant, all was confusion, and every report was extravagantly exaggerated. The regular garrison and the yeomanry, prepared themselves with the utmost animation but nobody knew his station, or could ascertain his duty. Orders were issued, and immediately revoked, positions were assigned and countermanded; more confused, indescisive and unintelligible arrangements of a military nature never appeared.

No probable point of attack was signified, and the only principle of defence appeared to be compromised in one sentence, "every man for himself, and God for us all." Lord Clare appeared the most busy and active, as far as his tongue was concerned. Confidence and bravery were recommended in all quarters; but a very serious uneasiness was perceptible throughout the metropolis; his Lordship's activity was confined to the council chamber, and to the upper court of the castle.

As night approached, orders were given that the yeomen, cavalry and infantry, should occupy Smithfield, which was, at length, considered as the probable point of attack from Santry, where the peasantry were reported to have collected in the greatest numbers. The yeomen, amongst them were nearly eight hundred attorneys, horse and foot turned out. Their infantry were effective, and their cavalry excellent. The gradations of their discipline were, however, extremely amusing: those who had imbibed their quantum of generous fluids, were the most fierce and enthusiastic; others who had dined on substantial matters, were as steady as posts. But those who had been paraded before dinner, after standing under arms for some hours, could endure it no longer and a forced loan of cheese, tongues, and bottled porter, from a Mr. Murray of Great George's street, was unanimously decided upon, and immediately carried into execution. The barristers, commanded by Captain Saurin, were from their position likely to sustain the first onset of the pikemen; and as night closed, such a scene of military array never was, and probably never will be witnessed. Smithfield is a long and very wide street, open at both ends, one of which is terminated by the quays and the river. It is intersected by narrow streets, and formed altogether one of the most disagreeable positions in which an immense body of semi disciplined men and horses were ever sustained in a solid mass, without any other order than, "if you are attacked, defend yourselves to the last extremity."

The cavalry and infantry were, in some places, so compactly interwoven, that a dragoon could not wield his sword without cutting down a foot soldier, nor a foot soldier discharge his musket without knocking down a trooper. The cavalry being elevated, could breathe freely in the crowd; but the infantry could scarcely avoid suffocation. A few hundred insurgents, with long pikes, coming on rapidly in the dark, might, without difficulty, have assailed the yeoman at once from five different points. The Barristers' and Attorneys' corps occupied these points. So much for General Craig's tactics.

The danger was considered imminent, the defence impracticable; yet there was a cheerful, thoughtless jocularity, with which the English nation, under grave circumstances, is totally unacquainted; and plain matter-of-fact men can scarcely conceive that renovating levity which carries an Irish heart buoyantly over every wave, which would swamp, or at least water-log, their more steady fellow-subjects. All the barristers, attorneys, merchants, bankers, revenue officers, shopkeepers, students of the University, doctors, apothecaries, and corporators of an immense metropolis, in red coats with a sprinkling of parsons, all doubled up together, awaiting in profound darkness, not without impatience, for invisible executioners to dispatch them without mercy, was not a situation to engender such hilarity. Scouts now and then came, only to report their ignorance, a running buzz occasionally went round that the videts were driven in — and the reports of distant musketry, like a twitch of electricity, gave a slight but perceptible movement to the men's muscles. A few faintly heard shots from the north side also seemed to announce that the vanguard of Santry men was approaching. In the meantime, no further orders came from the general, and if they had, no orders could have been obeyed. It appeared at break of day, that both the Santry and Rathfarnham men had adjourned their main assault till some other opportunity.

The different corps got more regular, and the bands struck up "God Save The King," the danger of the night in all its ramifications, re-occupied the tongue of every soldier in Smithfield: and at length an order came from General Craig to dismiss the troops, and to parade again in the evening.'

The last brigade to be formed by the Irish army in the 1940's was the 8th, and although incomplete it was charged with the defence of Shannon airport and composed of a mixed group of units: a fighter squadron, two infantry battalions, an anti aircraft artillery regiment and a squadron of Ford and vintage Rolls Royce armoured cars. The tragedy for the fliers in this grouping was that no allowance was made by the brigade administration for their specialist function, and there was a continuous demand for manpower for "fatigue duties": camp cleaning, turf cutting, cookhouse chores etc. etc. This meant that ground crews were being taken away for long periods from the maintenance work on the fighters, generally resulting in only a small number of machines of the squadron being serviceable; this would not occur today, since the whole concept of soldiers' and airmens' duties and assignments has changed. Fortunately the pilots were reasonably well exercised in the tactics and operation of their few fighter aircraft, and from the day that their flying training had finished and they were posted to the few operational units, they were proficient in the use of machine guns, cannon and bombing equipment, attending the range of exercises in

Gormanston each year where they blazed away and bombed, admittedly on a small scale compared with the exercises and the reality of the belligerents.

Gormanston was the ancestral home of the Preston family, the premier title in Ireland and, like the Norfolks in England, they were Catholic. When Cromwell came their way and halted at the gates, he demanded to know who was the owner of the castle, and the Preston of the day replied, 'My Lord Gormanston's today sire, my Lord Cromwell's tomorrow.' The Lord Protector left the lands and the castle untouched.

The Prestons had a tradition of the foxes howling eerily around the castle walls when a member of the family died; young Lord Gormanston of the Irish Guards was killed on the beaches at Dunkirk during the British evacuation in the debacle of 1940, but the foxes had howled in the demesne long before the official telegram arrived. We were in that castle many times as guests of the family, and as a carousing lowly second lieutenant I wore the ermine and mink robes and the coronet of a peer of the realm.

As the conflict in Europe progressed through its years and increased in its ferocity, with aerial combat claiming men and aircraft on a scale never reached in the previous war, the Air Corps was able to husband its pilots and their aircraft, and from my logbook of those years which would be typical of other pilots in my squadron, no interception of foreign aircraft was made by my unit during our two years at Shannon. At the end of this time, with the war drawing to its inevitable conclusion and all risk of invasion disappearing, the army commenced to wind down, and as part of a massive tattoo spectacular in Dublin the squadron flew its last wartime formation, and we considered ourselves very lucky, because out of our original cadet group of twenty, only one was killed in a flying accident.

I think that of all the military aircraft that I flew during that period, the Gloster Gladiator was the most memorable. This fighter was built by the British aircraft manufacturer Gloster, and first flew in 1934; it was the last of a long line of biplane fighters and was of the usual type of structure predominant since the first war — an aluminium alloy skeleton covered with doped - linen fabric. Nevertheless, it was unusual for its time because it possessed an enclosed cockpit fitted with a heater, and landing flaps. Two Browning 303 machine guns were synchronised to fire through the propeller arc and two more were underslung from the bottom mainplane. Powered by an 830 hp. Bristol Mercury radial engine of nine cylinders, it had a service ceiling of 33,000 feet with a top speed of 250 mph.

This biplane was a delight to fly, from the captivating rumble of the Mercury to its capacity to barrel roll all day if one so desired — it was like winding it around a large corkscrew with the ailerons. The Gladiator did precisely the same thing in the vertical axis in a spin, with the nose circumventing the same spot on the ground, the machine almost vertical, the spin fast and the radial engine grunting delightfully as the aeroplane rotated. It had two objectionable features — if the pilot was overenthusiastic in a dive it was easy to strip the fabric from the centre section, that portion of the top mainplane just forward of the cockpit; the fuel tank situated just behind the engine was not particularly robust either and monotonously developed leaks. To remove it was a major job and those four Gladiator fuel tanks nearly broke the heart of the flight sergeant, "Daddy" O'Keefe — his anguish was worse when they were scrapped — the quartermaster discovered new tanks in the technical stores.

Another endearing feature of that aeroplane was its stability and its docile acceptance of its wing being tucked in behind the flight commander's in formation flying, at a distance of perhaps six feet, and remaining there in perfect safety provided the pilot kept his eye on his end of Dessy Johnston's moustache. Dessy was my flight commander on Gladiators and Hurricanes, and he was a superb fighter pilot by any air force standards, the "Butty" Carr was usually on the other side in the standard formation of three. Johnston had a slight stammer but he never faltered in the air on the radio, and when you were tucked in there behind his wing he flew his aeroplane almost as if he were alone and we followed him, in close.

Formation keeping was an essential part of the military aviation role; the birds in their graceful groupings had obviously set the scene, as they stayed tight together or in loose but definitive flock patterns for discipline, protection, navigation, identification and comradeship. The same reasonings pertained to the formations of bombers and fighters, although during the first world war, it was the Germans who realised that large formations were not always really successful, because the absence of radio communication limited their command response to hand signals relayed from machine to machine; this inhibited spontaneous reaction and rendered them unwieldy. There were many instances of one or two brave men dashing headlong into large formations of enemy fighters and wreaking havoc. The most famous event of that war in this context was the last, though not fatal combat of the Canadian, Major William Barker; posted home from France in October of 1918, Barker was flying a Sopwith Snipe with full tanks. He was already an ace of 41 kills, but a juicy target in the shape of a Rumpler two seater observation plane lured him down to the attack — he destroyed the

Rumpler but a hail of bullets from behind brought him to his senses, and the reality that the sky was full of Fokker D 7's, in fact sixty of them from Jagdeschwader 3. Barker attacked head on into the Jastas, and although his cockpit was awash with blood, his legs shattered and the Snipe riddled with over three hundred bullets, he shot down three German fighters before crash landing in an almost unconscious condition behind the British lines.

Strangely enough the dispute about the tactical use of large groups of fighters, although for different reasons, had not been fully resolved even in the RAF of the Battle of Britain in 1940. Right through the heat of that crucial combat, the chief of Fighter Command was under continuous pressure from his Group Captains, some of whom advocated the use of large formations and others who favoured smaller compositions.

In the bomber squadrons of that second world war, it was the United States Air Force which perfected the "box" type of formation, that placed the Fortresses and Liberators in tight groups at different levels in the bomber stream, and afforded their gunners the maximum field of fire. The reality of the matter was that if a bomber was forced to leave its formation of whatever type, for whatever reason, it was easy meat for preying fighters.

The Luftwaffe responded to these formation tactics in different ways: either the mad dash of the single fighter into the box pack, or the "Jazz Music" for ordinary bomber streams or the lower echelons of box formations. The weak spot of all bombers was the belly, and although usually protected by twin guns in a ventral turret, it was the favourite target area for an attacking fighter.

"Schräge Musik" — jazz music, was the name given by the Germans to the installation of two vertical cannon behind the rear canopy of the ME 110 twin engined fighter bomber; the weapon set up was so devastating against Lancaster bombers that it was then fitted to the JU 88's. A special sight above the windscreen enabled the pilot to manoeuvre to any chosen position beneath the bomber, and loose off a hail of cannon shells, initially with catastrophic consequences to both the attacked and the attacker, because the stream of projectiles was of such intensity that either the bomber's fuel tanks blew up, or its bomb load exploded blowing both aeroplanes to eternity. The attacking technique was modified and the night fighters worked further up along the belly, so that their first burst blew off either the four propellers or the four engines — neither mattered, the bomber was doomed. I have a friend who was a flight engineer on a Lancaster during the massive but abortive raid on Nuremburg; as tranquil as one can be in such circumstances he was peering out of his observation window at the glinting arc of the two

155

starboard propellers in the moonlight, when all four were suddenly blown off by gunfire.

Tactic and counter tactic, fighter versus bomber all came to an end for the Luftwaffe when the Allied fighters, using drop tanks, stayed with the bomber groups all the way to the targets, and all the way home.

In December of 1945 with our war games over, my logbook shows a transfer to the national airline, Aer Lingus, with the blessing of the army and a six months secondment or "trial" period. Not enough of the pilots of the Air Corps, and particularly senior pilots transferred at that time, yet even if they had, the majority of the recruitment would still have had to come from the demobilised ranks of the RAF, most of whom selected were Irish, but with a considerable number of British, augmented by others who had qualified in civilian schools.

Sophisticated pilot selection methods had not yet evolved and the key credential to obtaining a civilian flying job was the logbook, usually a service one — the hours, the types flown and the experience. Such a facile method of qualification produced from time to time a highly mixed result — forged logbooks, or genuine qualifications confirming pilots of immense experience, but who could occupy no place in domestic flying. Yet the system at that time was no different in any European airline company — the ex-service pilot was simply accepted on face value. Aer Lingus led the way in early 1960, by introducing its own cadet pilot selection and training scheme; I was Chief Pilot at the time, and insisted that the same selection techniques be applied to any pilots, regardless of their source, if they were hired outside our own training programme.

Those early years then for Aer Lingus produced some cookies in the guise of pilots and assorted ground personnel, and it took some time to filter them out. Nevertheless, the majority of the mix was reminiscent of what had happened in earlier years during the foundation of the Air Corps, from which a homogeneous group of pilots and engineers had finally emerged around that common denominator — an Irish aeroplane. The Air Corps — RAF undertones continued down through the years, not a healthy ingredient in my view, but then human endeavour is born of difference and varied allegiances, and the mix produced without a doubt the finest collection of professional airline pilots operating in western Europe.

Half a dozen highly skilled civil pilots of the old school composed the nucleus of Aer Lingus at this time, some of whom had been in the company almost from its foundation in 1936; to this elite group then was added a small number of Air Corps pilots — many more were to follow down through the years, and that large number of ex-

RAF personnel. I had but 5 hours of twin engined Avro Anson time, little of it at the controls, and was pitchforked into the stern tutelage of a Captain Wilkins, a TWA pilot of great experience who had been a colonel in the United States Air Force. Not possessing even the vaguest idea of the peculiarities of multi engined aeroplanes, having been seduced during my army career by the charm of Gladiators and Hurricanes, I proceeded to see-saw the arse off the colonel's DC-3, with heavy inputs of rudder in response to the simple tasks that were given to me. Years afterwards when I was Chief Pilot, I saw my file and I realised that he was really a kind man — he had annotated my lack of progress as being due to "girl trouble" — maybe he was right.

I flew the colonel's big Douglas twin for the first time on 18 December 1945; the aircraft was in reality a C-47, the military version of the DC-3, the most widely used transport in aviation history. Aer Lingus also owned an original DC-3, delivered just pre war — it was a 21 seater, powered by two Wright Cyclone 1100 hp. radial engines; the military C-47's had Pratt and Whitney Twin Wasps of 1200 hp, which gave improved performance and became the standard engines of the aeroplane. Although an incredibly reliable aircraft with no vices, its climb capacity on one engine was appalling; it was licenced to operate under a category D tabulation, which accepted an individual aircraft's performance provided it conformed to a "fleet rate of climb" graph. This meant that each machine was taken out of line each year and subjected to a gruelling test flight, which really did nothing except prove that it was a magnificently reliable aeroplane with a lousy to sometimes negligible rate of climb on one engine. Those Pratt and Whitneys were the essence of mechanical integrity and never gave trouble, and in all of their years service with Aer Lingus, there was only one near thing: a passenger DC-3 taking off from Dublin, sustained an engine failure just at lift off into a low ceiling, but it gained height and was safely landed at Baldonnel. The tragic loss of the airline's DC-3 in the Welsh mountains had nothing to do with engine failure.

The C-47 was the aerial workhorse wonder of the Allied armies, and was modified and used in a multitude of roles; the total US production, primarily from Douglas factories, came to 10,000 — some of which are still flying today. In 1936 the Japanese acquired a licence to build the type, and almost 500 of a slightly modified version, engined with 1300 hp. Kinseis, were produced for the navy; the Allies assigned it the rather quaint and affectionate name of "Tabby". A Russian aerodynamicist, Boris Lisunov, who had been seconded to the Douglas plant in Santa Monica, later supervised the licenced Soviet version, the Li-2, of which 500 were built.

Its most spectacular accomplishment during World War Two

was a take off from a high altitude strip in China, with 75 evacuees on board, and on the night of the invasion, D-Day 6 June 1944, C-47's made over 1000 flights to France, dropping parachutists and supplies and towing gliders laden with troops and their equipment.

The Douglas C 47 was of all metal aluminium alloy construction except for the control surfaces which were fabric covered for lightness of response, but conventional as it may have seemed by latter day standards, it was novel in the fact that the strength of the wing to fuselage attachment did not depend on the traditional spar structure system. This orthodox method of aircraft assembly was usually designed around a wing containing two main support spars or beams running through it; these in turn were bolted to the ends of similar spars which protruded on either side from a box frame to which the fuselage or body was attached. With the C-47 or DC-3, the wing to fuselage attachment did not depend on the traditional spar of peripheral bolts which were positioned through a massive flange fitted to, and corresponding to the shape of the inboard section of the wing. Such was the strength of the union, and the perfection of the Douglas machining, that years after the date of their original manufacture, and with thousands of hours in the air, when the time came for a major inspection necessitating the dismantling of the entire airframe, the bolts always reluctantly withdrew in the condition that they were inserted. They never failed to reveal the attachment sections in the pristine state in which they were originally tooled, and that too in addition to tugging gliders and being generally abused by wartime usage.

*   *   *

The methods of protecting modern jet engines and their airframes from the ravages of ice accretion or ingestion are radically different from the somewhat basic devices used in the past to cope with wing, carburettor and propeller icing, on an aircraft like the DC-3. Pulsating rubber sleeves, or "boots", ran along the leading edges of the wings and tailplane, and the idea was that a coating of ice would be allowed to build up before the air inflated boot was switched on; by pulsating in irregular patterns the rubber cracked the ice deposit which in turn was blown away by the slipstream. The system was reasonably effective and did not suffer from one of the disadvantages of a more modern method as was designed into the Vickers Viscount. When this aircraft was flown in icing conditions, the leading edge of the wing could be heated, but sometimes, in unusual circumstances, the result of such heating caused "run back," where the resultant water from the melting ice gradually flowed back along the top surface and built up into smooth, but damaging frozen layers — its influence played havoc with the aerodynamic properties of the wing, because the major portion of the lift capability of any aircraft develops from its upper surface.

The carburettors of the Pratt and Whitney engines of the DC-3 were protected against ice ingestion and blockage, either by the use of a ducted hot air supply, or an independent system which sprayed an alcohol preparation into the throat of the air intakes. The problem here being, that the accidental use of carburettor heat and deicing fluid together was a disastrous mix, and would result in engine failure — correct usage of either one or the other was totally effective.

The propellers of the DC-3 also used an anti-ice alcohol spray, the fluid being conveyed to the blades by small pipes attached to their surface which ran up a short distance from the hub, which was the focal point of the distribution supply.

The system was totally ineffective against heavy icing, because, when it accumulated, it destroyed the aerodynamic efficiency of the propellers by depositing itself upon them in irregular patterns, which in turn set up an imbalance; the results were conveyed to the aeroplane and its occupants as a vibration, and a bombardment of the fuselage by the ice particles flying off the blades. This unpleasant experience was usually accompanied by airframe icing, and whilst the boots did their job in breaking off the wing ice once it formed, the very weight of the accretion across the surface of the aeroplane had a marked effect on its performance. It was possible to aid the propellers in their distress by rapidly altering their pitch and thus varying their speed; this helped in the shedding of the ice.

The problem of heavy icing was a dangerous one for aircraft of that era and the preceding generation, because, once having encountered the hazard, it was not always possible, owing to degradation of performance, to climb up out of the conditions, or for terrain reasons to fly lower. There was also the added complication of taking an already ice coated machine into a further new environment of cloud, temperature and humidity which could be lethal.

The critical temperature range hovered just around zero centigrade, which, when encountered in cloud of sufficient humidity, would cause the formation of dangerous glazed icing, comparable in appearance to its sugary counterpart on a cake; lower freezing temperatures would cause rapid rime deposits, but it was not as dangerous and was easier to handle. Pilots used a basic rule of thumb in determining their reaction to ice formation: this was a rounding out of the simple fact, that for each 1,000 feet of altitude, up or down, the temperature decreased or increased 2 degrees centigrade. As a guide to the possibilities of collecting ice in cloud, the assumption was fairly accurate, except in the presence of frontal conditions, or in a worse situation, where such conditions existed in the proximity of, or over mountain ranges. In such circumstances "orographic lifting" could occur, where strong frontal winds rammed into the mountain face and forced the air mass upwards inducing temperature changes of unpredictable magnitude, and the associated risk of heavy icing. Within such an air mass there generally lurked another meteorological phenomenon, which could also be encountered in less complex circumstances: supercooled water droplets. These were large globules of unfrozen moisture existing at very low temperatures, which, by all the laws of nature should have transformed themselves into ice pellets; but it had to take the reactionary effect of an aeroplane flying through their cloud to set off their natural processes, where they, as if in resentment, then encumbered the metallic intruder with an almost instant coating of glazed ice.

On 9 February 1949, my logbook recalls that I had reached a total flying time of 2,600 hours, and had transported 11,800 passengers; on that morning I operated the early flight to London, and a strong wind on the way gave us a flight time of one hour and fifty minutes to Northolt. The Dublin-London route those days was via Nevin and Barmouth on the Welsh coast, with a safety height of 4,500 feet over the mountains; despite the presence of the hills and the prevailing westerly winds, this route was not excessively turbulent unless those winds were very strong, or a frontal system was straddling them. If conditions were unfavourable for a direct flight, then an alternative track was across the sea to Liverpool, and then down over the relatively flat English countryside, via Birmingham into London.

We flew the outward sector at 5,500 feet and only experienced slight turbulence and light icing. On the return, with the strong winds in mind, and particularly so over the mountains, we chose to flight plan to Dublin at 6,500 feet — presuming that the basic conditions would not have altered greatly in the intervening three to four hours; but they did, and the entry in my logbook reads: "Nearly bought it — props would not deice."

Brian Noble, an ex RAF flyer of considerable experience was my co-pilot, and as we entered the mountain region, we double checked the preparations for what had been but routine on the way out: seat belt sign on, carburettor heat at the proper temperature, and a small trickle of anti-icing fluid to the propellers to coat their surface and make the blades unreceptive to ice. We only had six passengers on board, and the air hostesses, Nuala Doyle and Terry Finn were having an easy time; then, as the saying goes, the ice hit the fans.

160

Supercooled water droplets or heavy natural icing — two degree temperature spread for every thousand feet up or down, minus, or plus, dependent upon your choice — all of the theory became irrelevant, because Ralph Greene was coming in the opposite direction at 5,500 feet, and Tom Cregg, with twenty one passengers was overhead at eight and a half and there was crossing traffic at seven five. Our DC-3, EI-ACH was stuck with 6,500 feet; Noble got out of his seat and switched on the Gee Box to confirm our position; the propellers of the Pratt and Whitneys had started to vibrate, and I turned the rheostat up to increase the flow of anti-icing fluid; one had to be careful here, because, if the delivery rate was excessive the supply could be rapidly exhausted. Nuala Doyle came into the cockpit to ask what was happening, because, as she said, 'the passengers are getting very frightened.' So were the pilots!

The fluid delivery was at "Full," and I was attempting to aid its influence with rapid movements of the propeller pitch control but to no avail, because all hell had broken loose in the aeroplane. The fuselage was shuddering badly, the vibration coming from props that were evidently heavily coated with ice; ominously, there was no sound of ice pieces banging against the sides of the cockpit. The carburettor heat setting was correct, the wing boots were flaking off their ice, and there was an ample supply of alcohol in the anti-ice tank, yet the aeroplane was about to shake itself to bits. The speed started to fall off because of the ineffeciency of the propellers, Noble was still at the Gee Box, and now Terry Finn came in and said 'God, Aidan what's wrong?' It seemed to me that our only hope was in the mechanical reliability of those piston engines, because, regardless of the distorted shape of the propeller blades, those motors would continue to drive them until they vibrated themselves out of their nacelles. As we progressed further west, the intense earphone crackling static started to diminish, and now, according to the Preston controller, Greene and Cregg were clear of us — 'did we wish to ascend or descend?' We decided to go down to 4,500, and in the descent broke clear of cloud, on track, and in the vicinity of Nevin — the frontal mass gave way to isolated cumulus and sunshine; the propellers divested themselves of their lethal coating, Finn brought us coffee, and we coasted smoothly home towards the faint outline of Dublin city. That flight was all of two hours and thirty minutes, but it felt like twice that time.

Modern jet aircraft spend most of their time above the weather, but because their speed is so fast, even at the lower levels, skin friction from the passing air brings a huge increase in body temperature, and whilst the leading edges of the wings can be heated by means of hot air, the airframe is almost immune from heavy icing. This, of course, is a totally different set of circumstances from those prevailing in a number of tragic accidents, where takeoff has been initiated in icing conditions with, either inadequate airframe deicing, or with a coating of ice already formed on the critical areas of the machine.

Despite the freedom from most of the risks of serious icing of today's aircraft, the jet engine is even more unforgiving of ice injection or accretion than its predecessor, the problems here being multiple. An intake of large particles of ice will cause blade damage to the engine compressors, and ice accumulation seriously affects the continuity of the airflow into the turbines by fouling by intakes and guide vanes — in a relatively short time the blades of the compressor, or front engine section, become inefficient, get out of balance and cause serious vibration; ingestion will cause blockage of internal power sensing probes; and then the ultimate indignity can occur, when for the listed reasons, together with the effects of supercooled water, the thermodynamic efficiency is effected and a flame out occurs: the engine continues to rotate at high speed, but with no thrust.

All of these perils are removed by the proper usage of the devices built in to combat such conditions: multiple internal hot air bleeds, sensing probes and continuous firing ignition plugs. In this context it is worth while recalling the unfortunate circumstances surrounding what could have been the most successful and outstanding passenger aircraft of the '50's — the Bristol Britannia.

The Britannia was a four engined turboprop long range transport, first flown by the Bristol Aircraft Company on 16 August 1952; with a fuel capacity of 8,500 gallons of kerosene, and a maximum takeoff weight of 185,000 pounds, it had a range of 5,334 miles at a cruising speed of up to 405 mph, carrying 133 passengers in superb comfort. These performance figures were far in advance of the aeroplanes with which it would have competed, outclassed and outsold: the Lockheed Super Constellation and the Douglas DC-7C, but for one devastatingly detrimental factor - its Bristol Siddley Proteus engine. A reverse flow turboprop power plant, highly susceptible to even mild icing conditions. The ducting of ram air into the engine was thwarted by having to reverse itself before it reached the compressors, and this was the Achilles' spot which dogged the engine, caused multiple flameouts and damned the aeroplane. Instead of writing off the Proteus and re-engining with a Rolls Royce, Bristol stuck with it, and when eventually a fix had arrived, time and demand had passed them by.

Heavy icing then, was the terror of the era of relatively low powered unpressurised passenger aeroplanes, operating in the winter skies of Europe where dense cloud cover and winter temperatures were nearly always conducive to its formation. It was of course; possible to fly above the overcast, provded frontal conditions did not exist because that influence could stimulate cloud formation and extend it for hundreds of miles, reaching heights of 30,000 feet or more, but prolonged flight above 10,000 feet in an unpressurised aircraft was uncomfortable.

On the majority of the over water routes in Europe the pilots generally operated in visual flight conditions, safely and pleasantly beneath the clouds, and their passengers were the more appreciative of the journey, because of being in sight of the sea surface, or the coast for the duration of the flight. Provided cloud did not obscure dangerous terrain, it was also possible to fly inland services without risk beneath the overcast, although this in itself could physically be an unpleasant experience due to the turbulence of strong winter winds, or in the summer, from the thermal up and down draughts caused by the heating of the sun.

We flew the Isle of Man, Liverpool, Manchester and Glasgow runs for years, mainly in visual conditions during the day, and there was splendid scenery on the way. We had an almost regular clientele on the routes, most of whom were known to the pilots; from time to time some of the passengers would express a wish to view the scenic delights of the flights at closer range. These requests were usually joyfully acceded to, and were supplemented by the individual flair of the pilots, who, from time to time, would deviate anyway in altitude and course to highlight the more outstanding features of the terrain beneath.

Gradually, the random choice of "instrument flight rules" flight at an assigned level on a specified route, or "visual flight rules," by the pilot in command was removed by reason of the increasing density of the traffic, generated when the nations of post war Europe had finally set aside their arms and sought to establish themselves in the developing world of civil aviation. The military remained, for obvious reasons, a law unto themselves, and their aerodrome deployment and exercise areas, their stated right to an almost unbridled unilateral possession of the skies for defence purposes, heightened the re-think by the civil authorities. Far too many "near misses" were occurring between passenger and military aircraft, and indeed between the aeroplanes of the operators themselves, and this ominous trend forced the administrations to develop set airway routes, where traffic was tightly controlled and the military forced to accept and avoid the disciplined flow of civilian flights in the regulated airspace. It was still possible to fly by "visual flight rules" in uncontrolled airspace, but with increasing risk; finally, the European air traffic control centres, almost synonymously, introduced "instrument flight rules" at major airport zones, which meant that no aircraft could enter the designated airfield controlled airspace, unless it had been assigned a level to fly at, and a specific entry point.

The result of these refinements, whilst removing the joie de vivre of free flight in what was uncontrolled airspace, tightened up air traffic discipline, removed most of the risks of collision but forced the pilots to fly at unpleasant levels in unpressurized, piston powered aircraft, susceptible to icing and all its hazards. Fortunately the scales of balance, influenced by improvements in the manufacturing industry, were tipping at the same time in a compensatory direction, and the emergence of pressurized, albeit piston engined aircraft, removed most of the hassle of the icing and permitted the generously powered machines to cruise at high levels, above the weather, to their destinations.

Aerial navigation of the late '40's was still relatively primitive, and most of the transports carried a radio operator whose dual function was to provide morse code wireless telegraphy communication with ground stations, and to obtain radio bearings for the purpose of establishing the aircraft's position or progress. The air routes, whilst being spelt out in considerable detail on topographical and navigational charts, were but ill defined by radio beacons, all of them low powered and usually located with considerable distance between the stations. Their reduced output was necessary in order to prevent overlap interference, and hence the signals received from them on the automatic direction finding apparatus of the aircraft could not be relied upon until within close proximity of the facility. Reception could be further hampered by icing conditions or radio static.

The main aid on the London route was not really an approved navigational utility, but the poweful BBC station at Daventry; the problem here being that high powered commercial radio transmitters were often part of a synchronized chain, where, although the stations were widely separated, they would be on the same frequency. This factor could feed confused information into the direction finding equipment, and influence it to indicate false bearings.

Fortunately Aer Lingus aircraft of the period were provided with a navigational aid of exceptional accuracy that had been developed during the war: this was the "Gee Box," a visual receiver of high frequency radio pulses that were continuously transmitted from multiple ground stations in an overlapping grid. It was simple to operate and almost totally free from interference: when its signals were plotted, and that in a matter of seconds, on the appropriate charts, it provided very accurate position information. The lattice system was not intended to extend into Europe, and was therefore a navigational aid primarily for use in the airspace over England, but, because its propagation could not be precisely defined it produced reasonable guidance data extending to the borders of western Germany. The chain was almost totally British subsidised; as more area intensive aids evolved, the network was gradually phased out.

The landing aids serving the civil airfields varied in sophistication in direct relationship to the importance of the terminal. The most advanced aid evolved during the war, was the radar based "GCA," or "Ground Controlled Approach". The radar operators were housed in caravan complexes close to the runway in use; if the wind direction changed it was a simple matter to rapidly reposition the units to their special pads adjacent to the new landing direction. The system was composed of two gradated radar screens comprising a vertical and horizontal scanner; both of these screens were matched to the obstacles, or the variation in the contour of the terrain on the approach lane of the runway, and each of them were marked with the ideal descent and approach paths. The radar equipment received a very distinct image of the aircraft, but to avoid confusion with other reflections the pilot was always instructed to execute a number of special heading changes to confirm positive identification. When recognition was absolute the landing sequence began, and the aircraft was guided down along the proper path by the voice of the radar director, who constantly broadcast height and lateral corrections or instructions, until the pilot was in visual contact with the runway.

Wireless telegraphy was also available as a main landing guidance at lesser airfields, and during its usage for this purpose, the aircraft received a series of uninterrupted bearings, whilst it manoeuvred itself in timed patterns and on special headings to coincide eventually with the "safe" bearing on which it descended into the airfield.

Similar use could be made of a radio beacon if it was sited close to an airport, and the various headings and heights necessary for an accurate let down could be flown by reference to its signals displayed on the dial of the automatic direction finding receiver.

"Standard Beam Approach," or "SBA" was the British term, or "Lorenz Blind Landing System" if it was German — this was a landing aid with which most of the airports of Europe were equipped. It was an audio device which emitted a narrow diverging beam and was located at the audio device which emitted a narrow diverging beam located at the runway; when the pilot intercepted its on-course signal on the approach it transmitted a continuous note; if the aircraft deviated to the left, the steady signal gradually became the morse code letter "A," to the right it was an "N." There were two marker beacons in line with the beam, one close to the boundary of the airfield and the other at a distance of a couple of miles, and when these markers were passed they emitted a pulsating note. The landing procedure required precise heights to be flown over the markers as the aircraft progressed down the steady signal.

The "Radio Range" was an American developed facility and was based on the transmission of the same type of signals as the SBA, but it had multiple beams and higher power, and doubled as an area navigation aid in addition to providing multiple let down patterns to the airfields it served.

Within a relatively short time the aural transmission of the Standard Beam Approach had been replaced by a visual display; this was produced by the very accurate interference free signals of the "Instrument Landing System," the ILS. This transmitter was precisely located in line with a main runway, and it provided visual guidance on a cockpit display, indicating descent path, and horizontal adherence or deviation from the centreline as the aircraft made its approach. The ILS now has its signals integrated into modern flight deck instruments and is still the main landing facility in worldwide use.

In the era preceding the introduction of machines like the DC-3 aircraft were not fitted with powerful landing lights - in fact they had no lights at all, and therefore in night operations they arrived in total darkness, on a grass strip defined by a line of paraffin fed "Goose Neck" flares. This "seat of the pants" technique was refined by the introduction of large mobile searchlight type lights, that illuminated the entire landing area. With the construction of proper runways, electrical lighting was incorporated into their surface, and the simple white lead-in light arrangements with which the runways were first supplied developed into complex patterns of a few further colours, which provided the pilot with badly needed, positive guidance in the approach zone. Calvert, a British scientist, was the major contributor to this technology, producing a cruciform, elevated type of lighting system that revolutionised approach designs, and provided a high intensity guidance path of unique formulation that made a tremendous contribution to safety.

Other developments of his ideas added "sequence flashers" which further improved the critical area; the flashers comprised a short line of single lights, rapidly pulsating in sequence and pointing the way to the end of the runway. Further illuminated approach guidance came to be used by day or night, in the form of high candle power glide path indicators: light transmitters placed close to the ideal touch down point on the runway, where a steady combination of two colours of their beams indicated a safe descent angle.

Glancing through an old logbook of 1946 I can see that we were grateful for the tolerance of the old landing system. Coming into Croydon in a snowstorm, and when eventually catching sight of the goose neck flares, I realised we were on the wrong side of the lights, but I knew the extent of the grass swathe of that aerodrome like the back of my hand, and I put the DC-3 safely down on that left side. A Belgian DC-3 behind us, short on fuel, missed six times and had to get in on his seventh try.

On 13 July 1946 I was crewed as copilot to Capt. Brian O'Daly, an ex-army mate of mine who was later to leave Aer Lingus and join the Dutch airline, KLM. We were flying back from London on a sultry day; the trailing aerial of El-ACE was extended: almost fifty feet of cable, terminating in a large pear shaped leaden weight which ensured that the antenna dangled well below the aeroplane. Soon the heat of the sun had bred a huge crop of towering cumulus and cumulonimbus; the cumulus type cloud was a typical product of the benign summer sun of Northern Europe — fat and woolly white puff balls of moisture in an infinite variety of shapes and sizes. Occasionally, when the formation processes got out of hand, the innocent cumulus proceeded to swell uncontrolledly into towering masses of boiling overhanging cloud called cumulonimbus; now a major electrical trap was being sprung, either directly between the cloud participants themselves, or individually from any one of them to the earth's surface. These energy laden creatures of the heavens are either positively or negatively charged, and in certain circumstances too, it only requires the stimulus of a catalyst, such as an aeroplane in their proximity to trigger off a lightning bolt.

To cope with such a magisterial expression of nature's wrath, the simple linen fabric — metal framework of bygone aeroplanes was protected against the consequences of attracting such emissions by a bonding system based on the "Faraday Cage" principle. With an aircraft, this required an elaborate wiring scheme, whereby each separate part of its structure, or its components were connected to each other by wire, and the integrity of the relationship was challenged by testing, on a regular basis, to ensure that the continuity was faultless. If an undetected short developed, it would cause a localised build up of static electricity which could eventually spark across the gap with serious consequences to the aeroplane. The charge accumulated by such a flying "Faraday Cage" had in itself to be safely disposed of, and the trailing edges of the wings were fitted with static dischargers: electrically conductive streamers of approximately six inches in length. The residual potential was dissipated on landing, by a similar streamer from the tail which earthed to the runway; the discharge system was later refined by the introduction of electrically conductive tyres.

Most of these refinements were negated on that day in July by the fact that our trailing aerial was extended — or at least partially extended, because O'Daly, having observed that the sky had lost its innocence, had ordered his wireless operator to wind in the cable. With just a few feet to go, the aerial of the DC-3 attracted the energy of the nearby storm cloud, and the massive flash of electricity bonded the leaden trailing weight to the bottom of the aeroplane in a shapeless fused mass; the clap of the accompanying thunder and the acrid smell seemed to me as if we had flown into the mouth of an exploding cannon — it was my first experience of a lightning strike.

Despite the awesome destructive capability of such a discharge, it is almost unbelievable to realize that aircraft containing hundreds, if not thousands of gallons of volatile and explosive high octane petroleum in their tanks, contained it in perfect safety — almost. There were a number of fatal accidents where the tank venting and bonding systems were incapable of coping with the enormous amount of electricity generated in a lightning strike. In modern aircraft the fuel used, kerosene, is relatively inert and their tanks possess inbuilt static discharge protection systems.

The presence of static electricity manifests itself in many ways on aircraft in flight, all of them highly spectacular, definitely intimidating but mostly harmless. It might zig zag across the windshields in devilish patterns of blue and intense white, or define propeller arcs in an eerie corona, or even bathe the wingtips with soft blue tongues for minutes, or even hours; the phenomenon is known as "Saint Elmo's Fire."

The visible discharge of static electricity is not peculiar just to airborne contraptions, it is seen and feared by fishermen, playing across the rigging of their vessels, and was the precursor of thunderstorms. Mediterranean sailors used to invoke the protection of Saint Elmo, a fourth century bishop of Formiae, whose miraculous powers were supposed to ward off the thunderstorms; from this practice the display acquired its name. The phosphorescence is due to the positive and negative potential of billions of electrons interacting with each other in an electrically charged field, which has been created by forces erupting in a nearby thunderstorm.

There is another type of lightning presentation called a "Fire Ball," — a huge roly poly nebulous thing that ambles along in the sky like a massive loose ball of hay. I had heard of one appearing in the cabin of a Super Constellation; rolling all the way down the aisle to disappear through the tail section as mysteriously as it arrived, causing no harm to anybody or anything. I met one of these Fire Balls years later, approaching to land at Kennedy Airport, New York, on a thundery afternoon. The storm was some distance away, but as our 747 came closer to the runway, this large, round, hay-like object detached itself from beneath the cloud and rolled towards us, enveloping the nose of the aircraft; but it parted and passed harmlessly along its sides. The scientific definition of the Fire Ball explains it as a creeping corona discharge that advances along a path which is an intense portion of an electric field.

Lightning does of course strike aeroplanes many times each year but, with an all metal surface its effect is usually minimal, generally only leaving behind a carbon smudge on the surface of the metal, but whose formation is accompanied by an explosive sound; the reality being that, whilst its energy potential is measured in millions of volts, the actual current is extremely small. When aircraft are destroyed in thunderstorms, fortunately a diminishing statistic, thanks to radar, their destruction is not generally attributable to the formidable contact with nature's electricity, but rather to the devastating effect of the extreme turbulence generated in the storms which impose on their structures, forces out of all proportion to the safety margins incorporated in their design.

Violent agencies are at work within the cumulonimbus, and their influences radiate from it: updraughts and downdraughts, icing, electricity, hail and torrential rain — the downdraughts have squashed into the ground, many an unwary aeroplane foolish enough to fly beneath them. Thunderstorms can be safely circumnavigated, or even penetrated in certain circumstances by the use of radar, which points up the soft spots in the cells and highlights the core. Lightning flashes and accompanying turbulence can be very frightening for airline passengers, particularly at night, but they are usually due to the proximity of the cells and the reflections of their discharges, as the pilot navigates in a safe area to circumvent the hazard. All in all then, that great thermodynamic engine of the heavens, the cumulonimbus cloud, is best avoided and left entirely to its own infernal machinations.

*　　*　　*

Clear air turbulence, or in abbreviation, "CAT," is another sign of nature's dynamic and thermal disagreements. Wind direction and velocity can change and vary sharply in emphasis over a relatively short distance, both in the vertical and horizontal plane; this fact alone can induce turbulence into the flight path of a high flying aeroplane. The matter may be further aggravated by a rapid variation in temperature over the same route, which plays havoc with stable flight. The existence of jet streams at upper levels, those narrow bands of strong winds snaking through the clear skies of the atmosphere, may also cause a rapid onset of turbulence that can be continuous, dependent on whether or not the aircraft is positioned in the core of the jet, or just flying along its burbling edges. If the jet stream is unaccompanied by continual temperature changes, and the course of the aeroplane coincides with its core, then the passage will be smooth. I have flown in jet streams of over 150 mph for hours on end with hardly a tremor and yet, for that again, encountered wind flows of considerably less speed of the same height that have heaved us across the heavens.

Turbulence in cloud is a more understandable happening, since the very physics involved in the creation of the cloud itself influence any object within it: up and down currents, temperature changes combined with, and causing the formation of moisture vapour, both allied to the consequent variation in air density. The bumps and jolts often experienced on the approach, even on a fine summer's day, are attributable to the heating effect of the sun on the varying composition of the earth's surface beneath the aircraft, the rays stimulating ascending air currents of differing densities and temperatures. The more robust side of approach turbulence is caused by the eddies and swirls of strong winds, induced by the physical features of the land and the buildings underneath.

*   *   *

I note from an old logbook that I flew one of the airline's DC-3's, "St. Kieran" for the last time in late December of 1952. On New Year's day of 1953 that aeroplane was on a routine scheduled flight to Birmingham — it carried a crew of two pilots and one air hostess, and there were 22 passengers on board. The aircraft was cruising in cloud approaching the Birmingham area, when one of its Pratt and Whitney engines cut out; the captain descended immediately to a lower level but moments later the second motor suffered a power loss. The pilots were unable to restart the engines and the captain prepared for a forced landing. They were fortunate to have in the cabin, an air hostess of superb quality, who did not panic in those desperate circumstances, but who went about her business calmly, preparing the passengers for a landing that she well knew could more than likely prove to be fatal for them all.

Losing height rapidly, the captain maintained the aeroplane at a safe speed; he was a very methodical man and possessed a fair knowledge of the terrain immediately beneath them. Breaking out of a very low cloud base, they were in open country, and fast approaching one of the fields of Newlands New End Farm, Spernall, 16 miles southwest of Birmingham. The crew got it down on that field, but the surface was ploughed and it ripped away the two

170

engines; the machine continued to slide and bored through a hedge, then across a road and into another field, where collision with an oak tree tore away the tailplane and the starboard wing, leaving some of the wreckage suspended in the tree. The aircraft finally came to a halt straddling a ditch, approximately 50 yards from another road. The fuselage had suffered relatively little compared to the rest of the machine and, providentially there was no fire. Almost as a tribute to the skill of the captain in getting it safely down, that magnificent Douglas construction cocooned its occupants against injury. The cockpit crew were not so lucky, and the copilot had to be taken to hospital. The farmer who owned the fields, Sam Pritchard, was first on the scene and said that the passengers had left the machine so quietly and calmly that "they might have been getting off a bus."

A public inquiry was held in Dublin to investigate, and determine the cause of the accident, but controversy has surrounded its findings ever since.

* * *

In 1956 I was appointed as a flying instructor on DC-3's, Fokker Friendships — that delightful Dutch turboprop twin, and the four engined Vickers Viscount, the aeroplane that revolutionized the industry with a new concept of speed, comfort and reliability, and over-the-weather flying. That beloved DC-3 was a real pain in the ass when it came to flying training; its performance in the climb on one engine was so miserable that any such flying was a tiring business, and if by chance the ball in the turn and slip instrument was marginally off centre, indicating an out of trim condition, in the critical stage of an engine cut on takeoff, the machine would not climb at all. Worse still for the instructor, since such failures had to be simulated by pulling back the throttle, the cylinders cooled down rapidly and much valuable time was wasted in keeping the engine alive. A turboprop like the Viscount or the Friendship had adequate reserves of power in the event of a failure, and if one of their Rolls Royce Darts was shut down, it responded instantly to the throttle when relit.

The more interesting part of the work concerned the conversion of pilots to new aircraft types. The trainees had to make a lengthy scholastic preparation before reaching the actual flying stage; ground school was the place where engineering teachers unveiled the mysteries of new engines, airframes and associated systems; their lectures were supplemented by slide presentations, cutaway engine sections and ancillaries, and the pupils were provided with textbooks of extraordinary detail, usually supplied by the manufacturers.

A state written examination had to be passed before the actual flying training began, and in those early years, it was then straight onto the aeroplane from the word go. The simulator concept was still in the embryo stage, and airlines were only equipped with the rudimentary "Link Trainer".

The "Link" was purely a procedural trainer, but it was realistically articulated in the three axes of flight to simulate reality; the planes of motion being: rolling, yawing and looping; the movements were limited to a set number of degrees, except in the yawing plane, where there was a 360 degree capability. The machine was equipped with all the blind flying instruments of an aeroplane; it had a control column, throttle, flap and landing gear simulation, and extensive radio apparatus; it did not resemble any particular aircraft type and was not designed for flight training, but it was here that the pilot practiced blind flying, and learned to perfect the varying approach and let down procedures specified for different airfield locations. The instrument displays: speeds, heights, rates of descent and compass heading were repeated on the instructor's panel; travel across the ground was imitated by an electrically powered "crab" with ink on its leg, which traced the movements of the "aeroplane" across a chart of the exercise area; it traversed at an infinitely reduced rate, but its progress was in direct proportion to both the speed of a real aircraft and the scale of the charts.

During the conversion courses to new types, the captains occupied the left seat - this was where they were normally located in their day to day work; the instructor sat in the right, but with the copilots, he moved over to the left seat. Introduction to a commercial aeroplane of some complexity was, even for experienced pilots, a prolonged and daunting process, where every nuance of the new machine had to be demonstrated to each individual with infinite care. Once the pupils had grasped the fundamental characteristics, they embarked upon a programme of intense flying workouts; the multiplicity of exercised was in direct relationship to the number of engines on the aircraft - two or four, and the sequence of tutorial progress would depend on the aptitude the novice displayed in absorbing and mastering the flight techniques associated with those engines.

This advancement was initially concentrated on the serious business of learning to takeoff and land the aeroplane; the instructor intervening only if things looked to be going seriously wrong. The aeroplane was kept moving by the use of "rolling takeoffs" - this drill kept the sequence dynamic because, after a practice landing, instead of rolling all the way towards the end of the runway, and having to taxy back to the point of takeoff, and there perhaps to have to wait in turn - the moment the pupil put the aircraft down, the instructor readjusted the trim, reset the flaps and the trainee advanced the throttles for takeoff. The air traffic controllers for their part, kept feeding the detail into the pattern, and would advise when it was necessary to stand off because of circuit congestion or confliction with commercial flights.

When the trainee achieved competence in handling the aircraft in a normal configuration, the exercise would progress to the assymetric condition, with the instructor simulating engine failures in varying flight profiles. With a four engined aircraft such as a Boeing 707, this required some safety precautions, and when it came to handling two engined landings, only one of the "failed" engines would be shut down, with another throttled fully back but alive; the pupil would be permitted the use of the two designated engines. Satisfactory progress was then challenged by the introduction of further breakdowns of electrical, hydraulic and pressurisation systems - and of the actual flight instruments themselves; through the sequences the instructor reacted as all good teachers do, and where there was a difficulty the exercise was repeated until the problem had been mastered. Inevitably there were disappointments along the way: captains and copilots who were very safe and competent operators of other aircraft, but for whom adaption to the new type, was just not jelling. To eradicate the possibility of a personality incompatibility with a particular instructor, the backward pupil was switched to a new man, and if there was no further progress at this stage, the conversion training would be discontinued, and the pilot would then revert to the aircraft type previously flown. This was a sad and disappointing business for the individuals concerned, but apart from their fortunes, the constant and repetitive exercises were also demanding on the aeroplane structure, and costly in fuel and tyres; historically too with all flight training, there was a risk, and many aircraft and crews were lost in perfecting the very manoeuvres that were supposed to prepare them for such emergencies if they happened for real on the line. An Aer Lingus training Viscount crashed and all the crew were killed; and in another of the many incidents, the ridiculous detail involved recovery of a four engined Boeing 720 from an unusual flying position solely by reference to basic instruments. The pupil misread the dials and put the aircraft into an almost terminal velocity dive, where there was no response from the elevators or the stabilizer; only the consummate skill of the instructor saved the machine, when he opened the power levels to the stops, and the resultant massive surge of thrust brought the nose of the machine up sufficiently to regain control. Every one of those training courses brought its mishaps, and further dangerous situations would crop up during the routine mandatory biannual flight checks.

This dangerous practice of practicing for danger was almost totally removed by the introduction of flight simulators, where, even the most complicated exercises and flight emergencies could be realistically carried out in perfect safety. The simulator was an extremely expensive piece of equipment, and not all of the airlines could afford them, but they could rent the time from others, and every moment of that time was so totally rewarding that it resulted in raising pilot standards and skills to a level that could never have been achieved by the old methods. When my group of pilots converted to the Boeing 747 in 1971, we spent 16 hours each in the simulator, and approximately $3\frac{1}{2}$ hours on the actual aeroplane - flying a few fundamental but basically safe exercises.

Instructors are born - not made, and although I knew I wasn't a bad one, I found the whole business a tiring chore, and after two years I was pleased to return to line flying.

Chapter Six

JET LAG

Desynchronisation of bewildering complexity
– oh sleep, where is thy balm?

Poet and peasant, creatures large and small, all beings of God's creation require the balm of sleep, which Shakespeare described as the 'chief nourisher in life's feast.' The rotation of the earth around its axis veiled portion of the globe in darkness, as segment by segment it turned away its many faces from the life giver, the sun, and shrouded all its species in a veil of night and a pattern of sleep; and as the centuries advanced until the advent of the jet aeroplane, insomnia and sleep disturbance were blamed on the complexity and the pace of modern living.

Across the established norms of sleep, or lack of it for whatever reason, tore the high speed jet, imposing upon the metabolism of its occupants traumatic changes never before experienced — changes that were heightened in intensity when the traverse was in an East to West or West to East direction. The disturbance is commonly referred to as "jet lag," that desynchronisation of the body rhythms, combined with sleeping problems that compound the difficulty of decision-making made in a daylight ambiance, where those rhythms are in the night phase and the body less efficient.

In the matter of long range flying, the major cause of fatigue is held by many experts to be sleep disturbance and deprivation, inextricably linked with the desynchronisation of the normal rhythms of the body systems. I was on long range flying for eighteen years, most of it on the North Atlantic route, and despite the obvious disadvantages of that sleep deprivation and of sleep displaced into a different time zone, lack of humidity in the aircraft, the variation in food, and the partaking of such food at odd and reversed times — I found that I was able to wedge a block of adequate sleep into each 24 hour period, albeit at the wrong times; I was fortunate because the ability to sleep out of phase with the body rhythms varies between individuals. I suffered from no dietary problems, and quite obviously, as with thousands of other aviators, men and women in long range flying, my systems had levelled off to a fairly stable plateau by reason of the number of years they were exposed to such changes. This is not to say that those of us who adapted to the problem did not experience fatigue; during the years of the late sixties, Aer Lingus' Boeings operated a very long and commercially successful "summer" programme, extending from April until October. By the time the crews reached the beginning of the autumn, the "lag" had begun to tell, they were fatigued and eagerly looking forward to leave and the respite of a comparatively easy winter schedule.

The single most important factor that contributed more than anything else to alleviating the environmental discomfort, was the cockpit humidifier fitted to the later Boeing 747; it was not a practical proposition to have such an amenity serving the main cabin, because of the large quantity of water that would have to be transported to satisfy the demands of the equipment. The relative humidity of the air on board a large jet on a long flight may fall to five per cent or lower from a norm of around fifty five, and so, the installation of the humidifier in the cockpit restored that almost total absence of water to a level of twenty per cent or even higher. Low humidity in the cabins of pressurised aircraft causes discomfort, from dehydration of the upper respiratory tract and skin, but does not necessarily cause overall body dehydration if sufficient liquid is consumed.

The original Boeings — the 720's, were fitted with an inefficient and inadequate pressurization cum air conditioning system, which

176

was, for all practical purposes, a facsimile of existing systems in Super Constellations, and DC-7's etc. It was unsatisfactory, temperamental and unable to cope with the ventilation demands of the much larger passenger cabin. Temperatures in excess of 110 degrees, plus high humidity and accompanying fumes of kerosene were the norm when taxying in a queue of fifty or more other aircraft — all of them similarly afflicted, and awaiting their turn for take off out of New York on a summer's night.

Airborne, where the humidity then dropped to almost zero, and where, despite the consumption of innumerable cups of tea or glasses of mineral water during the five hours or so of flight, the crew deplaned at Shannon feeling like dried out prunes, and with the inside of the men's trousers powdered with dry skin. The replacement 707 had a much improved system, and the complex and well designed equipment of the modern wide bodied jet provides a full temperature range of conditioned air, either in flight or on the ground, even in the most extreme conditions, although it still does not remove the kerosene fumes ingested in busy airport taxi areas and is generally not a cabin humidifier.

To ensure that optimal sleep facilities are available to flight crews away from base, most hotels endeavour to comply with airline requirements: bedrooms are assigned in a quiet part of the building, away from street noise and elevators but, despite the best arrangements, different rooms in different hotels constantly brought sleeping difficulties to those destined to occupy them during a busy summer season: the ineffective or noisy air conditioning unit, the rowdy party next door, "sorry wrong room number" on the telephone, a housekeeper checking room occupancy, the plumber banging away on the pipes of the floor above at a not unreasonable time for him — between the hours of perhaps ten to four during the day, the noise of fire engines hooting down the streets, or police sirens in the distance.

These were only minor irritations to the random occupant, but to airline crews they assumed enormous importance, because the total absence of them ensured reasonable rest after, and prior to a long flight. It was in this context that I approached the custodian of my regular room at a New York hotel: a very large, friendly African lady, extremely well endowed and wearing a blue polka dot head scarf. We met in the corridor of the hotel outside my room, as I was leaving to operate the evening service back to Shannon. I had not slept well and I conveyed my complaint to the lady, by telling her that it was impossible to rest on the mattress due to some loose spring within the frame, that kept making a jingling noise. Madam placed her hands on her hips and said to me: 'Jeez Captain, ah knows zactly how youse feel, everytime you moose in the bed, youse athinkin', people athinkin', business is happnen!'

The normal symptoms of fatigue: diminished attention, slowed and flawed perception, impaired thinking, decreased motivation — this decline in performance arises from the two basic classifications of the expenditure of human energy in physical or mental tasks. Each of those categorizations requires sleep, but such slumber differing in its quality — relatively easy rest as a result of the physical activity, but often slow and difficult after mental exertion. Either of these states, or a combination of both can be visited upon the trans meridian passenger as a normal consequence of travel, but when these fairly routine facts are further burdened by disturbed body rhythms, the resultant is commonly called "jet lag," something of a misnomer in view of the complexities with which it is associated.

All of the creatures of the earth exist in a wider world of rhythms: the tides, the interplanetary relationships, the seasonal orbit of our world around the sun, the movements of the galaxies; but it is the rotation of our planet — those 24 hours of light, shade or darkness that affects most of life.

The biological processes of all species incur sequences of events that repeat themselves constantly in simple or complex patterns — patterns that occupy individual time spots ranging from micro seconds to years. The rhythmic changes in themselves relate directly to time, peaking or valleying or levelling in a very direct affinity to the hour of the day or night. Blood characteristics, chemical passage, hormone levels, body temperature, even pain sensation all change during the 24 hours; Russian research revealed, that the total bioelectric intensity of the various brain wave forms show a daily pattern, with a peak at about five o'clock in the afternoon falling to the lowest point at around five in the morning. The circadian rhythm of human temperature peaks at nine during the evening, with its low also between four or five am. The body then, being an integral unit, reacts to the unbalancing of its chemical processes by producing fatigue, possibly exacerbated by the fact that the systems are reacting to the time change factor at different speeds and thus may become uncoupled and desynchronised from each other.

Sleep disturbance is inevitable in long range aviation, where the irregular working periods break into what should be the normal "body nights" — and where many people simply cannot subsequently persuade their frames to continue sleeping in an endeavour to make up their normal quota of hours. Usually in these circumstances, the sun has long since risen, and every iota of the weary traveller's metabolism is signalling, though admittedly, in some confusion, "get up — get up, I am reacting with my daylight signals!" The problem then of disturbance, or the inability to sleep a full quota, is compounded further by the basic fact that even if a sleep period is displaced by two to four hours, although with the amount of sleep remaining constant, vigilance and calculation in tasks can be significantly impaired, and the mood of the individual adversely affected. Long range crews have experienced all of these complexities, and there is some plateauing of their metabolisms which at least enables them to tolerate the constant changes; but pity the infrequent traveller who arrives back home from New York, or from other places far west, usually bewildered by the feelings experienced, and who blames it all on "jet lag," which, almost describes it.

Goethe rhapsodised: 'Sweet sleep, thou cometh like pure happiness, most willingly if uninvited, Thou looseth the knots of rigid thoughts and, wrapped in graceful madness, we cease to be.' Oh ethereal poet, I wonder what thou wouldst have penned after your jet return from a twenty eight hour stopover in ye olde New York, and thou notst knowing thine arse from thine elbow?

Chapter Seven

WOMAN'S WAY

Welcome dear creature
to activity –
prior province of man.
Grace these happenings
with femininity.

During the year of 1892 my grandfather received a very tempting proposition in the nature of an unusual job in the woollen business, from the South African government, at the then princely salary of £400 per year. He decided against it:

'I stayed in Foxford and I heard Maggie Brennan sing at the old harmonium in the little wooden chapel — I listened and looked. It was her lovely voice that first attracted me; no doubt beautiful singing can be a source of uplift in the church, but I am afraid that I found the voice of the brown haired, brown eyed girl a distraction. May I be forgiven if sometimes my mind strayed from my prayers to vague wondering as to what manner of a girl was this, who sang like a very angel. I had not much time for such musings, because I began my working day at six thirty and ended it when I laid my head upon the pillow, or even carried the problems of the day there. To wonder how our small percentages on the flannel was going to be made to pay, or worse problems — where were the next orders going to come from? I remember occasions when I said to the Reverend Mother: "We may close down, we have no orders." She had the answers ready; "But I have an order for you, Frank; I want flannel for the poor. Make it and God will do the rest." She called that "bribing the Lord." '

Maggie Brennan continued to distract him: 'When I began to take surreptitious peeps at her bright face and brown eyes, I could not but feel that they matched her voice. I courted her with my eyes, not daring speech. In fact I had no opportunity or time for speech, even had I dared. I think she knew I was courting her all the same. I had no idea of how I would ever break the silence between us. Mother Morrogh Bernard, full of the idea of encouraging workers to invest in the mill came to talk to me about it one day. She mentioned a number of people that were going to put money in. I had already signified my intention of doing so. Maggie Brennan, she mentioned, was desirous of investing. "Maybe my bit could go in with hers?" I said. Here is where you modern young things get a laugh. The nun asked me if I would like her to ask Maggie if she would marry me — I said I would, and the answer was favourable. From that time Maggie and I had an hour together each evening — that was our courtship. Looking back, I cannot find in my heart the slightest trace of envy for the emancipated moderns, with their movie going and dancing expeditions — Maggie and I were deeply happy.' That was grandpa in 1892, and a great deal of what he wrote is so innocent and refreshing, when compared with the total permissiveness encouraged by modern society.

It was not in a woollen mill, but in a DC-3 five hundred feet above the waters of Loch Lomond, and miles away from the scheduled route, that I first met the girl who is now my wife; ahead of time on the way to Renfrew in Scotland, I had deviated to show some of our regulars that famous loch. The view from our "high road" was magnificent, so I called the hostess, a Miss Keegan, to the cockpit to admire the scenery; the radio was on, but not tuned to a directional beacon — we were listening to an Irish tenor singing "Paddy Reilly;" I gave her the earphones as we flew over the waters of that fabled lake. The next day was not quite so romantic: she mistook me for another pilot.

In 1939 Aer Lingus had purchased a new modern aeroplane for service on the busy route to Liverpool — this involved a completely new concept of passenger comfort, and a cabin attendant was necessary. Miss Eva Toner from the publicity department was chosen for the job, and she wore a black costume, with matching glengarry hat; she stitched a pair of pilots' wings to the dress — she was the first Aer Lingus air hostess. In thirty six years of commercial flying I kept my eye on the brand image of an Irish airline hostess, and I found them generally charming, good looking, efficient, well trained and compassionate flight attendants.

In leafing through the pages of an old logbook where I listed the names of my crews, I can see the youthful pretty faces of the girls who were hostesses when I was young: their personalty and appearance, and some of their perfume is still impressed in those leaves. As the pages turn, so do those lovely faces and the years, the stopovers, the romances and the broken hearts; the escapades and the dances and the parties — the Don Juans and those that courted their Maggies with almost their eyes alone........

A simple plaque on the wall of the hostess training centre at Dublin Airport commemorates the world's first airline stewardess, Ellen Church Marshall. The inscription is a moving tribute to a remarkable woman:

"Humanitarian, war heroine, and aviation pioneer, Ellen Church Marshall dedicated her indomitable spirit to the service of mankind."

Ellen created a new and exciting profession for young girls of the 20th century, and also, as a much decorated Air Force nurse, she had helped thousands of American soldiers who were wounded on the battlefields of Europe. She was born on 22 September 1904, on a farm near Cresco, Iowa, and her life was dominated by her gifted imagination combined with intense dedication and a warm personality. As a young nurse she had walked into the offices of Boeing Air Transport, a small company, later to become United Airlines, and asked for a job as a stewardess on their passenger planes; the year was 1930 and such a request was unique, because no airline or aeroplane had ever carried a female flight attendant. An enlightened official of that little company accepted the unusual challenge which Ellen had made to a world of aviation dominated by males; she was given a job. She was rapidly joined by seven other girls who were also nurses, and it was this qualification which was highlighted: they wore white nurse's uniforms when on board the aircraft; it was considered that their medical training was an invaluable asset towards the comfort and well being of passengers, but soon they became maids of all work, carrying the baggage on and off, cleaning the interior of the planes and helping to bucket the petrol into the tanks; they even pushed the aircraft into the hangars. When all of the seats were occupied in flight, the girls had to sit on the mailbags, and in total contrast to today's pleasant relationship, they were unpopular with the pilots. These were tough old characters who for years before had flown the postal services in antiquated ex service biplanes; they wore sidearms to protect the mails, and found a woman's intrusion into their world rather unsettling, and also jealously resented by their own womenfolk!

With the exception of some smaller jobs in aircraft factories, women were not really involved in flying until an American girl, Amelia Earhart, pioneered the way ahead; even in those early days she had surveyed the role of women in aviation with a view to securing equal employment opportunities. In 1928, Amelia was the first of her sex to fly across the North Atlantic; Mrs Frederick Guest, the American wife of a former British Air Minister had sponsored the venture, and the machine chosen was a Fokker trimotor, the pilot of this seaplane, the FRIENDSHIP, was Wilmer Stultz, with a navy veteran, Louis Gordon as the mechanic.

A contemporary of Miss Earhart's, Helen Richey, succeeded in obtaining a job as a copilot, but she was refused entry to the pilots' union, and could not obtain an instrument rating from the Department of Commerce! In England, another flier, Amy Johnston had made some spectacular flights, and amongs her achievements was a solo trip to Australia in 1930; she was a ferry pilot in World War Two, but lost her life after bailing out of a Spitfire over the Thames Estuary.

Airlines were slow to copy the example of United, and it was not until 1945 that career opportunities for women in civil aviation expanded dramatically; now well over 50,000 of them are employed as flight attendants. The Russian carrier, Aeroflot, has made a number of record breaking flights flown by an all female crew. An important aspect of this transition into an alien field, was that the women participants did not lose their femininity, a facet of their biology which too often has sadly disappeared in many misguided efforts by feminists, to emulate or surpass the opposite sex in spheres of human endeavour that could never be common to both, but existed as complementary or parallel accomplishments to other activities that were manifestly female. The sky was no discriminator of the sexes for whatever reason — it was enriched totally because of their presence.

In April of 1978, at a commemorative ceremony in Dearborn, USA, an Irish honour party, composed of government, army, airline, and diplomatic representatives made a presentation to the Ford museum to mark the fiftieth anniversary of the pioneering flight of the BREMEN. Unsuccessful attempts had been made by the Irish government to secure a loan of the Junkers' monoplane from Fords for display in Ireland; when later discussing with the curator their refusal to loan the machine, he said to me, 'Well, you must admit the BREMEN is in good company' — so it was. The museum covers fourteen acres, and whilst the vast majority of the exhibits were vintage motor cars of Ford manufacture, there were many other vehicles of historical interest; the BREMEN was displayed near the famous trimotor of Admiral Bird, and it formed part of a collection of airborne contraptions that had conquered the skies over the earth.

The BREMEN memorial plaque — a rectangular base of Connemara marble ornamented with an inscribed silver plate, carries an aircraft tail of bog oak, inlaid with an Aer Lingus shamrock also styled in silver. The inscription reads:

50 Years Later.
Presented by the Irish Air Corps on April 13, 1978. This plaque marks the visit here by Ireland's Minister for Defence, Robert Molloy T.D. to commemorate, on the fiftieth anniversary, Ireland's part in the historic first east to west crossing of the Atlantic by an aeroplane, THE BREMEN.

The co-pilot was Colonel James C. Fitzmaurice, commanding officer of The Irish Air Corps, from whose headquarters at Baldonnel the flight took off.

I was part of that honour party, and when the ceremonies concluded I was invited to accompany the military in their arranged visit to the United States academy at West Point — part of a fact finding mission set up by the Department of Defence to evaluate the problems involved in the integration of women into the armed forces.

West Point in 1978 was commanded by an officer who, heretofore, had been the commanding general of NATO. Now as a Lt. General he was commanding at West Point, his situation being unique in the chapters of American military history because he was recalled from retirement, and to a lower rank, to redeem the academy from the scandal to which it had been exposed — cadets cheating at exams. A most charming man, but, although not that elderly, he reminded me very much of my grandfather; he arrived a few minutes late for the conference and remarked that 'even God takes no account of mans' time spent fishing;' he went on to attribute the quote as being directly from the bible, but reminisced that when he had made the same excuse at a NATO meeting, a Turkish colonel had stood up and said, 'Excuse me General, but that quotation appears in the Koran!' General Goodpaster and his staff confirmed that they had experienced no difficulty in integrating

Presentation ceremony at Dearborn. At the podium – The Irish Minister for Defence; directly behind Mr. Molloy is Brig. General J.B. O'Connor, OC Army Air Corps.

Photo – Aer Lingus

One day – perhaps, it'll be me.

Photo – Air Lingus, and Bestick Williams

Photo – Aer Lingus

The **BREMEN** in good company at Dearborn.

female cadets into what was, very traditionally, an all male preserve. In the matter of arms drill, the only concession made to women, because of their smaller stature, was the provision of a lighter carbine than the standard training issue, and in self defence exercises, for the same reason, the course for women was more comprehensive; a surprising fact emerged from the physical training exercises, where it was discovered that the PT had developed muscles on the chest cage of the female cadets that were not supposed to be there!

A special parade was arranged for the visiting party — '78 was still the year of the relatively long hair styles, and so it was impossible to distinguish the boys from the girls, but certainly one thing was obvious — they were very small in stature by the standards of the Irish Army.

The academy is very old, and consequently so is its decor; but although festooned with brass and bronze mementoes to old soldiers and battles long ago, its ambience was not devoid of humour. General George Patton, that famous character of World War Two, was not renowned during his cadetship for his literary interests, and when he died, they sited his bronze statue plonk in front of the library. From Patton's statue we went to visit the mess hall where the dining room of the original West Point building had been incorporated in its enlargement, and the conducting officer informed us that the hall had a capacity of 4,000, who were served a four course meal in twenty minutes — I thought to myself that those cadets must be suffering from permanent indigestion, even ignoring the fact that they sometimes engaged in the calisthenics of eating a West Point "Square Meal".

I returned from that visit, not thinking of the competence of female soldiers, because I knew that their integration was successful from the experience of the Israelis and others, whose ladies could put a bullet straight through the centre of your head as accurately as any old sweat, yet, who for reasons of delicacy were usually employed only in support of the battle area. I was thinking of female pilots: the possibility of women in the cockpits of commercial aircraft had never entered my mind in my years with Aer Lingus; I was well aware of the very valuable contribution they had made to aviation, and there was certainly no bias amongst the men — it simply did not arise. I came to the realization that they have to be, and are, extremely good, coming as it were from behind in what was again a predominantly male orientated area. Biologically, the only factor that could possibly differentiate their work plateau from that of a man would be to me, the effect or otherwise of their menstrual cycle, a physical fact in the life of a woman, experienced by most as a routine part of their lives, but occasioning distress and emotional upset in some.

The commercial success achieved by Aer Lingus was in large measure attributable to its policy of having only female cabin staff — Irish girls who usually graced the workplace of their aircraft with charm, efficiency and beauty, in contrast to many "coffee, tea, or me" varieties found in other airlines; equal job opportunity rules now apply, and stewards are employed. I would consider that a male is a most necessary part of the cabin crew of a large aeroplane, primarily for the function of dominating the drunks and their braggadocio, or the assertives in the cabin, and for contributing physical strength to situations where his opposite might be frail — pulling down and launching of liferafts, assistance of incapacitated passengers or manhandling heavy equipment in the cabin. These considerations may be contradictory, in view of the heroism and the demonstrated capability of airline hostesses in many difficult and demanding circumstances. All of this seems light years away from the granny I met some time ago, admittedly almost 35,000 feet below us and coming the other way, eighty years of age but flying solo and delivery a single engined aircraft to a purchaser in Europe!

Chapter Eight

SOME MATTERS IN CONTRAST

Improbable projection to galaxy,
Vague nebulae of the night.
Fantasy responds with image
Of man on fantasy flight.

Captain Bartley O'Connor will confirm the date; I am almost certain that it was sometime in October 1967. Bartley has been a friend of mine for 25 years, and I know he is psychic. A frail old lady frequently used to appear in his house — her ghostly transparency terrified his dog, and scared gaping mesenger boys who viewed the spectre over Bartley's shoulder when he opened the hall door. None of the family made any attempt to communicate with the woman; she came and went at varying hours of the day and night. I had no encounter with this spirit, since my own experience of the supernatural was limited to a mild but active poltergeist who haunted a block of flats in which I spent my early married life. He swung the pictures on the wall, creaked phantom footsteps on the stairs and finally flaunted his impish talents by splitting our two crystal glass ash trays.

Whether or not these experiences have anything to do with the events of the night — I will leave up to you.

During October 1967, I was taking a flight out of Chicago to Dublin. There was a shortage of first officers, so O'Connor and I were crewing the aeroplane as captain and co-pilot, alternating on the duties.

It was a beautiful night and we flew serenely along at 37,000 feet with stars and gentle thoughts for company. The senior hostess came into the cockpit and said: 'Captain, we are two dinners short. I have two passengers in row four who were not there when we left. They're not listed on the seating form, and I think there's something very unusual about them!'

Bartley said nothing but I got out of the seat, put on my cap and jacket and went back to the cabin. My initial concern was that there was now insufficient food on board; we had 122 passengers and the flight kitchen had provided meals for only 120. The problem was later solved by making up two extra trays with some food filched from the crew catering; nevertheless it seemed strange to me that these two people were not listed on the passenger manifest, so I presented myself to them and explained my problem. The man in turn introduced both himself and the woman in a foreign accent with an inflection totally strange to my ear.

'My name is Vaalkar and this is my wife — my sincere apologies to you, Captain, if you were concerned about our presence, but we joined the flight at a late stage.'

He continued to talk to me in a precise tone, each word perfectly pronounced, each sentence beautifully phrased. Our flow of conversation was colloquial and ranged over politics and world affairs, but when he questioned me about the aeroplane the query was straight to the point. The man gave the impression that he was filing the answers as if they were being fed to a computer. 'Of what metal is this vessel composed? Why relate your speed to that of sound? Are you limited to this method of space travel? Are you confined to jet thrust for propulsive force?'

His wife, who had remained silent, spoke now in a similar metallic voice: 'Sergi, you must not question so. What will this man think of our manners?' This was my cue and I made a polite excuse and walked back to the cockpit.

'What was that all about?' said Bartley. 'You were a long time. Was she a good looking bird?'

I made no reply but sat into the co-pilot seat, fastened the safety belt slowly, and stared ahead in silence. This time it was

O'Connor's turn to look across at me. He jabbed me with his elbow and said: 'Give!' He still remembers clearly what I said to him: 'Just go back in a few minutes and have a peep at that couple in row four — no, I'm not going to tell you anything else about them — just go back.'

I continued to look ahead into the night and waited. Twenty minutes went by and I passed our "Forty West" position to Gander. It took me nearly as long to transmit it since static interference was heavy and the frequencies on both radio sets were plagued by a faint background whistle. Communication was bad all night, possibly due to the unusually heavy Aurora Borealis — the Northern Lights. However, there must have been another disturbance as well, for some moments later the navigator said: 'I have been monitoring the radar scope since I picked up the weather ship, and there has been a continuous interference trace. The last time that I saw that signal was during the war.'

Bartley O'Connor came back into the cockpit.

'Well?' I asked.

'I don't know quite what to think. Did you notice their skin?'

'Not particularly. The lights in that area are low.'

'Well,' he said. 'It has the most unusual texture. Both of those characters have the smoothest, whitest skin; no pores, no blemishes, no creases. I am absolutely sure of that because the woman dropped a book and I picked it up for her. In fact we all picked it up together, and their hands were directly beside mine.'

'So?' I said, 'they might have been Egyptians or high caste Indians.'

'That's possible,' Bartley replied, 'but did you study their clothes? The tailoring was perfect. It was a strange material and cut angularly; no curves at all, even on the bird. The whole set up reminded me of a tailor's dummy.' He told me that the woman spoke to him for some time and asked the most peculiar questions, showing herself to be a person of unusual intelligence.

I lost interest in the incident as we flew across the lonely ocean — O'Connor reverted his gaze to the side window and drew me over to look at the Northern Lights. There was an arc of white intensity stretching along the polar horizon and the light was changing in colour within itself like a reflection in the heavens from a vast amphitheatre; searchlights within the core were impatiently sweeping through the brilliance, the display was endless and if one glanced away for a second and then looked back, a myriad of changes were taking place within that seemingly symmetrical pattern. Apart from the splendour, there was something very unusual going on but even Bartley could not be sure as to what precisely it was, although he had been watching for two and a half hours.

We flew on into the dawn with the cabin curtains closed and the lights switched off. All our passengers slumbered, including the couple in row four. "Thirty West," the positions went by until at "Fifteen West" the night was over and we had caught up with the sun. Its rays focused on the temperature sensor in the corner of the cockpit, and the false signal triggered the air conditioning unit and chilled the air.

'How are our friends in row four?' I asked.

'They're not in their seats now,' Bernice replied, 'I presume that they have gone to the washrooms.'

They were not in the washrooms, nor indeed in the aeroplane. The Northern Lights were gone and with them the sweeping searchlights and the strangeness which Bartley had seen in the night sky. We went back separately to where they had been sitting. There was an extraordinary exotic odour about their seats, and the white linen headrests were now flecked with a fine graphite deposit.

'They'll never believe us,' said Captain Bartley O'Connor. They never did.

I dismissed the whole business from my mind, only recalling it a short time ago when the Russians released a news bulletin on their cosmonaut Vaalkar, whom they had been unable to recover from a polar orbit.

*   *   *

We lined up on runway 31 Left at New York. The aeroplane was heavy, and I opened up all four engines to the maximum power and allowed it to soak for a few moments before releasing the brakes.

'V 1' called the co-pilot. This was the speed at which it was safe and prudent to continue the take-off even should an engine fail.

'V 2' — the speed at which the aeroplane was self sustaining, in full control aerodynamically.

'Positive climb.'

'Gear up.'

At four hundred feet and V2 plus ten knots, namely a speed of 168 knots, we banked the Boeing 720 into a fifteen degree left climbing turn. This manoeuvre was one which did not endear itself to the pilots, but was carried out at the insistence of the authorities to diminish the noise effect beneath. In the turn, the New York tower controller called and directed us to change to the departure frequency. The co-pilot selected the new channel and made contact, he also acknowledged a new climb out heading; just as he checked the accuracy of the flight instruments by comparing their readings, the machine started to Dutch Roll in the climbing turn. A quick glance ensured that the yaw damper switch was engaged, so I damped out the movement with the controls and continued in the climb.

"Dutch Roll", a flight peculiarity first experienced with the swept wing design, that familiar sweep back of the wings of a modern jet, was so named because the movement resembled that of a fat Dutchman swishing and rolling from side to side on skates. The movement in an aircraft is one of rolling and yawing, starting off imperceptibly but increasing in intensity. The swept wing aeroplane is therefore fitted with an anti yaw device, a "yaw damper" which uses the rudder control channel of the auto pilot. The yaw damper senses the start of such a movement and quickly stifles it. In the event that the yaw damper is unserviceable, the pilot has been trained to dampen out the movement by the use of the flight controls.

We climbed uneventfully to 33,000 feet and levelled off to cruise. On the way up there had been a little more roll than usual, but neither of us thought much of it. Half an hour later we flew into cloud and through a frontal system running east west Bermuda to Florida; the weird tales of the Bermuda triangle were far from my mind. The turbulence increased and so did the rolling; I knew now from the behaviour of the aircraft that all was not well at the back end; air traffic control gave us an immediate clearance to a lower level.

I disengaged the auto pilot, and even though the speed was nearly 300 knots, the wings were swishing as the roll increased. Down went the starboard wing; I watched it go on the artificial horizon and waited until it changed direction and commenced to come up — now! I hit it with a firm input of starboard aileron, but the input was too late and the rolling only diminished slightly.

Concentrate again on the artificial horizon — left wing commencing to rise — now! Down with the control to the left, a shudder through the airframe as the ailerons bit and the spoilers rose; the rolling died away and I kept the wings level.

We flew with the seat belt sign permanently switched on, the turbulence continued and the intermittent "Dutch Roll" had to be dampened out as before — no point in turning back now as we are halfway there and the weather ahead is clear. Things were not too bad in the cabin according to the senior hostess, and the passengers had presumed that the rolling motion was in some way connected with the turbulence.

'Piarco Control: this is Flight 416 — I am overflying Barbados and proceeding direct to Trinidad.'

There it was on the horizon. Down now over the beach and the rain forest in the descent; a ninety degree turn over Port of Spain, landing flaps already at twenty degrees.

'Flaps thirty.'

'Flaps thirty — moving on the gauges.'

'Gear down.'

Flaps forty — flaps fifty and the wind as it always was, zero seven zero degrees at twelve knots. No roll on the approach.

'V Ref plus ten, sink rate seven hundred feet per minute.'

'Clear to land.'

Some adjustments on the stabilizer trim kept her smoothly in the groove and the power setting was just right. I disengaged what there was of the yaw damper.

'Final check complete, Skipper.'

I kept her going down the slot, flaring gently as we approached the runway and sat on top of that magical ground cushion of air that supports a Boeing 720 all day until you cut the engines. Nose level — not up, and at the right height and moment I pulled back the power and it sat onto the runway at Port of Spain in Trinidad.

Easing the nose forward with my left hand, I pulled the speed brake up with my right, pushed on the toe brakes with both feet, transferred my right hand to the thrust reversers and pulled them up and back into reverse. At eighty knots I tranferred my left hand to the steering wheel and guided it clear of the runway.

'Jock,' I spoke to the co-pilot — 'a large rum and coke for me at the hotel........'

*   *   *

The Canadian air traffic controller rotated his chair away from the radar screen and faced his supervisor. 'There's something wrong out there,' he said, 'but I'm not quite sure what its all about. Sir, watch this.' He pressed the transmit button and spoke into the microphone; 'Flight 912 — squawk ident on code 0321.*

There was no verbal reply from the flight, but its little strobe on the radar screen was duplicated for a few seconds in response to the controller's request.

'Now look at his height read out' — the supervisor watched the digits of the counter twirl around, 'like crazy' as he said afterwards at the investigation. When he looked at it, the read out was 50,000 feet and increasing rapidly.

'What level is that guy supposed to be at?'

---

* The expression "Squawk ident" is an instruction to a pilot to transmit a radio signal on that assigned frequency, for the purpose of radar identification. Height is transmitted from the aircraft automatically and continuously.

'Flight level 330 — thirty three thousand feet for the ocean crossing on track X-ray' said Bud.

'There must be something radically wrong with his altitude read out' — ' and his transponder' replied the controller. 'I've asked him to squawk ident on several different codes in the last ten minutes, and the damn signal keeps coming in from the same place; it's uncanny but that airplane does not seem to be moving at all.'

'Put out an alert on this 747, Bud, and I'll scramble one of the search and rescue boys from Goose Bay.'

The supervisor picked up the red telephone to talk to the base commander at Goose. Bud heard the voice of the group captain shrilling into the receiver: 'Are you telling me, Charlie, that one of your 747's appears to be stationary one hundred miles out from the coast' — the voice had become even more penetrating 'and that his height is now 70,000 feet. Nothing in your part of the sky could get up there........

'Listen sir, we don't understand it here either, but there is no voice reply from him on any frequency, and yet he acknowledges every request for a transponder ident.'

'OK, OK Charlie, I'll send up one of my boys.'

The Gander civil controller changed to the rescue frequency and listened to his military counterpart at Goose directing the intercepting jet. He wondered what the air force was thinking about that height counter which was now accelerating rapidly through 100,000 feet.

Five minutes later the height read out from the 747 ceased to function, but the blob remained on the screen and duplicated frequently to the requests from the military controller for a signal transmission; still there was no accompanying voice reply. The atmosphere had become eerie in both control rooms, but the radio chatter of the interceptor jet pilot and his radar man came crisply through the speakers as they flew the search pattern: they flew a diminishing square procedure around the radar echo of the Boeing 747 and dropped parachute flares over the water, but saw nothing; yet the signal continued and always in the same position.

After thirty minutes of fruitless work in the lower levels the search plane proposed spiralling up to maximum altitude around the large blob that occupied the centre tube of his close range intercept precision radar. He climbed rather slowly and came out of the haze layer at 30,000 feet into brilliant moonlight, where the task became more pleasant; still there was no contact with the elusive owner of the echo. At 41,000 feet the airframe was shuddering and Goose ordered him back to base.

He eased the interceptor down in a dive, and the glorious

canopy of the Milky Way disappeared from view as the jet sank down through the wispy darkness of the light summer cloud.

Before the searcher's wheels touched the runway at Goose, the read out from the big Boeing was 33,000 feet — the figures had reversed their count instantaneously, and miraculously the radar echo was moving slowly and normally towards the position of 52 degrees North latitude and 50 degrees West longitude.

The strong accent of Captain Bartley O'Connor was testy over the radio: 'Gander Centre, I have identified on my transponder about twenty times in response to varied requests. Do you read me?'

'Gander is reading you loud and clear. How me Flight 912.'

'Five square' came the reply, 'is anything the matter down there?'

Bud and the supervisor were still on the same watch, and the chief grabbed the mike and replied as calmly as he could: 'Flight 912, this is Gander Centre; you have been out of communication for one hour. The estimate passed by you for the position of 50 West appears to have been totally inaccurate. Check your present position and give me a revised estimate.'

Bartley looked at the inertial navigation systems, and the three positions shown agreed to within three miles; both altimeters read 33,000 feet and the speed indications were normal. He passed this information to control, and added 'Sorry about the estimated time of arrival for 50 West — I gave you 0302 hours but 0306 would be closer.'

'You mean 0406?' queried Gander.

'Standby one' replied the captain, and as he replaced the microphone the co-pilot drew his attention to the three cockpit clocks: each one of them displayed a time of 0300 hours. So did Bartley's watch and those of his two crewmen. Every watch, whether quartz crystal or conventional spring, belonging to every single person on board that plane was reading one hour slow — somehow one hour of time had been totally lost, or had it?

The pilots adjusted the aircraft chronometers to the Gander check, and the captain apologised to the controller for the incorrect setting. He expressed his regrets with reservations, because the aircraft clocks were the finest available and he had set them on the second to the Washington time signal before take off.

Bartley knew that there would be an inquiry, so he reached down towards his briefcase and withdrew a little book in which he made notes about the time queries raised by control. He called Gander again and informed them that Flight 912 would make a full report on return to base, and he asked for his apologies to be sent to the boys at Goose for having to scramble.

Flight 912 flew on towards the dawn in the eastern sky, and its pilots pondered on the strange events of the night.

'You have been involved in something like this before?' the co-pilot asked.

'The unknown you mean?' said Bartley, 'yes I have, but this beats Banagher. A few years ago the Russians lost one of their manned space ships to a perpetual polar orbit, and believe it or not two of its incarcerated occupants paid a visit to the cabin of my 707, on the way from Chicago. Appeared in the bloody seats from nowhere, and after a few hours disappeared like the proverbial thieves. The aurora borealis — the Northern Lights, were very active that night, more so than usual.'

The engineer pilot had prepared a special fuel check, and whilst they appeared to have been airborne for one hour in excess of the planned time to that point, the burn off did not reveal it; the engines had not consumed extra fuel.

A long dark golden edged cloud bank straddled the skyline up ahead as the cabin supervisor entered the cockpit. She admired its splendour and then sighed in a very low voice in Bartley's ear: 'Oh what a shame, the Milky Way is gone for tonight.'

The captain answered, 'The last time that you were in the cockpit, Kathleen, I had this most extraordinary sensation of floating upwards in space towards the Milky Way — in this aeroplane of all things!; then I heard Gander calling on the radio and I replied.'

He recounted the search and rescue alert, and all the fuss that had been made about an incorrect time check. She in turn told him that something somewhat unusual had happened in the cabin, yet the flight had been one of the most enjoyable that she had experienced. Some of the passengers, she said, had complained that they could not understand what all the bright lights and the banks of stars had to do with the cowboy movie that was being screened.

'That's bloody funny' said Bartley, 'I wonder was there any connection? — never mind, but let me continue with the rest of it.'

He said that he felt a soaring sensation as the jumbo accelerated up towards the Milky Way, and as they got closer, the galaxy became an enormous mass of storm clouds in torment; but yet they flew onwards and upwards, through the hydrogen gas and the star dust, apparently without ill effect. He checked the engine performance and the cabin pressure repeatedly, and everything was normal. Then they entered the core of the galaxy itself, and flew along corridors of countless stars whose lustre and colours surpassed the reflections from the finest jewels. He saw the bomb bursts of dying stars and the gaseous birth of others, and all the while he had the eerie feeling of gliding down along the passage of time towards eternity. They traversed the belt from the bright star Altair to Cassiopeia; then as quickly as it had begun the illusion vanished when he heard Gander calling.

There was total silence in the cockpit of the big jet.

'That's odd' said the third pilot, but I had that very sensation.'

'I had it as well, but I don't recall anybody dozing off, least of all you fellows;' the words came from Kathleen as she left the flight deck.

Apparently the coincidence of the phenomena had reached the cabin crew, because when Kathleen checked with her girls all of them knew that they had been flying beside huge banks of brilliant stars, and each of them thought that it was some unusual display associated with the Northern Lights, which they had seen many times from the cockpit. The passengers knew nothing of the dilemma of their pilots, but it transpired later than the only people that were not affected by the strange incursion of the stars were those who had fallen asleep. Some blamed it on overeating, others attributed it to an excessive indulgence in alcohol and the majority insisted that it spoiled a good cowboy movie, but — the coincidence could not be denied.

Nothing emerged from the subsequent inquiry, as the facts were irreconcilable. Nobody would believe the controller's story, that a radar signal, positively identified as belonging to a Boeing 747, would or could remain in an absolutely fixed position one hundred miles out over the Atlantic ocean for a period of one hour. The confirmation of the same story by the military at Goose added nothing one way or the other to the total disbelief evidenced and recorded by those on the official board........

I met Kathleen some few months ago; she had left the airline to get married.

'You know,' she said, 'I have often thought about the strange flight, and I think I can explain my own experience. My family is of very old Danish-Irish stock, and we were one of the last great tribes to be converted to Christianity. We believe in the power and the influence of the heavenly bodies on the affairs of man, and the predictions recorded by the astrologers in our ancient annals have all come to pass.'

'Anything in those vellum sheets about a flight of fantasy to the Milky Way in a giant metal bird?'

Her answer was vague and I had the feeling that she was holding back something. I asked the question again, but she became more evasive, and rather than embarrass her by continuing in the same vein I changed the subject.

When we were parting I tried a different tack. 'Are you psychic, Kathleen' I asked.

'You could say that' she answered, 'but so what, that's the way of all of our family for countless generations.'

There were many theories about the incident, but I had formed my own which I advanced subsequently to Bartley. 'A load of garbage' he replied.

'Like all that unusual dust that was found in the engine filters and the air conditioning system, when you got back to base. Where did it all get to anyway, Bartley?'

'The last I heard was that it just disappeared from the test laboratory.'

'Why not ask Kathleen about it?' I queried mischievously.

'I'll do that some day' he grunted the answer.

'There's a pair of you in it' I said as I walked away.

You see Bartley was the man who had the doomed Russian cosmonauts in the cabin of his Boeing 707, and Kathleen was the senior hostess on the trip. Bartley was also with Kathleen on her honeymoon in Honolulu.

*　　*　　*

A genuine event, unique in the annals of aviation, took place on board a Boeing jumbo jet at 35,000 feet on 14 Aug. 1977: an American dance studio presented me with a medal for free style dancing with one of my hostesses. I opted for the 747 foxtrot.

The plane had been chartered from Aer Lingus by the Arthur Murray Studios, who had decided in that year to hold their annual dancing competition high up in the sky. Our engineers had removed all of the seats in one of the passenger cabins and installed a maple floor, complete with a full recorded programme of suitable dance music. The happy voyagers had tripped the light fantastic throughout the night, and as we crossed the 40 west meridian I responded to the invitation to joint the dance-o-rama.

This interesting flight opens up immense possibilities for would-be record breakers or enterprising airlines who wish to attract maximum publicity. Some American operators have a piano bar in the upstairs lounge of their 747's — Irish could respond with a similar set-up, but augmented by four separate ballrooms, each one specialising in different dance tempos. The opulence of the first class area is reflected in its regal name, the "TARA" room, and this would be ideal for the soft-light-after-dinner touch; the more unruly music could be confined to our provincial cabins — the Ulster, Munster,

201

Leinster and Connaught rooms. A music director would of course be required, and this responsibility could be vested in the aircraft commander!

I thoroughly enjoyed this unusual flight, and the charming people who had chartered the plane, but with apologies to the late James W. Blake and Charles B. Lawler, their song kept running through my mind:

East Side, West Side, all across the sky,
The crew sang "Ring-a-Rosie", and the miles flew idly by –
Boys and girls together, Me and Mamie O'Rorke,
Tripped the light fantastic – on the airway from New York.

*   *   *

The Boeing 747 was heavy, and although 33L at Boston was a long smooth runway, the jet was taking its time in the humid July night. Bartley was tensing slightly, waiting for his co-pilot to call 'rotate'; when the call came they were well down the runway, and he eased the nose up to 13 degrees on the attitude direction indicator, and the 747 came clear and penetrated into the damp night. The departure procedure called for a right turn onto a heading of 100 degrees just prior to the marker for the reciprocal runway, but before he made the turn the cabin supervisor came into the cockpit followed by a man in a nylon mask holding a gun to her back. The man brushed Kathleen aside, made his way towards Bartley's seat and stuffed the gun into the captain's ribs and said in an American accent, 'Bartley, I can fly this ship if I have to; if you don't do precisely what I tell you, I'll kill you;' before the pilot could reply the masked man placed his hand down on the pedestal and turned the transponder to another code. He now spoke to Kevin Courtney in the right hand seat: 'You tell ATC that you're hijacked, and we are not coming down — we'll be coming out in our own time.'

Bartley O'Connor was a shrewd man, and although he was aware of some of the difficulties that lay ahead, he was acutely conscious of his responsibilities towards the 350 passengers on board his aircraft; his training and crew discipline and rapport would lead him into no action that would jeopardize their safety.

'"Bruno" is my name' said the slim man in the nylon mask,' and I have five more undisclosed backups in the cabin, but provided you behave, you will come to no harm.' He said it rather politely, Bartley recalled afterwards. O'Connor was not a man who normally perspired through the palms of his hands, but now they were wet —

202

very wet, until Bruno's words registered with him: he realised that Bruno was not unstable, and he appeared to be highly intelligent, and he felt that they would survive, provided they did as the hijacker ordered. He decided also, that although his total acquiescence was essential for the safety of the aircraft and its occupants, he was not going to be completely dominated by the hijacker, and he turned to his other pilots and said, 'Gentlemen we are being hijacked by this man and his companions, but our duty is to the passengers and whatever Bruno says we do, we do to the letter, provided I give the orders — OK Bruno?'

'OK man' said the man in the mask, and he shoved the pistol further into the captain's ribs.

'Tango 904, this is Boston Radar — make an immediate right turn onto heading 100, you are conflicting with Allegheny 142.'

'Do as the man wants' said Bruno. Bartley made the turn to the right and increased speed to retract the flap sections; Tom O'Brien on the engineering panel adjusted the power. At 24 years of age, Tom was a big man and his every instinct was to have a go at Bruno, but he maintained his composure and adjusted the power levers with more than usual care.

'Tango 904, this is Boston Radar, I am receiving your transponder code.' Courtney was about to reply, but Bruno took his mike and transmitted: 'Boston Radar, this is the hijacker speaking, we have commandeered Flight Tango 904; the crew have agreed to our plans and I have assured them that no harm will come to either the airplane or the occupants.'

'Tango 904, this is Boston Radar — your message received and understood.'

'Now Mr. Bruno' said Bartley, 'what do you want me to do?'

'Pick up the cabin address handset and tell your passengers that you have been hijacked in a worthy cause, and that the hijackers have assured you that they have no intention of harming anybody or the airplane, provided you do as you are told — and you are going to do just that Captain, aren't you?' Bruno had offered black Balkan Sobranie cigarettes to the crew, but Bartley was the only one to accept the gesture.

Kathleen had never moved from her position behind the pilots; she knew Bartley's form and what she saw and heard was good enough for her. With an almost defiant gesture she ignored Bruno and spoke directly to Bartley. 'What do you want me to do Captain?'

'Go back to the cabin girl, and leave the rest to me.' She turned to Bruno and asked 'OK?' He replied by pointing towards Bartley and saying 'OK, if he says so.'

When Kathleen left the cockpit the captain spoke to the hijacker:

'I've agreed to co-operate with you, you'll have no trouble from the crew but take that bloody pistol out of my back, I want to use the PA.'

'Go man' directed the laconic Bruno, now positioned on the jump seat. The 747 continued in the climb as its pilot reached up for the handset and dialled PA-PA.

'Ladies and gentlemen, this is your captain speaking —' Bruno had reached up and pressed the Flight Interphone switch and the strong Irish voice of the pilot came through the cockpit loudspeakers — 'we have been hijacked. The hijacker appears to be both rational and normal, but he has a pistol in my back. He is totally familiar with the 747; he has assured me that provided I co-operate with his demands there will be no danger to you. I have agreed to co-operate. The hijacker has also agreed to allow me to talk to you. You are in no danger.'

No sooner had he replaced the handset, than Kathleen was on the intercom. 'Come down Bartley for God's sake, all hell has broken loose.'

Bruno pulled the pistol back and nodded assent; the captain unbuckled, pushed his seat back, got up and walked down the spiral staircase into the main cabin. He turned into the tourist area with Kathleen behind him, and shouted above the din, 'Drinks are on the house; we have been hijacked as you know, but we are all going to be safe. You are going to be inconvenienced and diverted, but please, I would ask you for a full understanding of our position and your acceptance of the circumstances. I am still your captain and in command of this plane, and I believe that we will all be safe.' He walked the full way down the aisle, repeating the very loud announcement, and then did the same up the other side of the huge cabin. Anxious faces, distraught mothers, small children, elderly men and youths and young girls in jeans and sweat shirts faced him along the aisles; they plied him with questions which he answered slowly and truthfully, and when eventually he reached the first class compartment he picked up the handset and made another announcement: 'Ladies and gentlemen, the man who has hijacked us has guaranteed me that if I follow his instructions no harm will come to anybody. I intend to do just that — we have plenty of fuel and we will look after you. "Bruno" — that's the name of the leader of the hijackers, has told me to inform you that he has a backup team of five men and women in the cabin, who will only reveal themselves if we do not carry out his orders. His instructions are very specific: I am to set course for Birmingham, Alabama, and upon arrival there I am to circle over the main base of the Strategic Air Command for twenty minutes, at as slow a flying speed as we can at this height. I then alter course for Cuba, and on approaching Havana I descend to 1500 feet and depressurise the aircraft, then Bruno and his companions will leave us by parachute. We will then be free to resume normal flight. It will take us two hours to Birmingham — Bruno wants twenty minutes over the air base, and then it is just short of two hours to Cuba — that's four hours and twenty minutes, which according to my calculations will enable me to land you safely at Miami at seven o'clock local time. I regret the inconvenience and the worry caused to you all, but I have made arrangements with my company to have another 747 meet us at Miami to fly you onwards to Shannon and Europe. I may appear to be very matter of fact, but Bruno is holding a gun upon my crew in the cockpit, but I again repeat that he has assured me that no harm will come to anybody, provided we go along with their plans. The bar is now open, and all drinks are on the airline from here to Shannon.' Bartley returned to the flight deck to find Bruno sitting in his seat with his pistol pointing at Courtney's head. The third pilot made a gesture of futility with his hands.

'I've told them' said Bartley, and then, ignoring Bruno he addressed Courtney — 'What's happened Kevin?'

Courtney handed him a slip of paper — 'I wrote it all down Skip.' Bartley read the message:

Boston ATC clears Tango 904 to overhead Birmingham Air Force Base at flight level 330 direct INS. Clearance includes 20 minutes circling of the base at 330 with an onwards clearance direct Havana Cuba. No further communication necessary providing a listening watch maintained on 121.5. Maintain present transponder code.

By now the first of the F-16 fighters of Brig. General Otis L. Vandenberg's 960th Fighter Group were closing in on the jumbo; eventually there were four F-16's on either side — in tight, and Bartley, now back in his seat was looking out of the cockpit window straight into the eyes of Lt. Colonel Oscar J. Blasmitz whose wing tip was thirty feet away from Bartley's nose — the decal under the fighter's canopy bore the colonel's name. Bruno left the cockpit and the captain made a transmission on 121.5. 'Welcome Colonel Oscar, Bartley O'Connor here, captain of Tango 904 — there's shag all I can do except go along with this guy.'

'I understand' replied the colonel, 'my callsign is Air Force Seven, and we will remain with you in United States airspace — my squadron will be relieved in two hours by another unit — callsign Air Force Eight. Nobody will fire at you or make unsafe manoeuvres.'

'Roger Air Force Seven' replied Bartley.

Meanwhile, Bruno had gone down to the cabin area and opened up the electronics hatch; he climbed down the ladder into the bay, and from an attaché case produced a small steel saucer like object fitted with a heavy rubber seal around the periphery of its base; the top of the saucer had a protruding percussion cap. He placed the saucer against the hull, checked the rubber seal with his fingers to ensure it was snugly in place and then punched the percussion cap with a small tool. There was a sharp explosive sound, a momentary rush of expelled air as the hull was punctured and then silence; he took a long narrow metal tube from the briefcase, unscrewed the spent charge from the metal cup — there was a hiss of escaping air until he inserted the tube into the hole and pushed it through the hull. He screwed the small complicated looking camera to the probe, removed the back cover of the camera and peered through the lens to see what the camera was looking at: the countryside to the north of Baltimore was sliding peacefully by in the dawn haze. He replaced the back of the camera and loaded a film.

The cabin of a hijacked aeroplane is not a pleasant place, and Tango 904 was no exception. The acute anxiety of their situation was not altogether allayed by Bartley's honeyed words, but that captain was always in harmony with his cabin and he knew that the few drinks on the house would go a long way towards alleviating the distress, but he was to go down again and again amongst his passengers to talk with them and endeavour to reassure them of the continued safety of the flight. He prefixed his visits with PA announcements, calling their attention to points of interest beneath that would not normally be seen on the way to Shannon; speeds, heights, and — incredibly, an estimated time of arrival at Shannon were all given out in his matter of fact voice. Kathleen assured him that some semblance of calm had come to the cabin; meanwhile, Bruno had a steak and half a bottle of Beaujolais in the first class cabin; he was the only occupant. He ordered the movie on, and sat back to listen to and watch the film with the Luger twined around the index finger of his right hand; after a further one hour and thirty minutes, Bartley came down to him and said, 'We are approaching the Air Force Base at Birmingham.'

The hijacker left his seat and re-entered the electronics bay; as he disappeared down the hatch he said over his shoulder to Bartley, 'when you arrive over the field, circle in a left turn for precisely twenty minutes — precisely over the base you hear, no monkey business or I'll come up and blow your head off!'

Bartley circled for the required twenty minutes, and so did the
˙ ᶜ squadron; Bruno set the camera on continuous, returned
ɔr the remaining five minutes of the orbit and looked
window at the in tight F-16 group on the left who had
ιe abreast — the whole unit was bobbing up and down

206

in unison with the Boeing 747 in the wispy cirrus cloud. Bartley thought he heard the hijacker mutter, 'O God, why didn't I stay where I was,' but the moment passed and Bruno got back to business. 'Direct for Cuba now' he ordered, 'INS routing, and pump it in whilst I read out the co-ordinates, no intermediate positions or any horseshit like that.' Bruno read out the co-ordinates and Courtney inserted the position in the three navigation sets. 'Tell the escort' said Bruno, 'we are altering course for Havana.' Bartley made the transmission on 121.5 and the group turned for Cuba. At the limit of United States Controlled Airspace the F-16's broke away in unison — they disappeared down below as if by magic with an enormous surge of power, leaving behind a few twirled rings of jet efflux to mark their passing. Tango 904 continued towards Cuba.

At 200 miles they had contact with Havana on 121.5, and Bruno took the mike from Bartley's hand and spoke in Spanish to the controller. Bartley remained impassive, each syllable of the conversation registering in his brain. Cuba did not want Bruno, but acknowledged that he had something to sell that they might be interested in. 'Standby' replied the controller, 'I'll check.' He called back in five minutes with 'Permission granted to land by parachute at Havana.'

'Descend to 1500 feet' commanded Bruno, 'depressurise on passing through 10,000 feet. My group of five and I will exit through the number five left door. When the door "open" light comes on your panel, maintain a steady heading across the airfield for one minute — commence depressurisation.' The crew did as they were told, and Bruno left the cockpit for the cabin. Bartley waited until he had closed the door, and then he picked up the telephone and dialled the cabin attendant at the fifth door at the right side. 'Maureen, the captain here, I have only seconds, you know the score,' he spoke very slowly, 'that hijacker is going to go out 5 Left on the opposite side by parachute; I'm taking a chance he's on his own. Kathleen is too close to him for me to call her. As soon as you see him start to go out the door, dial the cockpit, but say nothing and leave the rest to me. Timing is essential. You understand?'

'Yes Captain' was the simple reply.

They were lined up on 23 at Jose Marti International. 'You know what to do, Kevin?' — the co-pilot nodded, and Bartley disengaged the autopilot and held the jumbo steady on course for the runway at 1500 feet. The door "unsafe" light came on, and the cockpit telephone chimed, Bartley shouted, 'Now Kevin.' Courtney snapped back the power levers of the number's three and four engines and the big jet gave a sickening lurch to the right. 'Bring the power up to normal — rapidly,' ordered Bartley as he picked up the telephone to

The 747 foxtrot.

answer Maureen — 'Thank you Maureen, is there anybody else trying to get out?'

'No' she replied. Tell Kathleen to leave the door open' he said, 'I'll send the third pilot down to close it.'

He made an announcement to the passengers that the emergency was over, and that they were all safe and would be landing at Miami in thirty minutes. He climbed the jet to 15,000 feet at reduced power, lit the last of the Balkan Sobranies and handed over control to Kevin Courtney.

On arrival at Miami the jet was impounded by the military; the passengers were screened for onward release to Europe, and Tango 904 was moved to a more discreet parking area. Portions of the harness, and shreds of the parachute were still entwined around the tailplane.

'Why?' asked Kathleen later, 'he was a nice man.'

'No hijacker is a nice man — or woman for that matter,' replied Bartley.

Chapter Nine

THE POPE IN THE SKY

Pastoral flight.
Passenger of Christ,
His pope in the sky.

When the possibility of a visit to Ireland by Pope John Paul II was still just a rumour, Aer Lingus became interested; traditionally popes flew with the national carrier Alitalia, and therefore it would be a major coup for the Irish if their offer was to be accepted. They had proposed to the Vatican, that they would fly the papal party, free, to Dublin and then subsequently to Boston; an expensive gesture for Aer Lingus, but it would enhance the reputation of the airline and increase the pride of the Irish people in its achievements; it would also provide the company with excellent publicity. The Vatican accepted the generous gesture.

The jumbo selected for the paper flights, ST. PATRICK, was withdrawn from line service well in advance of the programme and was given a comprehensive check, including a total cabin refurbishing. Extensive modifications were carried out to the upper deck lounge and these, in the main, consisted of the installation of a mini bedroom-cum-lounge; the bed was made up with Irish linen pillow cases and sheets, complemented by a tweed blanket of yellow shade. The normal tasteful decor of that area was further enriched by the addition of a wooden crucifix of traditional Tara design. Finally, the coat of arms of Pope John Paul was emblazoned on four prominent positions of the fuselage: TOTUS TUUS — totally yours, it was coincidentally a most appropriate motto in the circumstances, because that's what the airline was for those wonderful few days.

Radio Telefis Eireann were faciltated in the provision of a live radio broadcast from the aircraft as it entered VHF range of Dublin airport: one of the 747's transmitters had been assigned for their exclusive use, and its signals were relayed into the national grid by a select ground station.

The plans covering both the flight from Rome to Dublin, and the eventual departure out of Shannon for Boston were comprehensive and extremely thorough. Extensive briefings and conferences placed all of the facets of this important series of flights before the multiple agencies of the state; flight and cabin crews, ground engineers, airline security personnel and most of the departments of the airline were deeply involved in the perfection and structuring of plans designed to ensure that there would be no hitch in the handling of the papal party. The reputation of the national airline was at stake, and Aer Lingus was determined that no slip up would occur. Another of its 747's was delegated the task of back up, similarly catered to the ST PATRICK standard, and assigned around-the-clock reserve crews. As a final cover, a 707 was available should the need arise.

*   *   *

The flagship of the Aer Lingus fleet, state registration letters EI-ASI, under the command of Dublin born Capt. Thomas P. McKeown, was airborne from Rome's Fiumicino airport at 8am local time, 29 Sept. 1979; on board was His Holiness Pope John Paul II with an entourage of 25, and in addition to the papal suite there was a media corps of over 140; no seats were open for sale to the public. The cabin crew had been specially selected for the flight and amongst those hostesses were nurses and linguists fluent in French, Spanish and Italian. Captain Philip Russel, linguist extraordinary was stationed in the cockpit with, the total fluency to handle conversations in Irish, Italian, French, Spanish, Polish, German,

212

Some of the Aer Lingus pilots who were to operate the papal flights. L to R: F/OPF Kennedy, F/O R.K. Parkinson, Capt. T.P. McKeown, Capt. A.A. Quigley, Capt. J.L. McCarthy, F/O J.P. Morrissey, F/O F.J. O'Brien.

Photo – Aer Lingus and O'Reilly, Skerries.

Portuguese, Arabic, Greek and Turkish, and a working knowledge of some other languages. There was no doubt about it, since the Vatican was fielding a well known man of letters in the person of John Paul, Aer Lingus had responded handsomely, and we knew that when we got that pope into the sky, if he had chosen to speak in divers tongues, the airline was in a position to reply and up the ante.

The breakfast menu contained such succulent Irish delights as Black and White pudding, pork sausages, back rashers and brown and white bread. The menu cards were decorated in the papal colours of white and yellow, with the cover design featuring the pope's personal heraldic shield in gold.

The papal suite, located in the upper deck of the first class compartment, had its four-place table covered with a white linen tablecloth, into which had been worked a series of Irish scenes. The cutlery was of Celtic design, and the food was served on Galway-made bone china in the airline's traditional TARA design; the cut glass was of the Lismore pattern, and the centrepiece crystal dish of the dining table held freshly cut red roses. From the start, His Holiness endeared himself to his crew; he relished his breakfast, particularly the black pudding and established himself as a man well able to handle his food. Although the papal party had free passage, all of the passengers, including the pope, had airline issue tickets; this was necessary for insurance purposes; I have a copy of Karol Wojtyla's ticket issued in Rome on Sept. 26: it simply bears the name "H.H. Pope John Paul II", and it was valid for single route usage only, Rome-Boston with a transit through Dublin and Shannon.

McKeown's papal flight, for the purpose of air traffic control and identification was called AER LINGUS ONE. It received, as do all flights of this importance, priority vectoring from the European controllers, and after a smooth uneventful passage of the skies of western Europe it arrived in Irish airspace, 30 miles east of Courtown, to rendezvous at 18,000 feet with its escort of Irish fighters. Meanwhile, things in the cabin of AER LINGUS ONE were not that tranquil; the distinguished passenger, after breakfast, had come downstairs to commune with the representatives of media, and as was their modus operandi, and their duty, they nearly devoured him. Although he had his own aides to protect him from undue harassment, the pope, characteristically, made no attempt to impede the press, and treated them in his own easy way; however, there was one exception. An over-enthusiastic reporter, having already secured a fair amount of John Paul's time, ducked across the aisles of the jumbo, and once again confronted this special passenger, who by now had walked around the large cabin talking to other journalists, and was returning to his upstairs suite.

214

'Ah, my young friend,' spoke the pope in his slightly Polish accent, 'I believe that you and I haf met before,' and he walked gently past his enthusiastic interviewer. Archbishop Marcinkus, the pope's strong man, who was sitting closeby in an aisle seat and who had heard the conversation, composed himself to excellent timing and Yale precision, waited for John Paul to pass, and then came up-hard into the young man's crotch with his elbow. McKeown told me afterwards, that to his own certain knowledge, it was the first time he had ever heard of an archbishop giving a member of the press an elbow in the balls.

The day was wonderfully clear and calm and "St. Patrick" flew up over the Liffey at 1000 feet, spot on time; the Air Corps fighters, diminutive but deadly — they had orders to shoot at any unauthorised aircraft approaching the jumbo, were positioned on either side, as McKeown guided his magnificent aeroplane over the multitude gathered beneath in Phoenix Park - and all of Ireland went mad with joy.

*   *   *

In preparation for the papal visit, Irish Helicopters had leased two 24 seater Sikorsky S 61-N machines to supplement their 12 seater Bell 212, and the Bolkow 105. Six Aer Lingus hostesses had been specially trained in Ireland and Holland in the techniques of helicopter cabin crew operation, and they were on board each of the subsequent papal trips. The flights to the Papal Nunciature in Cabra, to Drogheda, Clonmacnoise, Galway, Maynooth, Limerick and Shannon were all flown in difficult circumstances, with the pilots having to cope with indifferent weather, low ceilings and fading light. The army helicopter unit had also been augmented for Garda duties: two Puma machines from the Bundes Gren Shutz - the aerial wing of the West German Border-guard had been seconded to the Air Corps. To monitor these operations, Aer Lingus established a 24 hour control centre, manned by their own personnel, army and Irish Helicopter pilots; the centre was directly in touch with police stations and the landing areas. The pope also travelled by helicopter to the Shrine at Knock - some few miles away lies the town of Charlestown.

Charlestown, planned, developed and built by a Mayo landlord, still preserves an air of grace not possessed by the general run of Mayo towns: certainly in the year of 1879 it was an elegant place compared to the nearby village of Knock, so typical of all congested rural areas in Ireland of the time. But it was at Knock in August of

215

that year that an apparently miraculous apparition of the Mother of God took place, which was reputed to have been witnessed by about twenty people, whose ages ranged from six to seventy five. The apparition consisted of three heavenly figures standing at the gable wall of the church — a small altar with a lamb and a crucifix was in the background, and the phenomenon remained visible for some considerable time; the figures were recognised as Our Lady, St. Joseph, and St. John the Evangelist. It was widely held later in the parish that the event was a supernatural recognition of the holiness of their saintly priest, Archdeacon Cavanagh; but the most contradictory and regrettable event was yet to take place, when the priest, on being informed by his housekeeper of the spectacle to be seen on the wall of his church did not think it worth his while to go and investigate for himself.

In October of 1879, the Archbishop of Tuam established an ecclesiastical commission to enquire into the happening at Knock. The canonical court took testimony from fifteen of those people who apparently saw the vision, and were satisfied as to their integrity; they reported to the archbishop that 'the testimony of all, taken as a whole, is trustworthy and satisfactory.' McHale, the archbishop, then 88 years of age, took no further action.

The archdiocesan administration neither approved or disapproved, and John McHale was succeeded by two other bishops who adopted the same policy - it was not until 1929 that an archbishop of Tuam participated in a pilgrimage to the shrine.

In 1936, Archbishop Dr. T. Gilmartin instituted a further commission, and amongst its tasks it heard testimony, under oath, from the three surviving witnesses; their story remained the same. The enquiry extended over three years, and in 1939 its report was sent to Rome by the archbishop, together with a request that a favour be granted to the shrine by the Holy Sea.

Benevolent tokens did indeed come from Rome down the years, climaxing in that visit of Pope John Paul II to Knock in 1979, but Rome does not give formal recognition to apparitions, and as Bishop Philbin had said in a special sermon in 1960 - 'Over several scores of years, this shrine, whilst officially unrecognised, established itself firmly in the Christian consciousness of the people who lived within a wide radius of the place.' He might have added - 'and many thousands overseas.' The bias against the belief of Knock was augmented by the exposure of many dubious divine happenings and miracle workers around the countryside in later years, but in the final analysis, true or false, one way or the other, Knock itself has evolved as a powerhouse for good, and a centre of prayer and devotion.

The Connacht Regional Airport, nearer to Charlestown than Knock, is situated on a plateaued hilltop commanding a splendid view of the barony of Costello, with its green pasture lands dotted with snug cottages and farmhouses. Northwards, Ben Bulben and its legendary mountain grave of Queen Maeve marks the beautiful Yeats' country, and to the west, Croagh Patrick graces the coastline near Clew Bay. At this site the bulldozing equipment removed the sodden carbonised moss from the hill, exposed solid bedrock, and built a modern runway for jet aeroplanes and a modern miracle for Knock. No runway today or its appurtenances — airport buildings, service roads etc., lies redundant unless it was a war necessity; no runway on the other hand is an ordinance of profit, rather it is a community service, a virtual honeypot drawing bees in the guise of aeroplanes, workers, merchants, tourists and pilgrims. I flew over those runways near the Arctic Circle, on the deserts, in remote areas of Canadian forestland and in the rich regions of the rural and urban civilised world, and all of those concrete ribbons far down below are human lifelines for commerce and travel, transforming their locations from austerity or isolation into prosperity and integration. Well might Cromwell say of today, 'To hell or to Connacht — not now by the sword, but by the jet!'

Monsignor James Horan, dynamic parish priest of Knock has this to say about their airport enterprise: 'In my view, and I have lived in this Province practically for the whole of my life, Connacht Regional Airport is the most important development that has taken place in the past hundred years. The Economic and Social Research Institute, a state-sponsored body, issued three important statistics in the past two years. One statistic stated that the average income of a family in the West of Ireland is 25% lower than the average income of a family in any other part of Ireland. I mean the province of Connacht.

The second statistic is that the unemployment figure for Mayo is twice the National average for the Republic. Low incomes and high unemployment is due to the deplorable lack of proper communications and infrastructure in Connacht. We have the worse roads in the whole country and our railways are almost non-existent; most of the link-lines have been closed for years. We have the most backward telephone system in the country; thank God, it is improving and will soon be fully automatic.

The third statistic issued by the E.S.R.I. was that it would cost £2,000 million to bring the roads of the country up to standard and, perhaps, a similar sum to improve our railways; but then the railways have already disappeared from the West of Ireland. The line from Shannon to Sligo has been closed for some years. I understand that the cost of the roads in 1983 would be more like £5,000 million. Commenting on the cost of the development of Roads and Railways, the E.S.R.I. advised the Government to develop regional airports and thus take the pressure off the road and railway systems. This would be a very wise economic decision, in the circumstances, and has come from a responsible body of experts. Unfortunately, when the Connacht Regional Airport is being discussed, this aspect of the case is never mentioned.

It is reasonable to suggest that an industrialist from Birmingham or Manchester would feel discouraged in establishing any project in the West. The reason is quite obvious. It would take two days to come to the West and two days to return; no industrialist or executive can afford that much time. The situation might even be worse if he happened to be from any part of the E.E.C. I am confident that with the advent of an Airport, the economic, industrial and unemployment situation in the West will improve. I can see a great industrial complex developing in the area; we have the outstanding example of the Mid-West Region. Surely, a prosperous Connacht will be an asset to the economy of the country, just as a depressed Connacht would be a drag.

From time to time, a Journalist or Engineer calls on me and asks to be shown around the Airport. They usually come with comic misconceptions of the whole project. When they see it, they are immediately impressed by the standard of the work carried out on the Airport. The Connacht Regional Airport Company is proud of the Contractor and his work-force; they have done a truly magnificent job. Instead of finding a bog-hole on top of a mountain, they find a beautiful Airport, 75% complete. It will be a tourist attraction in its own right.

The Connacht Regional Airport, the media insist on calling it Knock Airport, will be the most scenic Airport in Europe. It is built on a plateau and commands a view of a most beautiful and pleasant countryside, with its mountains, lakes, green pasture-lands dotted with snug cottages and farm-houses. To the North-East, you can see Ben Bulbin, Truskmore, marking Sligo and the beautiful Yeats' Country. Directly to the North you have the Ox mountains and the beautiful scenery around Ballina. To the North-West you have the Nephin mountains and the scenic Belmullet Peninsula. Directly to the West you can see the Partry mountains, and, of course, Croagh Patrick
‑‑ing as a proud monument to the faith of the Irish people. It is well
‑‑sts and pilgrims alike, as a place of pilgrimage. To climb
rings you nearer to Heaven, in more ways than one. To
, you have the Twelve Pins, the Maamturk mountains
Connemara wonderland. Only thirty miles away you

have Cong, the gateway to Connemara and the most beautiful scenery in Ireland. An Airport will open up this world of enchantment and beauty to tourists and pilgrims. The people of Connacht, the friendliest and the most hospitable in the world, want to share their scenic countryside with the outside world.

Unfortunately, not enough people have experienced it because there is too much hardship in reaching it. With an Airport, within an hour's journey, thousands and thousands of visitors will flock to the West. Knock Shrine is now known world-wide and thousands and thousands of pilgrims will take advantage of an Airport to make a pilgrimage. Of course, the Airport was not built for Knock Shrine, but Knock Shrine will be its best Customer. Knock Shrine may well be the dimension that will make the Airport viable and profitable.

You have the example of Lourdes; in 1947, when Tarbes Airport opened, they had 1,300 passengers. Aviation was then only in its infancy. By 1954 it has grown to 13,000 and the latest figure to hand, 357,000 for 1979. Looking to the future, I see a great influx of pilgrims to the Connacht Regional Airport. We are not interested in Jumbo Jets, as the media would suggest. We are interested in American pilgrims who can book their tickets to the Connacht Regional Airport, via Shannon. This can be arranged through medium-sized aircraft or even smaller planes.

Of all the provinces in Ireland, Connacht suffered most from emigration; its very life-blood was drained away by the mass exodus of young boys and girls in 1950's and 1960's. The scars of that 'scourge' can still be seen on the face of the country-side around the Airport; broken-down houses and neglected farms. I am proud to say that they prospered in the countries of their adoption; they made a tremendous contribution to the life and culture of other lands. I am certain that they and their families, of first and second generations, will use this Airport to visit the land of their forefathers.

Needless to say, they will receive a hundred thousand welcomes to the land of their birth. They will feel proud of the Airport and of the beauty of the surrounding countryside.

An Englishman, living in Dublin, called on me one day. He said "Monsignor, I don't want to take up your time but I really could not pass without telling you something. I visited the Airport. I saw, for the first time, a team of Irishmen doing a wonderful job, in their own country, that they have been doing in other countries for generations. They deserve an Airport," "Amen" say I.'

I agree with the monsignor, and I know that my dear grandfather would have too. I am also thinking of Jean Louis Jobit, captain of the Second Battalion of Grenadiers, 70th. Half Brigade of the Line of the French expeditionary force to Ireland in 1798, command of Major General Humbert — were he to pass that way but once again, his comments might be more favourable.

*　　*　　*

Raz jeszcze przypada nam honor i przywilej zlozenia na pokladzie samolotu sto tysiecy powitan jego swietobliwosci Papiezowi Janowi Pawlowi Drugiemu podczas jego podrozy z Shannon do Bostonu na pokladzie naszego Flagowegro Boeing'A 747 "Swiety Patryk" natchnienie, jakie przyniosla jego obecnosc w Irlandii zyc bedzie wiecznie w naszych apmieciach w imieniu zalogi samolotu oraz calego personelu Irlandzkich Linii Lotniczych.

*

Thar ceann fhoireann na heitilte seo cuirimid Céad Míle Fáilte roimh a Naofacht an Pápa, Eoin Pól II agus é ag dul ó Aerphort na Sionainne go Boston ar an mBoeing 747 seo, ár mBratlong Pádraig. Is spreagadh mór dúinn a chuairt ar Éirinn agus beidh cuimhne ag muintir na hEireann ar a chuairt go brách.

*

Once again it is our privilege and honour to convey a Hundred Thousand Welcomes on board to His Holiness Pope John Paul II as he journeys from Shannon to Boston on our Boeing 747 Flagship Saint Patrick. The inspiration of his presence in Ireland will live forever in the memory of all of us. On behalf of the crew of this flight and all the staff of Ireland's National Airline — and that address of welcome was signed by the Chief Executive of Aer Lingus, David M. Kennedy, and that conscientious ex-army officer, Captain Martin McGannon, in charge of security, slipped a very important note to me at Shannon:
Advising you that all equipment boarded at Dublin examined by me. Baggage, press and staff fully processed. Press reboarding at Shannon checked out and in by the Special Branch.
Your Garda officers on board, with our Chief of Security Liam Higgins, are Supt. Ned O'Dea and Inspector Don Boyle of the Special Branch.
'Where are their sweets, Martin?' I asked.
'In their holdalls' he replied........
On 1st October 1979 — the pope was continuing on to the United States for yet another official visit. This time the papal party was larger, but included as before, members of the Swiss Guard,

220

Aer Lingus security people, and armed Garda officers. Company officials from the American side had told us, that the chief of the United States Secret Service group at Boston, who were responsible for security measures there, insisted on referring to the papal group in his briefings, as the 'popal party,' and that is what we called it ourselves: the popal party. Since the consequences and implications of diverting such an unusual group of passengers to any of our regular alternate airfields on the eastern seaboard of the United States, would have been too upsetting to contemplate, the US Secret Service had designated Hanscom Field, Bedford, Massachussets, as a security diversion point in the event of Boston being closed with foul weather.

When the flight crew reported for duty that morning at Dublin, this possibility loomed large. A stationary warm front was lying along the eastern seaboard — the curse of the Boston — New York coastline where they hover in the same position for days, sometimes weeks, until the system rains itself out, the front had closed some airfields and imposed appalling weather on others, including Boston and the "popal alternate," Hanscom Field. When it came to the final briefing before leaving Shannon, the weather had worsened further, and anxiety about it during the subsequent flight, diminished to a certain extent our full enjoyment of the company of our distinguished guests.

To guard against a fuel shortage, and a distinct possibility of diversion, we carried double reserves, and in supplement a further 10 tonnes of kerosene, sufficient for another hour's flying. I was tempted to up the fuel even further, but decided against it because the runway at Shannon was wet, and if that heavy aeroplane had to abandon its takeoff at high speed for some unforseen reason it would not have stopped on the paved surface.

A formal group of state and company officials and members of my crew greeted the pope when he boarded the lobby in the first class section of the aeroplane. On being introduced to him, I saluted and then went to shake hands; he caught my outstretched arm in both of his hands and said to me, very movingly, 'now we are in your hands.'

The flight was planned for 31,000 feet, with an elapsed time of just over 6 hours, and after the ocean crossing it would overfly Gander in Newfoundland. We knew from experience that we would receive special treatment from the various control centres, and as we climbed up to cruising level a lengthy signal of felicitations to the pope crackled in on our high frequency radio, from the staff of the Irish Air Traffic Control Centre at Shannon. Levelling off at 31,000 feet the aeroplane was still in the cloud, and we were bumping along in turbulence with the seatbelt sign switched on; the co-pilot asked control for 35,000 feet, but the operator replied that the level was not available. 'Very well then,' I signalled, 'if we don't get the level, the pope doesn't get your message.'

'Stand by, I'll call you back,' he said.

Three minutes later the selcal chimed, and Shannon said, 'AER LINGUS ONE" — climb to and maintain 35,000 feet.'

A few miles further and the big transport had topped the overcast and bored smoothly along, with clear blue sky above and a glorious sun beaming down from the south. Our revered traveller had settled down in his special quarters, and my cabin supervisor informed me that there was a stimulating air of excitement throughout the entire aeroplane. Our cockpit door opened into the lounge, the papal suite, and we could see the Holy Father was relaxed and engaged in conversation with the Polish members of his staff; it transpired that whilst he spoke in English with most of his entourage, he was much more at ease with his own tongue and entered into animated chat with his Polish aides.

The flight kitchens at Dublin had prepared a superb menu for the occasion, augmented by Polish dishes, and John Paul did justice to it and the accompanying wines and Irish coffee. There were two Polish soups available, but he preferred the Bortsch — a broth prepared by cooking a roast duck in a rich beef stew; the potage had been strained and garnished with thin strips of red beetroot, shredded cabbage, slices of the duck's breast, beef and the juice of red beetroot; sour cream was served separately. The other soup, Kapusniak, was made from sauerkraut cooked in water with marrowbones, pork meat and pork sausages, carrots, knob celery, parsley roots and onions. The favourite dessert of the party proved to be our Bliny Kartofle, a dish from Krakow of old style potato cake made from sweet potatoes and garnished with hot plum and honey sauce.

The main group of people in the cabin had now eased into a relaxed mood; tensions and anxieties over the visit had been very real, and relief at its success manifested itself in many ways. The party was also totally exhausted because the schedule had been gruelling, with little or no sleep for some and long hours of worry for others. The pope had gone the pace too, but the main problem for his assistants had been to get the man to bed at a reasonable hour so that he could face the schedule of the following day in reasonable shape. Archbishop Marcinkus was an aggressive papal watchdog and one example of his form was evident in the hospitality tent some days before, where the group had gathered after the ceremonies in Phoenix Park. The pope as usual waded into the food with gusto, when the archbishop's strident tones rang out over the dignitaries, 'Hi, get that guy away from the roast beef — he's due in the nunciature in ten minutes.' Relief from such pressures gave us a cabin full of clerical benevolence and media bonhomie: Cardinal Casaroli, Papal Secretary of State, spilled the salad dressing on his sash, the Italian baggage master decanted his Irish coffee over an archbishop, and some journalists endeavoured to remove white paint, which they had caught from our rear stairs, from their lounge suits; meanwhile, an Italian pressman, despite continued assurances to the contrary, kept referring to one of our company officials, resplendent in morning suit, as the papal valet.

The red seamless papal cloak was hanging in the cockpit wardrobe, and the crew urged me to put it on, but I couldn't; I held that cape in my hands and said a silent prayer. Meanwhile Russel, my linguist, had drawn out on cardboard some large greetings in Polish, as he knew that I was going to bypass protocol and invite the Holy Father to the cockpit. When John Paul arrived — he was accompanied by Cardinal Casaroli, and he talked with the crew about the flight and the turbulence. I gave him the two little books that I had written on aviation, and I accompanied them with a remark to the effect that they were no great works of literary art, but I would be privileged if he were to accept them. Russel said, 'Holy Father, what the captain really means is, he knows that his books are not going to set the world on fire, but he also knows that they will be in the Vatican library! 'Our dialogue was totally in English, and although His Holiness did not say all that much, he understood our conversation and the humorous nuances which are so much a part of Irish talk; we felt that he was totally at home in our relaxed cockpit atmosphere. I asked him if he would like to sit in my seat and permit me to take a photograph; he was delighted to do so, and I took three in succession — by far the best of the take was one of the co-pilot describing the intricacies of the inertial navigation system to him, but, just as I pressed the button that beloved bloody Corkman, by accident withdrew his head from the viewfinder. Our guest returned to his suite and did not visit the cabin below at any stage of the flight; my chief of security was guarding the entrance to the first class area, and the cabin crew ensured that the pope's privacy was respected; I believe that, more as a gesture rather than a necessity he rested on the special bed for approximately 40 minutes.

The flight progressed, but not uneventfully — the weather at Boston continued to deteriorate although the gloom was dispelled by countless American and Canadian voices who said, 'Say ah, AER LINGUS ONE, have you got the pope on board?' We did not have time to reply because that pope on board was keeping us very busy and

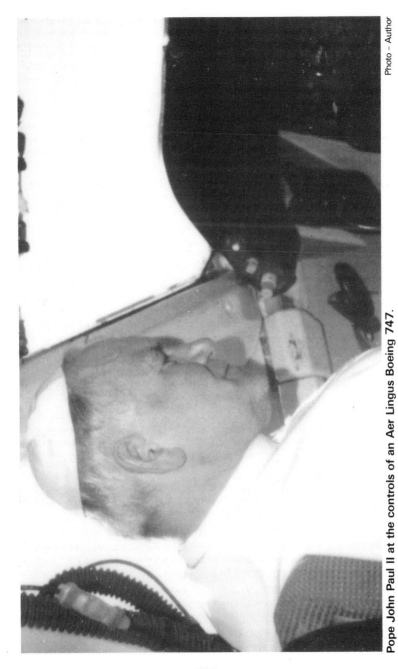

Pope John Paul II at the controls of an Aer Lingus Boeing 747.

we relayed his first message, to His Excellency Edward R. Schreyer Governor General of Canada, Ottawa:

AS MY JOURNEY TO THE UNITED STATES TAKES ME OVER THE GREAT LAND OF CANADA I WISH TO OFFER YOUR EXCELLENCY MY RESPECTFUL GREETINGS AND TO ASSURE YOU OF MY PRAYERS FOR YOURSELF AND ALL CANADIANS.
IOANNES PAULUS PP.II

That simple message was not that easy to transmit as the guy far down below had immense difficulty in getting the "Ioannes Paulus" bit. His next greeting was to the Honourable Jimmy Carter, President of the United States of America. 'Before I fire this one off,' said Morrissey the co-pilot, tell Plaisted the one about your confession — Paul Plaisted was my third pilot, manning the engineering control panel of the big jet. 'It was very simply this,' I said to Paul, 'a few days before the papal arrival, I went to confession, and as a penance the priest asked me to pray for the pope's safety on his flight to the United States,' Morrissey interjected and said 'Japers he doesn't know how right he was.' I continued to talk to Paul who had asked me, 'did you say anything to the priest?' — I replied that I did not, 'as if I did I would probably be in the box for a week.' Jimmy Carter got his message:

ON ENTERING UNITED STATES AIRSPACE I AM HAPPY TO SEND YOU MY GREETINGS AND TO ASSURE YOU OF THE PLEASURE WITH WHICH I LOOK FORWARD TO MY VISIT TO YOUR BELOVED COUNTRY. GOD BLESS AMERICA.
IOANNES PAULUS PP.II

We were now approaching Kennebunk, about twenty minutes out from Boston, and it was time to commence descent. Meanwhile the pope was using the public address system to the cabins; he thanked the journalists and the TV people for their kindness and courtesy, and he gave his blessing to all on board; it was a most moving experience listening to his voice coming through the cockpit speakers, and it contrasted sharply with what we knew we had to do: get him down safely in Boston in lousy weather. The 747 has a fully automatic landing system, and we planned to use that facility for an approach and landing on the special category 2 runway at Logan Airfield. The control tower was quite upset at this proposal, as apparently all the dignitaries were in formal position on the apron, close to runway 33L and the authorities wished us to use this runway. We reluctantly agreed to an approach on 33.

I coupled in the autopilot and it locked on accurately to the localiser — then to the glide slope, and whilst Paddy Morrissey made the safety calls I adjusted the power to meet the changing demands of the aeroplane — Paul Plaisted hovered in the background as overall supervisor; there was a crosswind of about twelve miles per hour and the runway was wet. At two hundred feet through the drizzle Morrissey called, 'runway in sight to the right,' — horizontal visibility was now down to half a mile. The autopilot had been crabbing the aircraft to cater for the crosswind, and when I disengaged it after Paddy's call, I maintained the same input; now I eased on left rudder to bring the nose around and applied right aileron to prevent the wing from rising, and we put that charming Polish man and his party safely down on runway 33 at Boston — there was no discernible reaction to runway contact, only a gentle kiss from the tyres. Motoring up to the tarmac we could see the impressive array of dignitaries, but this was their first glimpse of AER LINGUS ONE — visibility was so poor, they had not realised that we had landed. A message came to me in the cockpit that John Paul wanted to see me; I went back and he grasped both my hands as warmly as before and thanked me for the flight — he conveyed his appreciation, individually, to all the members of my crew in a similar way.

The address of welcome was given by Mrs. Jimmy Carter, and for the airline it was a marvellous boost, because the picture of our big aeroplane, with its crew smartly lined up in front, was transmitted on an uninterrupted basis for thirty minutes into most of the homes of North America. After the ceremony we were driven to our hotel in Boston, and whilst relaxing over a few drinks in the bar we were able to watch the subsequent events on television. At the Boston cathedral, there was a heavy preponderance of males, and the pope hesitated with a wry smile in the midst of his initial greeting — 'My brothers (pause) and several sisters.' More of the character of the man was to follow, when it became obvious that, as a nun was addressing him on the altar in formal welcome on behalf of the sisters of America, she was, as they say "speaking out." Instead of the usual pat on the head, and he was listening intently, he kept tapping her on top of her veil — continuously, as a father listening to his child, and perhaps not quite approving of what he had heard.

Unquestionably, for the preceding seven hours on the flight, we were in the presence of a remarkable human being who would have been equally successful in any chosen career — international banker, statesman, university professor, diplomat; but one thing was abundantly clear: he was using every facet of his God given gifts to promote the demands of the job his creator had ordained for him.

*   *   *

The 31 October of 1981 was the day that I finished flying, after forty one years in the service of Irish aviation, and looking back over those years I am privileged to reflect on those people who influenced me the most. The gentle and meticulously precise Colonel W.P. Delamer as commanding officer of the Air Corps, and later as the manager of Dublin airport; the courteous and highly efficient general manager of Aer Lingus for many years, Dr. J.F. Dempsey; the rough, swashbuckling Captain Jack Kelly Rogers; the jovial long service engineer Johnny Maher and his aggressive colleague, Frank Delaney.

Memory is a whimsical task master, playing tricks with the recall section of the mind if it is required to reproduce the images of the recent past, yet able to bring back with astounding clarity, events long since dimmed and filed away in the passage of time. That first droning sound of a Farman Salmson high wing monoplane seeping in through the open window of Foxford school in a summer afternoon of 1932, and the rapport of Martin Gavigan with his class, as the glasses slipped further down his nose and the blackboard problem became secondary when that sound transfixed him in wonderment, together with his boys — then the ecstasy of later discovering the aeroplane in a field near Pontoon. Mossie Quinlan clambering out of the cockpit of the Magister, and ambling away from that small wooden aeroplane as he sent me solo. The smell of the high octane exhaust fumes, and the uneven rumble of the Rolls Royce Kestrel engine of the Hawker Hind as "Daddy O'Keefe" gave it full throttle on the blocks and searched for the mag. drop. The glorious slow roll of that Gloster Gladiator fighter, challenging its mortal pilot to keep the roll going until they flew over the horizon, its Bristol Mercury engine grunting and growling at the pilot's whim. The thrilling, powerful whine of the engines of the Boeing 747, pushing that magnificent aeroplane into the blue skies of peaceful man.

The warmth of the handshake of Karol Wojtyla.

End.